Fathers and Paternity

Applying the Law in North Carolina Child Welfare Cases

Sara DePasquale

2016

UNC
SCHOOL OF
GOVERNMENT

The School of Government at the University of North Carolina at Chapel Hill works to improve the lives of North Carolinians by engaging in practical scholarship that helps public officials and citizens understand and improve state and local government. Established in 1931 as the Institute of Government, the School provides educational, advisory, and research services for state and local governments. The School of Government is also home to a nationally ranked Master of Public Administration program, the North Carolina Judicial College, and specialized centers focused on community and economic development, information technology, and environmental finance.

As the largest university-based local government training, advisory, and research organization in the United States, the School of Government offers up to 200 courses, webinars, and specialized conferences for more than 12,000 public officials each year. In addition, faculty members annually publish approximately 50 books, manuals, reports, articles, bulletins, and other print and online content related to state and local government. The School also produces the *Daily Bulletin Online* each day the General Assembly is in session, reporting on activities for members of the legislature and others who need to follow the course of legislation.

Operating support for the School of Government's programs and activities comes from many sources, including state appropriations, local government membership dues, private contributions, publication sales, course fees, and service contracts.

Visit sog.unc.edu or call 919.966.5381 for more information on the School's courses, publications, programs, and services.

Michael R. Smith, DEAN
Thomas H. Thornburg, SENIOR ASSOCIATE DEAN
Frayda S. Bluestein, ASSOCIATE DEAN FOR FACULTY DEVELOPMENT
Bradley G. Volk, ASSOCIATE DEAN FOR ADMINISTRATION

FACULTY

Whitney Afonso	Richard D. Ducker	Christopher B. McLaughlin	Jessica Smith
Trey Allen	Joseph S. Ferrell	Kara A. Millonzi	Meredith Smith
Gregory S. Allison	Alyson A. Grine	Jill D. Moore	Carl W. Stenberg III
David N. Ammons	Norma Houston	Jonathan Q. Morgan	John B. Stephens
Ann M. Anderson	Cheryl Daniels Howell	Ricardo S. Morse	Charles Szypszak
Maureen Berner	Jeffrey A. Hughes	C. Tyler Mulligan	Shannon H. Tufts
Mark F. Botts	Willow S. Jacobson	Kimberly L. Nelson	Vaughn Mamlin Upshaw
Peg Carlson	Robert P. Joyce	David W. Owens	Aimee N. Wall
Leisha DeHart-Davis	Diane M. Juffras	LaToya B. Powell	Jeffrey B. Welty
Shea Riggsbee Denning	Dona G. Lewandowski	William C. Rivenbark	Richard B. Whisnant
Sara DePasquale	Adam Lovelady	Dale J. Roenigk	
James C. Drennan	James M. Markham	John Rubin	

© 2016
School of Government
The University of North Carolina at Chapel Hill

Use of this publication for commercial purposes or without acknowledgment of its source is prohibited. Reproducing, distributing, or otherwise making available to a non-purchaser the entire publication, or a substantial portion of it, without express permission, is prohibited.

Printed in the United States of America

21 20 19 18 17   3 4 5 6 7

ISBN 978-1-56011-857-2

Contents

Chapter 3

Identifying and Locating Missing Fathers   27

Chapter 4

Determining When Paternity Is at Issue   39

Chapter 7

A Child's Primary Permanent Plan of Adoption: The Process and the Role of Fathers   117

Appendixes

Case Index

Table of Statutes, Regulations, and Policy Manuals

Introduction

A father is a member of a child's family and an integral part of a child's life. But, unlike a birth mother, whose identity is known,[1] a man's paternity is not so obvious. A father's identity may be unknown. Even when a father's identity is known, not every father is automatically identified at his child's birth and named on the child's birth certificate. A man who is named as the father on a child's birth certificate may still have his paternity challenged, either by his own initiative or by a person or agency with standing to raise paternity as an issue.

There are various statutes in North Carolina that address paternity and fatherhood. Rather than exist as one chapter in the North Carolina General Statutes, laws addressing fatherhood are scattered throughout various chapters of the General Statutes and have also resulted from a body of common law. Because of the various sources of authority, it is difficult to easily find and know the relevant laws addressing paternity and parentage in North Carolina. One of several purposes of this book is to identify the various North Carolina laws about fatherhood for judicial officials and practitioners who handle child welfare proceedings. Throughout this book, the term "child welfare" is used to encompass abuse, neglect, or dependency proceedings and related termination of parental rights and adoption actions for those children who have been adjudicated by the court as being abused, neglected, or dependent and who have a primary permanent plan of adoption.

Knowing who a child's father is or is not impacts a child welfare proceeding when a county child welfare agency[2] (hereinafter "county department") intervenes in a family to protect a child from abuse, neglect, or dependency. When a county department becomes involved with a family as a result of a substantiated report of a child's abuse,

---

1. A child's mother may not be known if an infant has been abandoned through the safe surrender statute and the mother's identity is not disclosed. Chapter 7B, Sections 500(b), (c) of the North Carolina General Statutes (hereinafter G.S.). *See also* G.S. 14-322.3.

2. G.S. 7B-101(8a) ("department" is defined as "[e]ach county's child welfare agency," which may be the county department of social services, a consolidated human services agency, or an agency referred to by another name).

neglect, or dependency, the county department must determine who the child's parents and relatives are. A child's parents and relatives should be notified of the county department's involvement with the child and, if appropriate, included in developing and participating in the child's case plan. In providing protective services to a child, a county department works with the child's parents and provides services that assist them in improving their parenting such that the child is safe and the family is stabilized and preserved.[3]

Courts presiding over child welfare proceedings must determine whether necessary parties have been identified and included in the actions before them. The role of the child's father is something the court must address in each child welfare proceeding. The North Carolina statutes governing abuse, neglect, or dependency actions require the court to inquire about the identity and location of any missing parents.[4] Addressing fathers specifically, the court must determine if paternity is an issue and may order that certain efforts to establish paternity be made.[5] The termination of parental rights statutes also focus on fathers. The court must hold a preliminary hearing to try to determine an unknown respondent father's identity and include him in the proceeding and, when unable to do so, to order service by publication on him.[6] In addition, the expectations of what a father of a child who is born out of wedlock must do to assert his rights as a parent are addressed in the grounds to terminate parental rights and the consent to adoption statutes.[7] The adoption statutes also contain a provision that requires the adoption petitioner to serve a notice that the adoption petition for the child was filed with the court on any biological or possible biological father who has not consented to the adoption, relinquished his parental rights, had his parental rights terminated by court order, or been judicially determined not to be the child's father.[8] A child's adoption may not proceed without all the necessary parental consents, relinquishments, or termination of parental rights orders. The court must determine whether such consent, relinquishment, or termination of parental rights applies to the child's father and, if so, ensure that it was obtained before granting the adoption.[9]

---

3. G.S. 7B-300.

4. G.S. 7B-506(h)(1), (2); *id.* §§ 7B-800.1(a)(2) through (4); 7B-901(b).

5. G.S. 7B-506(h)(1), (2); 7B-800.1(a)(3); 7B-901(b).

6. G.S. 7B-1105. Note that this preliminary hearing applies to an unknown parent, which may include an unknown mother.

7. G.S. 7B-1111(a)(5); 48-3-601(2)b.

8. G.S. 48-2-401(c)(3) (other exceptions to the notice requirement include a man who executes a notarized statement denying paternity or disclaiming interest in the child, who was convicted of certain specified sexual offenses where the criminal act resulted in the child's conception, or who the court determined is not required to consent to the child's adoption).

9. G.S. 48-2-603(a)(4).

In 2013 in North Carolina, 41 percent of births were to unwed mothers.[10] In 2014, more than one in four children lived in a single mother household;[11] and more than one in three children lived in a single parent household.[12] These statistics suggest that identifying and locating a parent and addressing paternity is often an issue that must be addressed in child welfare proceedings. Efforts must be made to find and include the child's noncustodial parent in an abuse, neglect, or dependency proceeding. The efforts to locate a parent apply to those parents whose identities are known or unknown. The early identification of, inclusion of, and involvement by a father enables a county department (1) to develop a case plan that works toward reunifying the child with each parent and (2) to also consider a child's paternal relatives as resources for placement and support. A child's permanency may be achieved sooner when the child's father is identified and involved early on in the action.

Despite the need to include both parents in a child's case plan, the 2007 federal Child and Family Service Review (CFSR) of North Carolina's child welfare system found that county departments lacked consistency with regard to efforts to support the relationship between children and fathers, to ensure sufficient visitation or contact between children and their fathers, to involve fathers in case planning, and to assess and meet the needs of fathers.[13] The 2015 CFSR report found that "families are not consistently engaged in [a child's] case planning, especially non-custodial parents" and that "stakeholders expressed concern . . . that diligent efforts to locate and serve notice

---

10. ANNIE E. CASEY FOUND., KIDS COUNT DATA CTR., *Births to Unmarried Women*, http://datacenter.kidscount.org/data/tables/7-births-to-unmarried-women?loc=1&loct=2# detailed/2/2-52/false/36,868,867,133,38/any/257,258 (last visited Feb. 8, 2016).

11. ANNIE E. CASEY FOUND., KIDS COUNT DATA CTR., *Child Population by Household Type*, http://datacenter.kidscount.org/data/tables/105-child-population-by-household-type?loc=1&loct=2#detailed/2/35/false/869,36,868,867,133/4290,4291,4292/427,428 (last visited Feb. 8, 2016).

12. Single parent household includes unmarried but cohabiting partners. ANNIE E. CASEY FOUND., KIDS COUNT DATA CTR., *Children in Single-Parent Familes*, http:// datacenter.kidscount.org/data/tables/106-children-in-single-parent-families?loc=1&loct=2# detailed/2/35/false/869,36,868,867,133/any/429,430 (last visited Feb. 8, 2016).

13. U.S. DEP'T OF HEALTH & HUMAN SERVS., FINAL REPORT: NORTH CAROLINA CHILD AND FAMILY SERVICES REVIEW 8–9 (2007), http://fosteringcourtimprovement.org/CFSR/ CFSR2Reports/NC/CFSRFinalReport2ndRoundCFSR.pdf. Note that the 2007 review is referred to as "Round Two." The CFSR is a federal review of a state's substantial conformity with certain safety and permanency outcomes that are required for federal funding under Titles IV-B and IV-E of the Social Security Act. The CFSR is conducted by the Children's Bureau of the U.S. Department of Health and Human Services. To date, there have been three rounds conducted in North Carolina: Round One in 2001, Round Two in 2010, and Round 3 in 2015. *See* CHILDREN'S BUREAU, CHILD & FAMILY SERVICES REVIEWS (CFSRs), www.acf.hhs.gov/programs/cb/monitoring/child-family-services-reviews.

of the proceedings to non-custodial parents were not made."[14] A second purpose of this book is to assist the courts and county departments in determining how to identify, locate, and include a child's father at the outset of an abuse, neglect, or dependency case.

A court may determine that paternity is an issue in a child welfare proceeding. If the court determines that paternity is an issue, it may adjudicate a man's paternity or non-paternity in the abuse, neglect, dependency, or termination of parental rights proceeding. A third purpose of this book is to assist the court in making its determination of whether paternity is an issue and, if so, to assist the parties and court in ensuring that the required steps to establish paternity are taken.

An adjudication determining that a man is or is not a child's father has a significant impact in a child welfare proceeding. The adjudication of paternity or non-paternity affects

- constitutional rights,
- a child's adjudication,
- a child's placement options,
- required reunification services,
- visitation rights, and
- a child's permanent plan of reunification, custody, guardianship, or adoption.

These issues are discussed throughout this book.

This book is organized into seven chapters that follow the stages of a child welfare case, starting with the commencement of an abuse, neglect, or dependency action and ending with the child's permanency. Throughout the chapters, the following questions that arise in child welfare proceedings but are not answered by the Juvenile Code are discussed:

- Which man is named as a party and why?
- What do efforts to locate a known father look like?
- When is paternity an issue?
- What efforts are required to establish paternity?
- How does the court establish paternity?
- Why does establishing paternity or non-paternity matter?

Note that the statutes discussed in this book reflect legislative changes made through the 2015 session of the North Carolina General Assembly.

---

14. U.S. Dep't of Health & Human Servs., Final Report: North Carolina Child and Family Services Review (2015) 15–16 (Dec. 2015). Note that the 2015 report is referred to as "Round Three" and is available on the North Carolina Division of Social Services website at www2.ncdhhs.gov/dss/stats/docs/child%20welfare%20docs/NC_ACF-CB_FinalReport_020216.pdf.

Chapter 1

The Abuse, Neglect, or Dependency Court Action: Naming Respondent Fathers

Commencing the Action

In North Carolina, a county child welfare agency is responsible for ensuring that children live in safe homes provided for by parents, guardians, custodians, or caretakers.[1] In the majority of North Carolina's one hundred counties, the child welfare agency is the county department of social services. Some counties have a consolidated human services agency or other entity that functions as the child welfare agency. In 2015, the General Assembly recognized that counties use different entities by defining "department" for purposes of an abuse, neglect, and dependency case as a county's child welfare agency [hereinafter "county department"].[2]

---

1. Chapter 7B, Section 101(19) of the North Carolina General Statutes (hereinafter G.S.) defines "safe home" as a "home in which the juvenile is not at substantial risk of physical or emotional abuse or neglect." *See also* G.S. 7B-101(3) (caretaker defined); 7B-101(8) (custodian defined); 7B-600 (providing for appointment of guardian); 35A-1202(7), (10) (general guardian and guardian of the person defined).

2. S.L. 2015-136 created G.S. 7B-101(8a) ("department" defined).

A county department provides protective services to children and families. Protective services involve

- receiving and screening reports of suspected child abuse, neglect, or dependency;
- completing assessments when a report is accepted (or screened in) for investigation;
- providing case work;
- arranging for services for parents; and
- initiating court actions when necessary.[3]

A court action is necessary when a county department determines that abuse, neglect, or dependency has occurred and the child's parent, guardian, custodian, or caretaker refuses to accept protective services, or when the child's removal from his or her home is needed to protect the child.[4]

The district court has exclusive, original jurisdiction over an abuse, neglect, or dependency proceeding.[5] A county department is the only person or institution with standing to initiate an abuse, neglect, or dependency action in North Carolina.[6] The action commences when the county department files a properly verified petition with the court.[7] The petition must include the child's name, address, and date of birth; facts that allege abuse, neglect, or dependency; and the name and last known address of each party.[8]

The Parties

The necessary parties in an abuse, neglect, or dependency action are the county department, the child, and the child's parents.[9] A parent is not a party when that parent has (1) had his or her rights to the child terminated by court order, (2) relinquished the child for adoption,[10] or (3) been convicted of first- or second-degree forcible rape, statutory rape of a child by an adult, or first-degree statutory rape and the criminal act resulted in the child's conception.[11] In addition to the county department, the child,

---

3. G.S. 7B-300.
4. G.S. 7B-302(c), (d).
5. G.S. 7B-200(a).
6. G.S. 7B-401.1(a).
7. G.S. 7B-405. For verification requirement, *see id.* § 7B-403(a); 7B-800.1(a)(5a).
8. G.S. 7B-402(a).
9. G.S. 7B-401.1. *See also id.* § 7B-601 (the juvenile is a party).
10. G.S. 7B-401.1(b)(2) (the court may order that a parent who has relinquished his or her rights to the child be made a party in the abuse, neglect, or dependency action).
11. G.S. 7B-401.1(b). G.S. 7B-401.1(b)(3) excludes parents convicted under G.S. 14-27.21 (first-degree forcible rape, formerly 14-27.2), 14-27.22 (second-degree forcible rape, formerly

and the parents, a child's caretaker, custodian, or guardian may also be a party to the proceeding.[12]

Parties are identified and named by the county department when it drafts the petition. As the court action progresses, parties may be added to or removed from the proceeding.[13] A party may be added through a motion to intervene if the person meets the statutory criteria for intervention, which is limited to a parent, guardian, custodian, caretaker, or another county department with an interest in the action.[14] If a man believes he is the child's father and is not named as a respondent by the county department, he may file a motion to intervene in the abuse, neglect, or dependency action. The court must decide if he is a parent, guardian, custodian, or caretaker when ruling on his motion to intervene. Factors a court may consider when determining if he is a "parent" and, therefore, a necessary party include

- the alleged facts that support his belief that he is the child's father;
- whether a different respondent father has been named and, if so, on what basis; and
- whether paternity is now an issue, requiring the court to obtain personal jurisdiction over him (for a discussion on determining when paternity is an issue, see chapter 4).

If his motion to intervene is granted, the court should determine paternity in the abuse, neglect, or dependency action (see chapter 6). If his motion to intervene is denied, he may file a separate action to determine his paternity (see chapter 4). If he is adjudicated as the child's father in that separate action, he must be added as a respondent parent in the abuse, neglect, or dependency proceeding because he is a necessary party.

The court may also remove parties from an abuse, neglect, or dependency action.[15] Before removing a party, the court must determine that (1) the person does not have legal rights that may be affected by the abuse, neglect, or dependency proceeding and (2) the person's involvement as a party is not necessary to meet the child's needs.[16] Removal of a party applies to custodians, guardians, caretakers, and any parent whose

---

14-27.3), 14-27.23 (statutory rape of a child by an adult offender, formerly 14-27.2A), and 14-27.24 (first-degree statutory rape, formerly 14-27.2).

12. G.S. 7B-401.1(c), (d), (e).

13. G.S. 7B-401.1.

14. G.S. 7B-401.1(h). *See also id.* § 7B-401.1(e1) (foster parents may not intervene unless they meet the criteria to initiate a termination of parental rights (TPR) proceeding pursuant to G.S. 7B-1103). Note that G.S. 7B-1103(b) authorizes any person with standing to initiate a TPR proceeding to intervene in an abuse, neglect, or dependency (A/N/D) action for the limited purpose of filing a motion to terminate parental rights in the A/N/D proceeding. Although not explicitly stated in the statute, the movant will be able to prosecute his or her claim to terminate parental rights in the A/N/D proceeding.

15. G.S. 7B-401.1(g).

16. *Id.*

rights are terminated or who relinquishes his or her rights to the child for the purposes of an adoption.[17] Removal of a party also applies to a respondent father who is later judicially determined not to be the child's father. Although he has been adjudicated not to be the child's parent, he may remain as a party if he is the child's guardian, custodian, or caretaker.[18]

Defining and Naming a Respondent Father

Identifying the child's mother and determining whether she must be named as a party in an abuse, neglect, or dependency action is not often an issue for a county department. The question of who should be named as a respondent parent arises more commonly with respect to the child's father. The uncertainty about who to name as a respondent father may be caused by a variety of circumstances. For example, the mother does not know who the father is because she either does not know anything about him or because there is more than one man who may have fathered the child. Or, a legal presumption or evidence of paternity applies to one man but another man has been identified as the child's biological father. Or, only one man is believed to be the child's father but no steps have been taken to acknowledge or establish his paternity. In these situations, the county department may not be able to identify any man or may be able to identify one or more men who could be named as the child's respondent father.

Neither the Juvenile Code[19] nor the North Carolina Administrative Code governing children's services[20] (hereinafter the Administrative Code) address who a county department should name as a respondent father when paternity is uncertain. As a result, there are various practices throughout the state, as each of the one hundred county departments exercises its discretion when determining who it should name as a respondent father in an abuse, neglect, or dependency proceeding. Some county departments name only "legal fathers"; some name "putative fathers"; some name "unknown father" or "John Doe"; and some name a combination of the three.

Defining "Parent"

There is no definition of "parent" in the Juvenile Code or the Administrative Code.[21] Federal child welfare regulations define "parents" as "biological or adoptive parents or legal guardians, as determined by applicable State law."[22] The applicable state law would be found in the Juvenile Code if there was a definition of parent.

---

17. *Id.*; *see also id.* §§ 7B-401.1(b)(1), (2); 7B-908(b)(1); 7B-1112.

18. G.S. 7B-401.1.

19. G.S. Chapter 7B is referred to as the "Juvenile Code."

20. Title 10A of the North Carolina Administrative Code (hereinafter N.C.A.C.), Chapter 70 regulates Children's Services.

21. Definitions are found at G.S. 7B-101; 10A N.C.A.C. 70A, § .0104; *id.* 70D, § .0102; *id.* 70E, § .0602; *id.* 70G, § .0402; *id.* 70I, § .0201; *id.* 70K, § .0101; *id.* 70M, § .0602.

22. 42 U.S.C. § 675(2).

Some guidance is provided by case law. The North Carolina Court of Appeals has recognized that the term "parent" has "varying definitions . . . for various purposes within the General Statutes," which requires the court to use a definition of parent that satisfies the intent and purpose of the applicable statute.[23] When determining a statute's intent and purpose, the court may look to the statute as a whole, including the purpose, preamble, title, and designated remedy.[24] A court should read the statutory provisions in context and together, so that the statute is one harmonious law.[25] In so doing, the court of appeals has held that the term "parent", although undefined in the Juvenile Code, the Sex Offender and Public Protection Registration Programs statutes,[26] and the name change statute,[27] does not include a stepparent.[28] The court of appeals has limited the definition of parent to "a mother or father" and found that "[o]ne is either a natural parent or an adoptive parent."[29]

Defining "Father"

The Juvenile Code, the Administrative Code, and federal child welfare statutes and regulations do not define "father."[30] North Carolina social services regulations governing programs apart from child welfare define "father" and may provide guidance to a

---

23. State v. Stanley, 205 N.C. App. 707, 709 (2010).

24. *Id.* at 709–10.

25. *Id.* at 710.

26. G.S. Ch. 14, Art. 27A.

27. G.S. 101-2.

28. *In re* M.S., ___ N.C. App. ___, ___ S.E.2d ___ (Apr. 19, 2016) (in holding that a stepparent did not have standing as a "parent" to appeal an abuse and neglect adjudication and disposition order, the court of appeals distinguished parent from stepparent by examining (1) the definition of caretaker found at G.S. 7B-101(3), which includes as part of its definition someone who is not a parent and expressly identifies a stepparent, and (2) the definition of stepparent as applied to adoptions and found at G.S. 48-1-101(18) as someone who is not a legal parent); *Stanley*, 205 N.C. App. 707 (looking at the definitions of "parent" found in Black's Law Dictionary, G.S. 51-2.2, and 108A-24(4b), the court of appeals held that the defendant, who was a stepparent, was not a parent who met the exemption for registering on the Sexual Offender and Public Protection Registry); *In re* Dunston, 18 N.C. App. 647, 649 (1973) (in a minor's name change proceeding, the court found that neither the requirement for parental consent nor the court's finding that a parent has abandoned the minor child applies to a stepparent).

29. *Dunston*, 18 N.C. App. at 649. *See Stanley*, 205 N.C. App. at 710; *see also M.S.* ___ N.C. App. ___, ___ S.E. 2d ___ (stepparent may not appeal as a parent in the absence of evidence in the record that the stepparent has become the child's parent through adoption).

30. *See, supra* notes 19, 20; 42 U.S.C. § 675. Note that the North Carolina Division of Social Services' Child Welfare Services Manual provides a list of common terms with "very brief definitions" that are used by legal professionals in a juvenile court proceeding. The purpose of providing a list of legal terminology is to assist child welfare case workers in understanding what is being said by the legal professionals in the court setting. "De facto father," "legal father," and "putative father" are included in the list, while terms such as "natural or biological father," "presumed father," "mother," "parent," or "adoptive parent" are not.

county department. The Administrative Code chapter regulating Work First[31] defines "alleged father," "legal father," and "natural father."[32] According to these regulations, an "alleged father" is a "man who is said without proof to be the father of a child" and includes a man who has admitted paternity without a court order establishing his paternity.[33] A "legal father" is the child's mother's husband at the time of the child's birth or a man who the court has determined is the child's father through a paternity, legitimation, or adoption action and is not necessarily the child's natural father.[34] A "natural father" is the child's biological father and may also be the alleged or legal father.[35]

Although regulations outside of the Juvenile Code provide guidance in determining how to label a "father," they do not address how an alleged, legal, or natural father should be treated in an abuse, neglect, or dependency action. A county department is left without direction as to whom it must name as a respondent father.

Defining "Legal Father"

A good general rule of practice for a county department is to name as a respondent parent in an abuse, neglect, or dependency action any man who is identified as the child's legal father under North Carolina law or any man who has been determined by another state to be the child's father.[36] The county department should look to common law and to the various North Carolina statutes that address parentage when determining who to name as a respondent father. Although there is no statutory definition of

---

1 N.C. Div. of Soc. Servs., Child Welfare Services Manual Ch. X, at 3–8 (2008), http://info.dhhs.state.nc.us/olm/manuals/dss/csm-67/man/CScX.pdf. The terms that are included are not based on definitions found in North Carolina law. For example, North Carolina law does not recognize the doctrine of de facto parent. Estroff v. Chatterjee, 190 N.C. App. 61, 76 (2008).

Note that chapters in volume 1 of the North Carolina Division of Social Services Manual that were last amended before 2013 are referred to as the "Family Services Manual," and chapters that were amended in 2013 or later are referred to as the "Child Welfare Services Manual." For consistency in this book, all chapters will hereinafter be referred to as the "Child Welfare Services Manual."

31. North Carolina's Temporary Assistance to Needy Families (TANF) program.

32. 10A N.C.A.C. 71W, § .0101.

33. 10A N.C.A.C. 71W, § .0101(14).

34. 10A N.C.A.C. 71W, § .0101(15).

35. 10A N.C.A.C. 71W, § .0101(16).

36. G.S. 110-132.1 (paternity determination by another state entitled to full faith and credit).

"legal father" in North Carolina,[37] for purposes of this book a "legal father" refers to a man who is recognized as the child's father under North Carolina law. A "legal father" includes

- the mother's husband at the time of the child's conception or birth;[38]
- a man who has executed along with the mother an Affidavit of Parentage at or near the time of the child's birth or as part of a child support case where the affidavit is filed with the county child support services agency and/or the district court;[39]
- a man who has been judicially adjudicated as the father through a legitimation proceeding,[40] civil paternity action,[41] criminal prosecution for willful neglect or refusal to provide adequate support and maintenance for a child,[42] child

---

37. Although policy and not a statute or regulation, note that 1 N.C. Div. of Soc. Servs., Child Welfare Services Manual Ch. XII, § XI.C.1. (2007), http://info.dhhs.state.nc.us/olm/manuals/dss/csm-75/man/CScXII.pdf, addresses Pregnancy Services and, as part of the Infant Born to an Incarcerated Mother Program, defines "legal father" as "the husband of the mother of the child at the time the child was born or conceived, or someone who has legitimated his child or has had his paternity judicially determined."

38. There is a rebuttable presumption that a husband is the father of a child born or conceived during the marriage. Eubanks v. Eubanks, 273 N.C. 189 (1968); Jones v. Patience, 121 N.C. App. 434 (1996); State v. White, 300 N.C. 494 (1980); State v. McDowell, 101 N.C. 734 (1888); *see also* G.S. 130A-101(e). Conception is presumed to have occurred ten lunar months or 280 days prior to the child's birth. Byerly v. Tolbert, 250 N.C. 27 (1959). *Cf.* G.S. 48-3-601(2)b.1., 2. A husband must be named as the father on the child's birth certificate unless a court order determined that another man is the child's father or unless the mother, husband, and biological father execute an affidavit of parentage that is accompanied by genetic test results. G.S. 130A-101(e).

39. G.S. 130A-101(f). The affidavit of parentage must be signed, under oath, by both the mother and father. The mother must (1) declare that the man is the father and that she was not married during the time of the child's conception through birth and (2) consent to the man's assertion that he is the father. The father must declare that he believes he is the natural father of the child. If the affidavit of parentage is signed at the medical facility, the father shall be included on the child's birth certificate. If an affidavit of parentage is signed after a birth certificate is issued, an amended birth certificate that includes the father's name is governed by G.S. 130A-118. An affidavit of parentage may also be executed pursuant to G.S. 110-132 as part of a county child support services case. See the following standardized form affidavits: DSS 4697 (Affidavit of Parentage); DHHS 1660 (Affidavit of Parentage for Child Born Out of Wedlock); AOC-CV-604 (Affidavit of Parentage), www.nccourts.org/Forms/Documents/266.pdf.

40. G.S. 49-10; 49-12.1. The putative father commences a special proceeding in the superior court by filing a verified petition seeking the declaration that the child is legitimate.

41. G.S. 49-14.

42. G.S. 49-1 *et seq.* G.S. 49-7 requires the court to determine whether the defendant is the parent of the child on whose behalf the proceeding is brought. *See also* G.S. 14-322.

custody action,[43] child support action,[44] divorce,[45] declaratory judgment,[46] or adoption;[47]

- a man who legitimated the child by marrying the mother after the child's birth;[48] or
- a man who is named as the father on the child's birth certificate.[49]

For a full discussion of the statutes and common law addressing paternity in North Carolina, see chapter 4.

Defining "Putative Father"

North Carolina statutes do not define the term, "putative father." "Putative father" is not mentioned anywhere in the Juvenile Code or Administrative Code. In contrast, "putative father" is used in the legitimation, paternity, birth registration, child support, and criminal failure to support statutes.[50]

North Carolina is in the majority of states that do not define "putative father."[51] One may look to the dictionary and other states' definitions of "putative father" for guidance. For example, the current edition of Black's Law Dictionary defines "putative

---

43. G.S. 50-13.1.

44. G.S. 50-13.4; 110-130; 110-131; 110-132; 110-132.2; 110-139; 52C-7-701.

45. G.S. 50-8; Helms v. Landry, 194 N.C. App. 787 (2009), *rev'd on other grounds*, 363 N.C. 738 (2009).

46. *In re* Williamson, 91 N.C. App. 668 (1988) (petition for TPR included claim for declaratory judgment that respondent was not the child's father); Mitchell v. Freuler, 297 N.C. 206 (1979) ("illegitimate" child of decedent brought declaratory judgment regarding his right to inherit from the estate); Batcheldor v. Boyd, 119 N.C. App. 204 (1995) (declaratory judgment to determine intestate heirs by determining paternity and possible legitimation of child born to decedent who married child's mother after child's birth).

47. G.S. 48-1-106(b) (an adopted child is the legitimate child of his or her adoptive parents).

48. G.S. 49-12.

49. G.S. 130A-101(e), (f); 130A-118; and 7B-1111(a)(5)e. (possible grounds for the termination of parental rights of a father whose child was born out of wedlock include the father's failure to establish paternity through actions that would name him as the father on the child's birth certificate). Subsection e. was added to G.S. 7B-1111(a)(5) by S.L. 2013-129, § 35, which codified *In re* J.K.C., 218 N.C. App. 22 (2012) (for purposes of a TPR on the ground of failing to establish paternity before the action was initiated, there is a rebuttable presumption that the man took the required action to establish paternity if he is named on the child's birth certificate). *See also In re* Crawford, 134 N.C. App. 137, 142–43 (1999) (respondent was legally recognized father through "Affidavit of Paternity and the birth certificate"; note that an Affidavit of Paternity executed in 1996 (as in this case) had a statutory presumption of paternity pursuant to G.S. 130A-101).

50. G.S. 49-10, 49-12.1, 49-14, 49-16; 130A-101(e)(2), 110-132, 110-132.2, and 49-5, respectively.

51. In January 2014, only thirteen states statutorily defined "putative father": Alabama, Arkansas, Florida, Indiana, Iowa, Maine, Montana, Nevada, Ohio, Oklahoma, South Dakota, West Virginia, and Wyoming. *See* U.S. DEP'T OF HEALTH & HUMAN SERVS., ADMIN. FOR

father" as "[t]he alleged biological father of a child born out of wedlock."[52] An Ohio statute defines "putative father" as a man (including a minor) who may be a child's father and to whom all of the following apply: (1) he was not married to the child's mother at the time of the child's conception or birth, (2) he has not adopted the child, (3) before an adoption petition was filed he was not determined by any state court or administrative agency to have a parent and child relationship with the child, and (4) he has not executed an acknowledgment of paternity of the child.[53] Using these sources as guidance to create a definition of putative father that incorporates the purposes of the various North Carolina statutes that reference putative fathers and/or possible biological fathers of children born out of wedlock, for purposes of this book the definition of "putative father" is a man who is not the child's legal father[54] but who claims or is alleged to be the child's father and has engaged in conduct that "is consistent with his right to care for and control his child."[55]

The Difference between a Putative Father and Possible Biological Father

The definition of "putative father," for purposes of this book, is tailored in a way that considers the man's conduct toward the mother during and after her pregnancy and toward the child. A putative father is more than a man who had sexual intercourse with the mother at or near the time of the child's conception. Such a man may be a possible biological father; however, the category "possible biological fathers" is broad and fails to take into account any actions taken by the man other than his sexual encounter with the mother near the time of the child's conception. A possible biological father has taken no action that is consistent with his right to care for and control the child.

The distinction between the terms "putative father" and "possible biological father" is based on the use of the term "putative father" in paternity, legitimation, and child support statutes and the use of the term "possible biological father" in the adoption of a minor child statutes.[56] The statutes that refer to a "putative father" have as part of

---

CHILDREN & FAMILIES, CHILDREN'S BUREAU, CHILD WELFARE INFORMATION GATEWAY, THE RIGHTS OF UNMARRIED FATHERS (2014), www.childwelfare.gov/pubPDFs/putative.pdf.

52. BLACK'S LAW DICTIONARY 724 (10th ed. 2014). See chapter 4 for a full discussion of what it means to be "born out of wedlock."

53. OHIO REV. CODE § 3107.1(H).

54. A man who is legally recognized as the child's father as described in the "Defining Legal Fathers" section above.

55. Rosero v. Blake, 357 N.C. 193, 208 (2003). For examples of conduct, see Lehr v. Robertson, 463 U.S. 248 (1983) and In re Adoption of S.D.W., 367 N.C. 386 (2014) (putative father must grasp the opportunity to develop a relationship with the child and assume the responsibilities of parenthood); G.S. 48-3-601(2)b. (consent to adoption); 7B-1111(a)(5) (ground to terminate a man's parental rights). See chapter 7 for a full discussion of these statutes.

56. The term "putative father" is used in G.S. 49-5 (prosecution for nonsupport of a child born out of wedlock); 49-10 and 49-12.1 (legitimation); 49-14 and 49-16 (paternity); 130A-101(e) and (f) (acknowledgment of parentage related to the child's birth certificate); 110-132(a) (acknowledgment of parentage related to child support); and 110-132.2 (genetic

their purpose either the establishment of the parent-child relationship or of rights and responsibilities over the child. In contrast, the inclusion of the term "possible biological father" in the adoption statutes is limited to receiving notice that an adoption petition was filed.[57] Even after receiving notice, a possible biological father's right to contest the child's adoption based on the need for his consent, relinquishment, or termination of his parental rights is allowed only if he has taken one of the statutorily proscribed actions, each one of which requires him to engage in conduct that would demonstrate his assertion of a right to care for and control the child.[58]

Including Putative Fathers in Abuse, Neglect, or Dependency Proceedings

The role of a putative father in the abuse, neglect, or dependency action is not specifically addressed by the Juvenile Code, Administrative Code, or the North Carolina Division of Social Services' Child Welfare Services Manual. North Carolina is not alone in its silence about the role of putative fathers in abuse, neglect, or dependency proceedings. A review of other states' child welfare statutes does not reveal a standard or preferred approach to addressing the role of putative fathers. States' statutory procedures range from the absence of any reference to a putative father to having specific provisions that require a putative father receive notice, have an opportunity to be heard as a non-party, and address when he is named as a party.

Arkansas and North Carolina represent opposite ends of the spectrum. Arkansas requires a putative father to be identified in the petition[59] but specifically excludes naming him as a party unless the court orders that he be a party after finding he established paternity through a court order or established significant contacts with the child such that putative parent rights attached.[60] Even if he is not a party, a putative father in Arkansas must still be given notice and an opportunity to be heard, and his paternity may be established in the dependency-neglect proceeding.[61]

In contrast, North Carolina does not require that a putative father be named as a respondent or receive notice and have the opportunity to be heard in the abuse, neglect, or dependency action. If a county department chooses to name a putative father as a respondent party, he will receive notice and have an opportunity to be heard. If the county department does not name the putative father as a party, he may

---

testing by subpoena from child support services agency). In contrast, G.S. 48-2-401(c)(3) uses the phrase "possible biological father of the minor" and G.S. 48-3-601(2)b. uses the phrase "any man who may or may not be the biological father of the minor" when addressing required notice of and consent to a minor's adoption.

57. G.S. 48-2-401(c)(3); 48-2-404.

58. G.S. 48-3-601(2)b. *See also id.* § 48-3-603 (consent is not required). See chapter 7 for a full discussion of the notice and consent to adoption of a minor child statutes.

59. ARK. CODE ANN. § 9-27-311(a)(6).

60. ARK. CODE ANN. §§ 9-27-311 (c)(2)(B); 9-27-325(o)(5).

61. ARK. CODE ANN. §§ 9-27-311(d)(2)(A); 9-27-325(o)(2), (6), (7).

file a motion to intervene if he is aware of the court action. Another party in the abuse, neglect, or dependency action may claim that a man is a putative father or possible biological father and seek to have him joined as a necessary party to the action. A court may also determine that a putative father must be named as a necessary party after making its inquiry and concluding that paternity is an issue.[62] For a full discussion of the court's inquiry, see chapter 3. For a full discussion of determining when paternity is an issue, see chapter 4.

The following questions remain unanswered by the applicable North Carolina laws, regulations, and policies. Should putative fathers be named as respondent parents in all cases where they are identified? Should putative fathers only be named as respondent parents in those cases where there is not a legal father named as a respondent parent? Should a putative father only be named as a respondent parent after he establishes or legally acknowledges paternity? If there are multiple putative fathers, should they all be named as respondent parents? Should a putative father who is also a child's caretaker be named a party only in his capacity as a caretaker? If a putative father is not named as a party, should he be included in the factual allegations of the petition? Should a possible biological father be considered a putative father and, if so, should he be named as a party or included in the factual allegations of the petition?

Because the laws and regulations do not address putative fathers or possible biological fathers in abuse, neglect, or dependency actions, practices vary throughout the state. Depending on the facts of the individual case, some county departments name the putative father and/or possible biological father as a party. Other county departments do not name him as a party but identity him and allege the facts supporting his status as a putative father or possible biological father.

Factors to Consider

There are several factors a county department may consider when deciding whether a man is a putative father who should be named as a respondent parent, including

- the facts that support or refute that he is the child's biological father;
- the likelihood that he is the child's biological father;
- the putative father's, mother's, or child's belief as to the putative father's paternity;
- statements the mother made to the putative father and/or others about the identity of the child's father;
- the steps, if any, the putative father has taken to acknowledge the child as his own (e.g., who he has told, how he refers to the child);
- whether the putative father has or attempted to have a relationship with the child;

---

62. G.S. 7B-506(h)(1); 7B-901(b). *See id.* § 8-50.1(b1).

- if the child knows the putative father, how the child refers to him (e.g., "daddy");
- whether the child resembles the father;
- whether the putative father has provided support for the child;
- whether the putative father has initiated a custody, child support, paternity, legitimation, or declaratory judgment action;
- how many putative fathers are identified; and
- whether paternity needs to be determined.

Although not an exhaustive list, these factors provide more guidance than simply naming every man the mother had sexual intercourse with at or near the time the child was conceived.

A good general rule is for a county department to name a putative father when he is the only man who claims to be or is alleged to be the child's father. This rule should apply even when there is a legal father, for example, when the mother was married at the time the child was conceived but she was separated from and had no physical contact with her husband during that time. A county department may also consider naming two putative fathers when the mother is unsure as to who the father is and when the two men who have been identified each believe they are the child's father. With both putative fathers named as respondents, paternity can be determined by the court (see chapter 5).

If a county department is concerned about naming multiple men as respondent fathers, it may name the one man who the mother or the county department believes is most likely the child's father. The county department may seek genetic marker testing and a determination of his paternity to resolve the uncertainty (see chapter 5). If the court enters an order that the one named respondent is the child's father, there is no need to name another man as a respondent parent. If the court enters an order that the one named respondent parent is not the child's father, the county department would have to amend its petition to name a different putative father as a respondent and seek the removal of the named respondent father as a party or, if applicable, reclassify his party status to caretaker, guardian, or custodian. The court would then need to proceed with determining paternity for this newly added respondent. The drawback to this approach is the delay involved in having the second putative father participate in the proceeding and, if he is determined to be the father, receive services and visitation with the child.

Summary

Determining whether to initiate a court action and who to name as a respondent father in an abuse, neglect, or dependency case are decisions that rest with the county department. In naming a man as a respondent father, the county department needs to consider North Carolina laws on parentage and give full faith and credit to other states' determinations of parentage. Legal fathers should be named as respondent parents. A county department must also determine who is a putative father, which involves an analysis that goes beyond who the mother had sexual intercourse with at or near the time of the child's conception. The county department should name identified putative fathers as respondents in the proceeding so that paternity may be addressed. Importantly, although the county department names respondent parties, the trial court reviews the county department's decision of who it named as a respondent father when the court identifies the parties to the proceeding and inquires about missing parents (see chapter 3) and whether paternity is at issue (see chapter 4).[63]

---

63. G.S. 7B-506(h)(1); 7B-800.1(a)(2), (3); 7B-901(b).

Chapter 2

The Impact of Naming a Man as Respondent Father

The county department's decision as to who to name as a respondent father in the abuse, neglect, or dependency proceeding affects the respondent's rights, the child's rights, and the court's jurisdiction to order certain actions related to the named respondent. This chapter discusses the differences in the rights that apply to a man who is named as a respondent father and a man who is merely alleged to be a putative or possible biological father but is not named as a party in the abuse, neglect, or dependency action.

Due Process

Parents have a constitutionally protected paramount right to the care, custody, and control of their children.[1] An abuse, neglect, or dependency action is a government action that intervenes in a family's life and interferes with a parent's right to care,

---

1. Stanley v. Illinois, 405 U.S. 645 (1972); Santosky v. Kramer, 455 U.S. 745 (1982); Troxel v. Granville, 530 U.S. 57 (2000); Petersen v. Rogers, 337 N.C. 397 (1994); Price v. Howard, 346 N.C. 68 (1997).

custody, and control of his or her child.[2] Because a parent's constitutional liberty interest is affected by an abuse, neglect, or dependency proceeding, the Due Process Clause applies.[3]

Notice and the Opportunity to Be Heard

After the county department files the petition alleging abuse, neglect, or dependency, the clerk of court must issue a summons for each respondent party.[4] The summons must provide notice of

1. the nature of the court proceeding;
2. the party's need to appear at the specified date and time for the hearing;
3. a respondent parent's right to a court appointed attorney;
4. the court's holding of a dispositional hearing to determine the child's needs and to enter an order to address those needs if the court adjudicates the child abused, neglected, or dependent as alleged in the petition;
5. possible dispositional orders, including a future hearing to terminate the parent's rights; and
6. the court's jurisdiction over the named party, which includes the court's authority to issue a show cause order for contempt resulting from the party's failure to comply with a court order entered in the action.[5]

The Juvenile Code[6] requires that each party, except the child, be served with the summons and a copy of the abuse, neglect, or dependency petition that was filed with the district court.[7] A respondent father will be served with a summons and, thereby, given notice of and a meaningful opportunity to be heard in the proceeding. Naming him as a party protects his procedural due process rights[8] and complies with one of the purposes of the Juvenile Code: to provide procedures that "assure fairness and equity

---

2. *In re* R.R.N., 368 N.C. 167 (2015).

3. *Stanley*, 405 U.S. 645; *Santosky*, 455 U.S. 745; *In re* T.R.P., 360 N.C. 588, 591–92 (2006) ("A juvenile abuse, neglect, or dependency action under Chapter 7B . . . frequently results in [the department of social services'] immediate interference with a respondent's constitutionally-protected right to parent his or her children.").

4. G.S. 7B-406(a). Note that the juvenile is the subject of the action and does not get served with a summons. *See id.* §§ 7B-407; 7B-408.

5. G.S. 7B-406. *See* Form AOC-J-142, Juvenile Summons and Notice of Hearing (Abuse/Neglect/Dependency), www.nccourts.org/Forms/Documents/481.pdf.

6. Chapter 7B of the North Carolina General Statutes (hereinafter G.S.) is referred to as the "Juvenile Code."

7. G.S. 7B-406(a). *See id.* §§ 7B-407; 7B-402(c).

8. *In re* L.D.B., 168 N.C. App. 206, 208 (2005) (" 'The fundamental premise of procedural due process protection is notice and the opportunity to be heard.' " (quoting Peace v. Emp't Sec. Comm'n, 349 N.C. 315, 322 (1998))).

and that protect the constitutional rights of juveniles and parents."[9] In contrast, if a putative father is not named as a party but is instead included in the factual allegations of the petition, he will not be served with a summons and will not receive notice or have a meaningful opportunity to participate in the proceeding.

Personal Jurisdiction

The court may proceed with hearing the abuse, neglect, or dependency action so long as there is proof of service on one respondent.[10] The summons that is served on a parent must "advise the parent that upon service, jurisdiction over that person is obtained."[11] Personal jurisdiction over a respondent parent will not occur until that parent is properly served with the summons, consents to the court's jurisdiction, or makes a general appearance in the action without objection, thereby waiving any defenses based on personal jurisdiction.[12] The court cannot obtain personal jurisdiction over an alleged putative father or possible biological father if he is not a party.

Personal jurisdiction over a putative father or possible biological father will be necessary if the court determines paternity is an issue that must be decided in the abuse, neglect, or dependency action. For a discussion of when paternity is an issue, see chapter 4. A putative father or a possible biological father is a necessary party to an action that will adjudicate his paternity or non-paternity.[13] If a motion for genetic marker testing is made, the court must have personal jurisdiction over the alleged father before ordering him to submit to that testing. For a discussion of genetic marker testing, see chapter 5.

A named respondent is subject to the conditions set forth in an order that is entered in the abuse, neglect, or dependency action. For example, the court may order the respondent father to engage in services, attend parenting classes, visit with the child, and pay support.[14] A respondent may be held in contempt for willfully failing to comply with an order.[15] In contrast, if a putative father is merely alleged as such in the petition, the court will lack the authority to order him to engage in any services, make any payments toward the juvenile's support, or submit to genetic marker testing.

---

9. G.S. 7B-100(1); *see also In re* Thrift, 137 N.C. App. 559, 561 (2002)("[T]he trial court must protect the due process rights not only of the child, but also of the parent").

10. *In re* Poole, 357 N.C. 151 (2003) (reversing the court of appeals based on the dissent in *In re* Poole, 151 N.C. App. 472 (2002)).

11. G.S. 7B-406(c); *see also id.* § 7B-200(b).

12. *In re* K.J.L., 363 N.C. 343 (2009); *see also* G.S. 7B-200(b)(ii).

13. A necessary party is a person who has a claim or material interest in the subject matter and whose interest will be directly affected by the outcome of the litigation. *See* Lombroia v. Peek, 107 N.C. App. 745 (1992).

14. G.S. 7B-904 (services, support); 7B-905.1 (visitation).

15. G.S. 7B-904(e); 7B-406(c).

Court-Appointed Counsel

Any indigent parent named as a party in an abuse, neglect, or dependency proceeding has a statutory right to appointed counsel.[16] Provisional counsel will be appointed to a parent when the petition is filed.[17] If the parent is indigent, provisional counsel will serve as the parent's counsel as long as that parent appears at the hearing, has not retained counsel, and does not make a knowing and voluntary waiver of the statutory right to counsel.[18]

If a putative father or a possible biological father is named as a respondent parent, it is unclear if he meets the statutory criteria for court-appointed counsel. The statute limits court-appointed counsel to parents,[19] and the Juvenile Code does not address whether "parent" includes a putative father or a possible biological father. If the court determines that a putative or a possible biological father who is named as a respondent parent is entitled to counsel, the North Carolina Indigent Defense Services will pay for that court appointment. Payment will be made because the court has either interpreted the word "parent" as it is used in the statutes governing abuse, neglect, or dependency actions to include a putative or possible biological father or the court has determined that the putative or possible biological father has a constitutionally protected interest that requires due process.[20] The court's determination that due process requires appointed counsel for the putative or possible biological father may be based on a finding that the putative or possible biological father's constitutional rights to the care, custody, and control of the child are implicated if he is subsequently adjudicated to be the child's father. In contrast, a putative or possible biological father who is only included in the factual allegations of the petition is not a party and is not entitled to appointed counsel.

Access to Confidential Records

To meaningfully participate in the proceeding, the parties must be able to adequately prepare. Part of the preparation involves obtaining information from an opposing party. The Juvenile Code requires that the county department maintain all information related to an abuse, neglect, or dependency case "in strictest confidence."[21] The

---

16. G.S. 7B-602.

17. G.S. 7B-602(a).

18. G.S. 7B-602(a), (a1).

19. G.S. 7B-602.

20. N.C. Office of Indigent Defense Servs., Appointment of Counsel for Non-Parent Respondents in Abuse, Neglect, and Dependency Proceedings (2008), www.ncids.org/Rules%20&%20Procedures/Policies%20By%20Case%20Type/AND-TPR/AppointmentsCounselNon-parentRespondents.pdf.

21. G.S. 7B-302(a1). Note that the child's guardian ad litem has access to all information pursuant to G.S. 7B-601, and the child may access the information pursuant to G.S. 7B-302(a1)(2). G.S. 7B-2901(b)(1).

parties in an abuse, neglect, or dependency action may access confidential information maintained by the county department through information shared by the county department or by a formal motion for discovery.[22] If a putative or possible biological father is named as a party in the abuse, neglect, or dependency action, he is entitled to request confidential information maintained by the county department. If the putative or possible biological father is only included in the factual allegations of the petition, he is not a party and is not authorized to move for discovery of confidential information from the county department.[23]

In addition to being served with the summons and petition, a party will receive copies of the pleadings and documents that are filed with the court.[24] The court records for abuse, neglect, or dependency proceedings are withheld from public inspection.[25] A respondent parent, guardian, or custodian in an abuse, neglect, or dependency action may examine and obtain copies of written parts of the record without a court order.[26] A named respondent father is entitled to examine the court records in the proceeding.[27] In contrast, if a putative or possible biological father is only identified in the factual allegations of the petition, he may not examine the court record without first obtaining an order from the court.[28]

Constitutional Rights to Care, Custody, and Control of the Child

Although a parent has a paramount constitutional right to care, custody, and control of his or her child, that right is not absolute.[29] A parent forfeits his or her constitutionally protected status when he or she is unfit.[30] In North Carolina, unfitness includes any of the grounds that are set forth in the termination of parental rights statute.[31] A parent may also lose his or her constitutionally protected status when he or she has acted inconsistently with his or her parental rights.[32] A parent's unfitness or acting

---

22. G.S. 7B-302(a1)(2), (5). *See id.* § 7B-700 for sharing information and discovery. *See also id.* § 7B-2901(b). Note that a party's access to information is not unlimited. A party may seek a protective order from the court. *Id.* § 7B-700(d).

23. G.S. 7B-700(c) ("Any party may file a motion for discovery.").

24. G.S. 1A-1, Rule 5.

25. G.S. 7B-2901(a).

26. *Id.* Note that a caretaker party is not included in this statute.

27. *Id.*

28. *Id.*

29. Stanley v. Illinois, 405 U.S. 645 (1972); Santosky v. Kramer, 455 U.S. 745 (1982); Troxel v. Granville, 530 U.S. 57 (2000); Petersen v. Rogers, 337 N.C. 397 (1994); Price v. Howard, 346 N.C. 68 (1997).

30. *Petersen*, 337 N.C. 397; Adams v. Tessener, 354 N.C. 57 (2001); Owenby v. Young, 357 N.C. 142 (2003).

31. *Owenby*, 357 N.C. 142.

32. *Adams*, 354 N.C. 57; *Price*, 346 N.C. 68.

inconsistently with his or her parental rights must be proved by clear and convincing evidence.[33] The father of a child born out of wedlock must take certain steps to acknowledge and take responsibility for his child before he may assert his paramount constitutionally protected right to care, custody, and control of the child.[34] A named respondent father's constitutional right to the care, custody, and control of his child are implicated in an abuse, neglect, or dependency proceeding.

The Child's Placement in Nonsecure Custody with His or Her "Father"

Upon or after filing its petition, the county department may seek an order for nonsecure custody.[35] An order for nonsecure custody is a temporary custody order that is entered before the adjudicatory hearing to protect the juvenile when specific statutory criteria are met.[36] The order for nonsecure custody must state who the child will be placed with or who has responsibility for the child's placement.[37] When a county department seeks an order for nonsecure custody, the court must first consider "release of the juvenile to the juvenile's parent, relative, guardian, custodian, or other respon-

---

33. David N. v. Jason N., 359 N.C. 303 (2005); *Adams*, 354 N.C. 57; *see also Santosky*, 455 U.S. 745 (a preponderance of the evidence standard in a termination of parental rights proceeding violates the Due Process Clause of the United States Constitution. Given the liberty interests involved, at a minimum, the standard of clear and convincing evidence is required).

34. Lehr v. Robertson, 463 U.S. 248 (1983) (an unwed father's constitutional rights are not automatically based on the mere existence of the biological link to the child; instead, an unwed father must grasp the opportunity which the biological link provides him to develop a relationship with and accept a measure of responsibility toward his child); *In re* Adoption of S.D.W., 367 N.C. 386 (2014) (a biological father's consent to his child's adoption was not required when he failed to grasp opportunities that were within his control to be on notice that the woman he had unprotected sexual intercourse with was pregnant with and gave birth to his child).

35. G.S. 7B-503(a); 1 N.C. Div. of Soc. Servs., Child Welfare Services Manual, 1201—Child Placement Services § I.F.2 (2015), http://info.dhhs.state.nc.us/olm/manuals/dss/csm-10/man/1201sI.pdf.

Note that chapters in volume 1 of the North Carolina Division of Social Services Manual that were last amended before 2013 are referred to as the "Family Services Manual," and chapters that were amended in 2013 or later are referred to as the "Child Welfare Services Manual." For consistency in this book, all chapters will hereinafter be referred to as the "Child Welfare Services Manual."

36. G.S. 7B-503 (criteria for nonsecure custody); *In re* O.S., 175 N.C. App. 745 (2006) (an order for nonsecure custody places the child in the temporary custody of a county department or a designated person pending the adjudicatory hearing). A child may not be held in nonsecure custody for more than seven calendar days (or with the consent of the parties up to ten business days) without a hearing on the need for continued nonsecure custody. G.S. 7B-506(a). *See also id.* § 7B-801(c) (an adjudicatory hearing must be held within sixty days of the filing of the petition unless the court grants a continuance pursuant to G.S. 7B-803).

37. G.S. 7B-505; 7B-506(h); 7B-507(a)(4). *See also* Form AOC-J-150, Order for Nonsecure Custody, www.nccourts.org/Forms/Documents/483.pdf; Form AOC-J-151, Order on Need for Continued Nonsecure Custody, www.nccourts.org/Forms/Documents/484.pdf.

sible adult."[38] Of the statutorily identified placement preferences, only a parent has a constitutional right to care, custody, and control of his or her child.[39] The purpose of the Juvenile Code includes preventing the unnecessary or inappropriate separation of a child from his or her parents, protecting the constitutional rights of children and parents, and providing for protective services that respect both family autonomy and the child's need for safety, continuity, and permanence.[40]

Unless there has been a determination by a court based on clear and convincing evidence that a parent is unfit, has neglected his or her child, or has acted inconsistently with his or her parental rights,[41] a court should first look to place a child with the parent from whose care the child was not removed. This parent is commonly referred to as the "nonremoval parent." The nonremoval parent may be the respondent father. A court will need to determine if the named father is a "parent" as contemplated by the Juvenile Code and, if so, whether he is unfit or acted inconsistently with his parental rights. For a putative father, that analysis may involve determining whether he grasped or attempted to grasp the opportunity to develop a relationship with and take a measure of responsibility for his child.[42] Note that a possible biological father (for purposes of this book) has made no attempt to acknowledge the child, let alone grasp the opportunity to develop a relationship with or take responsibility for the child.

If the court determines that the respondent father is a "parent" as that term is used in the Juvenile Code and has not found him to be unfit or to have acted inconsistently with his parental rights, the court should order nonsecure custody to him. The court may not, however, finally dispose of the action by ordering permanent custody to the

---

38. G.S. 7B-503(a).

39. Eakett v. Eakett, 157 N.C. App. 550, 554 (2003) ("The grandparent is a third party to the parent-child relationship. Accordingly, the grandparent's rights to the care, custody and control of the child are not constitutionally protected while the parent's rights are protected."). *See also* G.S. 7B-503(a) (placement preferences).

40. G.S. 7B-100(1), (3), (4).

41. Adams v. Tessener, 354 N.C. 57 (2001) (clear and convincing evidence); Price v. Howard, 346 N.C. 68 (1997) (a parent may forfeit his or her constitutional rights to parent when he or she is unfit, has neglected the child, or has acted inconsistently with his or her parental rights).

42. Lehr v. Robertson, 463 U.S. 248 (1983); *Adams*, 354 N.C. 57 (father acted inconsistently with his parental rights when he failed to follow up with and inquire about the child after the child's mother informed him that she was pregnant and when she informed him, after the child was born, that he would be contacted by child support services. Custody was appropriately based on the best interests of the child determination when the court ordered custody to the maternal grandparents); Rosero v. Blake, 357 N.C. 193, 208 (2003) ("[O]ur General Statutes recogniz[e] the legal relationship between parent and illegitimate child, [and] establish[] that an illegitimate child's father who has acknowledged or affirmed his paternity [by executing an Affidavit of Parentage] under [G.S.] 110-132(a) and whose conduct is consistent with his right to care for and control his child, no longer stands as a third party in relation to his illegitimate child.").

father at the nonsecure custody stage of the proceeding.[43] If a respondent father resides outside of North Carolina, the court must determine whether the Interstate Compact on the Placement of Children (hereinafter ICPC) applies to the child's placement with his or her father.[44] For full discussion on the ICPC and its applicability to an out-of-state parent, see chapter 6.

In some cases, a respondent father may not be located and served until after his child is placed in nonsecure custody. In those cases, the court should consider placing the child with his or her father at the next hearing on the need for continued nonsecure custody.[45] If a hearing on the need for continued nonsecure custody was waived, any party has the right to request a hearing to address the child's placement.[46] A named respondent father may request a hearing to determine whether the child should be placed with him. Without a successful motion to intervene, a putative father who is only named in the factual allegations of the petition does not have a right to file a motion for a hearing on the child's placement to request that the child be placed in his care.

If a court determines that a named or alleged father is not a "parent" as the term is used in the Juvenile Code, the court may still place the child in his home. A court may order placement in a home that it approves and designates in the order for nonsecure custody.[47] If a placement with a parent or relative is not available or in the child's best interests, North Carolina law allows the court to prioritize placement of the child with "nonrelative kin."[48] One of the definitions of nonrelative kin is an adult who has a substantial relationship with the child.[49] If a putative father has a substantial relationship with the child, the court may prioritize the child's placement with the putative father over a foster home.[50] The court may order placement with the putative father regardless of whether he is named as a respondent parent or not. If the putative father does not have a substantial relationship with the child, the court need not consider placing the child in his care.

---

43. *In re* O.S., 175 N.C. App. 745 (2006).

44. G.S. 7B-3800 (ICPC).

45. G.S. 7B-506(c) (referring to G.S. 7B-503).

46. G.S. 7B-506(f) (any hearing on the need for nonsecure custody after the first hearing may be waived); 7B-506(g).

47. G.S. 7B-505(a)(3); *see also* Form AOC-J-150, Order for Nonsecure Custody, www.nccourts.org/Forms/Documents/483.pdf; Form AOC-J-151, Order on Need for Continued Nonsecure Custody, www.nccourts.org/Forms/Documents/484.pdf.

48. G.S. 7B-505(c); 7B-506(h)(2a). Placement with nonrelative kin is discretionary with the court.

49. G.S. 7B-101(15a).

50. G.S. 7B-505(c); 7B-506(h)(2a). The preference for placement with nonrelative kin is discretionary rather than mandatory.

Placement in Nonsecure Custody with Relatives

If the court determines that the respondent father has acted inconsistently with his parental rights or is unfit, the court should look to the child's relatives, guardian, custodian, or other responsible adult when determining the child's placement in nonsecure custody.[51] A county department must, within thirty days of removing the child from his or her home, exercise due diligence to identify and provide notice to relatives, subject to exceptions for family and domestic violence.[52] The notice provided by the county department must explain that the child is in nonsecure custody and include the dates of hearings on the need for continued nonsecure custody; explain the options the relative has to participate in the child's care and placement; and describe how to become a foster family, with an explanation of services and supports that are available to the child placed in a foster home.[53]

Relatives include the child's grandparents, adult siblings, aunts, uncles, nieces, nephews, great grandparents, and other adult relatives suggested by the parents.[54] If the child has siblings, notice must also be provided to persons with legal custody of the child's siblings.[55] The county department must make efforts to contact and consider both paternal and maternal relatives.[56]

At each hearing on the need for continued nonsecure custody, the court must inquire about the efforts made by the county department to identify and notify the child's relatives, including persons with legal custody of the child's siblings, who may

---

51. G.S. 7B-503(a); 7B-505(b); 7B-506(h)(2).

52. 42 U.S.C. § 671(a)(29); Child Welfare Services Manual, 1201—Child Placement Services § IV.2, http://info.dhhs.state.nc.us/olm/manuals/dss/csm-10/man/1201sIV.pdf. *See* G.S. 7B-505(b).

53. 42 U.S.C. § 671(a)(29); Child Welfare Services Manual, 1201—Child Placement Services § IV.3, http://info.dhhs.state.nc.us/olm/manuals/dss/csm-10/man/1201sIV.pdf; N.C. Div. of Social Servs. (DSS), DSS Administrative Letter CWS-02-09 to County Directors of Social Services (Mar. 17, 2009), http://info.dhhs.state.nc.us/olm/manuals/dss/csm-05/man/CWS_AL_02_09.pdf (incorporating 42 U.S.C. § 671(a)(29)). Note that North Carolina does not have a kinship guardianship assistance payment program.

54. 42 U.S.C. § 671(a)(29); Child Welfare Services Manual, 1201—Child Placement Services § IV.2, http://info.dhhs.state.nc.us/olm/manuals/dss/csm-10/man/1201sIV.pdf.

55. 42 U.S.C. § 671(a)(29). Custodial parents of a sibling were added as notice recipients by the Preventing Sex Trafficking and Strengthening Families Act, Pub. L. No. 113-183, effective Sept. 29, 2014. G.S. 7B-505(b) expands the federal requirement to "other persons" with legal custody of the child's sibling. 42 U.S.C. § 675(12) defines "sibling" as an individual who is recognized by state law to be the child's sibling or who would have been considered a sibling under state law but for a termination or other disruption (such as a parent's death) of parental rights.

56. N.C. Div. of Soc. Servs. (DSS), DSS Administrative Letter CWS-02-09 to County Directors of Social Services (Mar. 17, 2009), http://info.dhhs.state.nc.us/olm/manuals/dss/csm-05/man/CWS_AL_02_09.pdf; Child Welfare Services Manual, 1201—Child Placement Services § IV.2, http://info.dhhs.state.nc.us/olm/manuals/dss/csm-10/man/1201sIV.pdf.

be potential resources for the child's placement and support.[57] The court should inquire about the relatives of each named respondent parent. If the county department has not identified and sent notice to the child's maternal and paternal relatives, a court must order the department to do so or make findings that notification to specific relatives would be contrary to the child's best interests.[58] If a putative father is only alleged as such in the petition, the court may not inquire about the efforts that have been made to identify and provide notice to his relatives of the child's placement in nonsecure custody.

If a maternal or paternal relative is willing and able to care for and provide a safe home for the child, the court must order placement with that relative unless the court finds that the placement is contrary to the child's best interests.[59] If more than one relative is willing and able to provide a safe home for the child, the court should consider the best interests of the child when deciding between multiple relative placement options. Factors a court may consider include the relationship between the child and relative, the relationship between the parent and relative, and the likelihood that the named respondent father is in fact the child's father such that the person available for the child's placement is the child's paternal relative. If a relative lives outside of North Carolina, the nonsecure custody statutes require compliance with the ICPC.[60] If the court does not order placement with a relative, the court may consider placement with an adult who has legal custody of the child's sibling.[61] A child may have siblings on his or her mother's side and/or his or her father's side. Unlike with the child's possible placement with a relative, the Juvenile Code does not require the court to consider the child's placement with a person who has custody of the child's sibling.[62]

Table 2.1 illustrates the statutory placement preferences for a child's placement in nonsecure custody.

Visitation with the Respondent Father

If a child is placed in nonsecure custody outside of the respondent father's home, the court order must address visitation between the respondent father and the child. The Juvenile Code requires that "[a]n order that removes custody of a juvenile from a parent . . . or that continues the juvenile's placement outside the home shall provide for

---

57. G.S. 7B-506(h)(2).

58. G.S. 7B-505(b).

59. G.S. 7B-505(b); 7B-506(h)(2). *See id.* § 7B-101(19) ("safe home" defined).

60. G.S. 7B-505(d); 7B-506(h)(2). *See also id.* § 7B-3800 (ICPC). See Chapter 6 for a discussion of the ICPC.

61. G.S. 7B-505(c); 7B-506(h)(2a).

62. G.S. 7B-506(h)(2a) uses the term "may," not "shall."

Table 2.1. Priority of Placement in Nonsecure Custody

(1) Non-Removal Parent

(2) Maternal or Paternal Adult Relatives: G.S. 7B-505(b), 7B-506(h)(2)
Adult relatives include the child's grandparents, siblings, aunts, uncles, nieces, nephews, great grandparents, and other relatives suggested by the parents.
   If the court finds that the child's relative is willing and able to provide proper care and supervision for the child in a safe home,* the court must order the child's placement with that relative, unless the court also finds that placement with that relative is contrary to the child's best interests.

(3)

Persons with Legal Custody of the Child's Sibling: G.S. 7B-505(c), 7B-506(h)(2a)		Nonrelative Kin: G.S. 7B-505(c), 7B-506(h)(2a)
The court may order placement with this person if the court finds that the person is willing and able to provide proper care and supervision to the child in a safe home* and that placement with this person is in the child's best interests.	OR	G.S. 7B-101(15a) defines "nonrelative kin" as an adult who has a substantial relationship with the child or, if the child is a member of state-recognized Indian tribe, an adult who is a member of a state-recognized or federally recognized Indian tribe. The court may place the child with nonrelative kin, if the court finds that the adult is willing and able to provide proper care and supervision to the child in a safe home* and that placement with this person is in the child's best interests.

(4)

Someone Else Approved by the Court and Designated in the Order: G.S. 7B-505(a)(3); 7B-507(a)(4)		County Department of Social Services: G.S. 7B-505(a)(1), (2); 7B-507(a)(4)
The court may order such placement if the court finds it is in the child's best interests.	OR	Custody and placement responsibility is ordered to the county department.

* Note that G.S. 7B-101(19) defines "safe home" as "[a] home in which the juvenile is not at substantial risk of physical or emotional abuse or neglect."

appropriate visitation as may be in the best interests of the juvenile consistent with the juvenile's health and safety."[63]

Section 1201 of the North Carolina Division of Social Services' Child Welfare Services Manual discusses the importance of visitation between a child who has been removed from his or her home and the child's parents.[64] Visitation is considered "an

---

63. G.S. 7B-905.1(a).
64. CHILD WELFARE SERVICES MANUAL, 1201—Child Placement Services §§ V. B.2, D., F., G., http://info.dhhs.state.nc.us/olm/manuals/dss/csm-10/man/1201sV.pdf.

essential component of work with children in foster care and their families"[65] and "is an opportunity to build a case toward a permanent resolution."[66] The Child Welfare Services Manual recognizes that parents and children have a right to visit one another unless the court orders otherwise.[67]

If a county department names a respondent father as a party, the court may want to determine whether he is a "parent" as defined by the Juvenile Code and, if so, address visitation with the child. A visitation order must specify the minimum frequency and length of visits and the level of supervision required.[68] In determining the appropriate visitation plan (including whether visitation is in the child's best interests), a court may consider whether the child and father have a pre-existing relationship. Depending on the relationship between the child and the respondent father, a court may determine that it is in the child's best interests for the initial visits to occur in a therapeutic setting.[69] If no visitation is ordered, the court must make the express finding that it is not in the child's best interests to visit with the respondent father.[70] If a putative father is not named as a party but is instead identified in the allegations of the petition, the court is not required to order visitation between the child and the alleged putative father.

Summary

A man who is named as a respondent father clearly has more rights in an abuse, neglect, or dependency proceeding than a man who is merely alleged to be the child's father. A respondent father's due process rights are protected, and the court will have personal jurisdiction over him once he is served with or waived service of the summons. Personal jurisdiction over a respondent father enables the court to order him to comply with certain conditions that may range from submitting to genetic marker testing to providing a safe home for the child. The court must determine whether a putative father or a possible biological father who is named as a respondent is a "parent" and, if so, whether he has acted in a manner that has impacted his paramount constitutional right to care, custody, and control of his child. The court's determination impacts the respondent father, the child, the county department, and other individuals who have an interest in the child's health and safety.

---

65. *Id.* § V.G.2, at 32.

66. *Id.* § V.G.4, at 34.

67. *Id.* §§ V.D., F., G.1.

68. G.S. 7B-905.1(b). Note that the AOC forms ordering nonsecure custody, AOC-J-150 and AOC-J-151, do not include provisions for visitation. *But see* DSS Form 5242, Contact and Visitation Plan, http://info.dhhs.state.nc.us/olm/forms/dss/dss-5242-ia.pdf.

69. *See* G.S. 7B-904(a), (b).

70. *In re* T.R.T., 225 N.C. App. 567 (2013); *see* G.S. 7B-905.1(a).

Chapter 3

Identifying and Locating Missing Fathers

Various statutes in the Juvenile Code[1] require the court in an abuse, neglect, or dependency proceeding to inquire about the identity and location of any missing parent.[2] Because this book addresses the role of fathers in child welfare proceedings, the discussion in this chapter focuses on identifying and locating a child's father.

The Court Inquiry into the Father's Identity and/or Location

Parents are necessary parties to the abuse, neglect, or dependency proceeding, which means that unless a parent has died or a statutory exception[3] applies, both parents must be named as respondents. When a respondent father is named in the petition,[4] the court must determine if he has been served with a summons and a copy of the

---

1. Chapter 7B of the North Carolina General Statutes (hereinafter G.S.) is referred to as the "Juvenile Code."

2. G.S. 7B-506(h)(1); 7B-800.1(a)(3); 7B-901(b).

3. G.S. 7B-401.1(b) (exceptions: parent's rights were terminated; parent executed relinquishment; parent was convicted of first- or second-degree forcible rape, statutory rape of child by adult offender, or first-degree statutory rape, and child was conceived through the criminal act). *See also id.* §§ 14-27.21(c); 14-27.22(c); 14-27.23(d); 14-27.24(c).

4. *See* G.S. 7B-402(a) (one of the required contents of the petition is the name and last known address of each party as determined by G.S. 7B-401.1).

petition alleging that the child is abused, neglected, or dependent.[5] If he has not been served, the court must inquire about his location and the efforts made to serve him.[6]

If a respondent father has not been named in the abuse, neglect, or dependency petition, the court must inquire into the father's identity.[7] The court's inquiry may start with determining whether the county department alleged that a specific individual or individuals may be the child's father.[8] If the petition alleges a man (or men) may be the child's putative or possible biological father, the court may inquire as to the facts that support or refute the likelihood of the man's paternity and the efforts a county department has made to contact the identified man or men. If the factual allegations in the petition do not identify a putative or possible biological father for the child who is the subject of the action, the court will have to obtain information about the father's identity at a hearing.

The court's inquiry into a father's identity and location occurs during different stages in the abuse, neglect, or dependency proceeding. If nonsecure custody has been ordered, the inquiry starts at the first hearing on the need for continued nonsecure custody and continues with each hearing on nonsecure custody held thereafter.[9] At the pre-adjudication hearing, the court must address the identity and location of any missing parent and whether the parent was served with the summons.[10] If the child is adjudicated abused, neglected, or dependent and the child's father has not been identified or located, the court must inquire into the missing father's identity and location at the initial dispositional hearing.[11] The court must make findings of the efforts that have been taken to identify, locate, and serve a missing father in each order on the need for continued nonsecure custody and in the initial dispositional order.[12]

In addition to inquiring about a father's identity or location, the court may order that specific efforts to identify or locate and serve the child's father be made.[13] The court may specify what a county department must do, such as conduct a public records search to either identify a legal father or determine the location of a father who has been identified, or interview the child's mother and relatives about the father's identity or whereabouts.

---

5. G.S. 7B-506(h)(1); 7B-800.1(a)(5); 7B-901(b). See chapter 2 for a discussion of the court's personal jurisdiction over a named party.

6. G.S. 7B-506(h)(1); 7B-800.1(a)(3), (5); 7B-901(b).

7. G.S. 7B-506(h)(1); 7B-800.1(a)(2), (3); 7B-901(b).

8. See chapter 1 for a full discussion of the difference between naming a man as a respondent father or merely identifying a putative or possible biological father in the factual allegations of the petition.

9. G.S. 7B-506(h)(1).

10. G.S. 7B-800.1(a)(2), (3), (5).

11. G.S. 7B-901(b).

12. G.S. 7B-506(h)(1); 7B-901(b). *See also* Form AOC-J-151, Order on Need for Continued Nonsecure Custody, www.nccourts.org/Forms/Documents/484.pdf.

13. G.S. 7B-506(h)(1); 7B-901(b).

Identifying Missing Fathers

The Juvenile Code does not address how to identify an unknown or missing father in an abuse, neglect, or dependency proceeding. Limited guidance is provided by the statute addressing the preliminary hearing for an unknown parent in a termination of parental rights proceeding:

1. ask the known parent to provide information about the unknown parent's identity or

2. order the petitioner to conduct "a diligent search" for the unknown parent.[14]

What constitutes a diligent search is determined on a case by case basis and does not involve applying a mandatory checklist of actions.[15]

A logical first step in identifying a father is to ask the child's mother for any and all information she has about who she believes fathered her child. The county department may have asked the mother about information related to the father's identity outside of the court proceeding and may also question her when she is under oath and testifying as a witness in the abuse, neglect, or dependency proceeding. A mother may provide information that ranges from the father's full name, date of birth, contact information, and social security number to a physical description without any identifying personal information and everything in between. A county department may benefit from using the "Locate Data Sheet"[16] when interviewing the mother about the identity and location of the missing father. Information fields on this form include the father's name; alias; physical description; place of birth; state that issued his driver's license; last known address; usual occupation; and, if married, his current spouse's name.[17]

A county department may also ask collateral contacts, such as the child's relatives, if they have information about who the child's father is or might be.[18] Depending on the child's age, it may also be appropriate to ask the child who his or her father is or who he or she refers to as "dad."

Other efforts to identify a father involve searching public records that address presumptions, adjudications, and evidence of paternity (see chapter 4). A child's birth certificate, a mother's marital status, affidavits of parentage, judicial determinations

---

14. G.S. 7B-1105.

15. Jones v. Wallis, 211 N.C. App. 353 (2011).

16. N.C. Division of Social Services (DSS), DSS-1168A, Locate Data Sheet, http://info.dhhs.state.nc.us/olm/forms/dss/dss-1168.pdf. This form was developed by DSS to assist a child support services agency in locating an absent parent (mother or father).

17. *Id.*

18. G.S. 7B-302(e) authorizes a county department to consult with individuals or make a written demand for information from individuals and agencies when arranging for the provision of protective services for the child. *See* 42 U.S.C. § 671(a)(29); G.S. 7B-506(h)(2); 7B-800.1(a)(4); 7B-901(b) (requiring a county department to identify and notify the child's relatives of the child's removal).

of paternity, and legitimation proceedings are all factors to consider when identifying a child's legal father. Records to search include

- the child's birth certificate maintained by the local register of deeds,[19] State Registrar[20] (or another state's equivalent), or the child's school,[21] along with any accompanying documents that are filed with the birth certificate, such as an affidavit of parentage,[22] court order,[23] or marriage certificate;[24]
- marriage[25] and divorce records,[26] which would address the marital presumption[27] of the child's legitimacy and post-birth legitimation;[28]
- criminal actions for nonsupport of a child;[29] and
- court actions for paternity, legitimation, divorce, child support, custody, and declaratory judgments.[30]

A county department may also contact a state or county child support services agency to inquire as to whether efforts to identify a father have been undertaken and, if so, if a father has been identified. A county department may also want to ask the child

---

19. G.S. 130A-99(a); 130A-118(e).

20. G.S. 130A-92(a); 130A-97(6).

21. G.S. 115C-364(c) (requiring a certified copy of the child's birth certificate or other satisfactory evidence of the child's date of birth to be presented to the school when the student is being admitted for the first time); 115C-402(b) (official student record shall include adequate identification data, including the date of birth). *See also id.* § 130A-109.

22. G.S. 130A-101.

23. G.S. 130A-119; 130A-118(b)(2), (b)(3). *See also id.* § 49-13.

24. G.S. 130A-110, 130A-118(b)(1). *See also id.* § 49-13.

25. G.S. 51-8 (register of deeds maintains marriage certificates for each marriage ceremony performed for which a marriage licensed was issued by the register of deeds); 130A-110 (register of deeds maintains a copy of the marriage certificate and transmits a record of each ceremony performed to the State Registrar).

26. G.S. 130A-111 (each month, the clerk of court files a report of each divorce and annulment granted by the court to the State Registrar); 50-8 (divorce complaints must state name and age of any minor child(ren) of the marriage or state that there are no children of the marriage); 50-11.2 (divorce judgment may contain provisions about the custody and support of children born of the marriage or state that there are no children of the marriage).

27. Eubanks v. Eubanks, 273 N.C. 189 (1968).

28. G.S. 49-12; 130A-118(b)(1).

29. G.S. 49-2; 14-322. Note that a county department may access the Automated Criminal Infraction System (ACIS) of the North Carolina Administrative Office of the Courts (AOC). *See* 1 N.C. Div. of Soc. Servs., Child Welfare Services Manual Ch. VIII, §1408, at 7 (2009), http://info.dhhs.state.nc.us/olm/manuals/dss/csm-60/man/pdfdocs/CS1408.pdf.

Note that chapters in volume 1 of the North Carolina Division of Social Services Manual that were last amended before 2013 are referred to as the "Family Services Manual," and chapters that were amended in 2013 or later are referred to as the "Child Welfare Services Manual." For consistency in this book, all chapters will hereinafter be referred to as the "Child Welfare Services Manual."

30. A county department can access the AOC's Civil Case Processing System (VCAP). *See* Child Welfare Services Manual Ch. VIII, § 1408, at 7, http://info.dhhs.state.nc.us/olm/manuals/dss/csm-60/man/pdfdocs/CS1408.pdf.

support services agency whether an affidavit of parentage has been executed and, if so, request a certified copy so that it may be introduced as evidence in the abuse, neglect, or dependency action[31] (see chapters 4 and 5).

Locating Missing Fathers

Neither the Juvenile Code nor the North Carolina Administrative Code specify the efforts that must be taken to locate and serve a missing parent. The North Carolina Division of Social Services' Child Welfare Services Manual requires a county department to make and document diligent efforts to contact an "absent parent."[32] The Child Welfare Services Manual also states that "it is the duty of the child welfare worker to make diligent efforts at the time of placement (if not accomplished before) to locate parents, including legal and biological fathers."[33] The actions that make up diligent efforts to locate a missing father are not addressed in the Child Welfare Services Manual except for one section discussing required documentation of attempts to locate missing parents or relatives that must be recorded during the first two weeks of a child's out-of-home placement. In that section, the Child Welfare Services Manual identifies the North Carolina Child Support Services Program, the Federal Parent Locator Services, and the Internet White Pages as "three useful sources to locate the addresses of missing persons."[34]

Additional guidance on what constitutes due diligence is provided by the Child Welfare Services Manual in its discussion of recommended efforts a county department should take when searching for a child's relatives and kin.[35] Due diligence is defined as "those efforts that are reasonably likely to identify and provide notice to adult relatives," which in this case would be the child's father, and includes

- interviewing the child, parents, caretakers, and relatives;
- asking participants in family decision-making meetings to help identify relatives;

---

31. G.S. 130A-101(f); *see id.* § 110-132. G.S. 7B-302(e) and 110-139(b) allow an authorized representative of a county department to access information obtained by the county child support services agency in order to locate a child's father.

32. "Absent parent" is defined as "a parent that does not typically live in the home where the child neglect, abuse, or dependency allegations are being assessed." Child Welfare Services Manual Ch. VIII, §1408, at 11, http://info.dhhs.state.nc.us/olm/manuals/dss/csm-60/man/pdfdocs/CS1408.pdf.

33. Child Welfare Services Manual, 1201—Child Placement Services § V.B.1. (2015), http://info.dhhs.state.nc.us/olm/manuals/dss/csm-10/man/1201sV.pdf.

34. *Id.* § V.C.7.

35. Child Welfare Services Manual Ch. IV, at xxxvii (The Children's Services Yellow Pages: Tools for Enhanced Practice), http://info.dhhs.state.nc.us/olm/manuals/dss/csm-10/man/CSs1201cYP.pdf.

- accessing internal agency databases, such as those in child support and child welfare agencies;[36] and
- using Internet-based tools.[37]

The Child Support Services Program[38] may be particularly helpful to a county department because one of its purposes is to "provide for the location of absent parents."[39] The Child Support Services Program has access to the North Carolina State Directory of New Hires;[40] information maintained and used by the Department of Transportation for driver's license issuance and motor vehicle registration;[41] and, upon written certification, otherwise confidential information from employers, utility and cable television companies, and financial institutions doing business in or incorporated under North Carolina laws.[42] An authorized representative of a county department may access the information obtained by the Child Support Services Program when trying to determine a father's location.[43]

In addition to the Child Welfare Services Manual, case law discussing service by publication provides guidance for what efforts constitute due diligence. Service by publication requires the plaintiff or petitioner to complete a due diligence search to

---

36. A child welfare social worker may want to access public assistance information as part of his or her efforts to locate the father. For programs governed largely by state confidentiality laws, such as Work First, Medicaid, and State-County Special Assistance, this type of information-sharing is authorized. *See* G.S. 108A-80 (allowing information-sharing for purposes directly connected with the administration of social services programs); Title 10A of the North Carolina Administrative Code (hereinafter N.C.A.C.), Ch. 69, § .0503 (allowing information-sharing with other government officials in order to facilitate program administration if disclosure is justifiable for such administrative purposes and if adequate safeguards are in place to protect the information); 10A N.C.A.C. 23H, § .0111 (similar provision applicable to Medicaid information). State guidance governing the Medicaid program explains that requests for information for abuse, neglect, or dependency cases must be evaluated on a case-by-case basis. N.C. DEP'T OF HEALTH & HUMAN SERVS., DIV. OF MED. ASSISTANCE, FAMILY AND CHILDREN'S MEDICAID MANUAL, MA-3500, § VI.A.1 (Apr. 2009), http://info.dhhs.state.nc.us/olm/manuals/dma/fcm/man/. A child welfare social worker should not access information from the Supplemental Nutrition Assistance Program (SNAP) for the purpose of locating a father because information from that program is governed by a more stringent federal confidentiality law. 7 C.F.R. § 272.1(c) (2015).

37. CHILD WELFARE SERVICES MANUAL, 1201—Child Placement Services § IV.2, http://info.dhhs.state.nc.us/olm/manuals/dss/csm-10/man/1201sIV.pdf.

38. The Child Support Services Program (also referred to as the Child Support Enforcement Program) is a program of the North Carolina Department of Health and Human Services, Division of Social Services.

39. G.S. 110-128; *see also id.* § 110-139(a).

40. G.S. 110-129.2.

41. G.S. 110-129.1(a)(2).

42. G.S. 110-139(c), (d). Note that *id.* § 110-139(e) exempts telecommunication utilities.

43. G.S. 110-139(b); 7B-302(e).

find and serve the missing party.[44] Due diligence in this context requires the use of all resources reasonably available to the petitioner in attempting to locate a respondent and includes a public records search.[45] Due diligence does not require an exhaustive inquiry of every possible means to ascertain the location of a respondent.[46] A court will examine whether the petitioner used all reasonably available resources when attempting to locate respondents.[47]

As noted in the Child Welfare Services Manual, a county department should interview individuals and access databases it has permission to access. A county department should also complete a public records search,[48] such as a property tax search (both real estate and vehicle taxes for registration) and a voter registration search. A county department may also send a "demand letter"[49] requesting information about the father's whereabouts from an agency or company whose records are not public records, such as the North Carolina Division of Motor Vehicles[50] or a private employer.

Due diligence should at least involve attempting to communicate with a missing father at his last known address, phone number, and/or email. If those efforts are unsuccessful, the county department should contact the U.S. Postal Service and/or check the telephone directory (directory assistance, paper copy of a telephone book, or Internet white pages). A county department may reach out to collateral contacts, such as relatives, co-workers, or acquaintances.

Federal law recognizes social media as one way to search for family members.[51] A search of social media sites, such as Facebook or Twitter, may provide information about the parent's location. Oftentimes, a city or state is listed in the member's profile. The father's relatives, friends, and, depending on the age of the child, the child may be "friends" of, or "followers" on, the father's social media sites and may be able to provide the location or contact information for the father. A county department may want to specifically ask the child, relatives, or others if they communicate with the father

---

44. Jones v. Wallis, 211 N.C. App. 353 (2011); *see also* G.S. 1A-1, Rule 4(j1).

45. *Jones*, 211 N.C. App. 353.

46. *Id.*

47. *Id.*; Dowd v. Johnson, ___ N.C. App. ___, 760 S.E.2d 79 (2014).

48. *Jones*, 211 N.C. App. 353; *In re* Clark, 76 N.C. App. 83 (1985).

49. G.S. 7B-302(e) authorizes the county department to make a written demand for confidential information maintained by a public or private agency to the extent permitted by federal law. A written request made pursuant to this statute is commonly referred to as a "demand letter."

50. 18 U.S.C. § 2721(b)(1), (4); *see also* G.S. 7B-302(e).

51. 42 U.S.C. § 675a(a)(1) (addresses an older (16- or 17-year-old) foster youth who will have a permanent plan that transitions him or her to independent living upon turning 18 (also known as Another Planned Permanent Living Arrangement/APPLA) and requires the state to show that it documented its unsuccessful efforts to locate the foster youth's biological family members, including using search technology that includes social media).

through social media and know of his location. A county department may also want to search social media directly to find and/or contact a child's father.

A respondent parent will be appointed provisional counsel upon the filing of the abuse, neglect, or dependency petition. A court may inquire into appointed counsel's efforts to locate his or her client and whether counsel was successful. If counsel was successful in locating the client, without the client's informed consent to disclose his location, the attorney may be prevented from notifying the county department or the court of the father's location because of attorney-client privilege.[52]

Summary

A county department should be prepared to respond to a court's inquiry into what efforts it has made to determine a missing parent's identity and location. A court will expect a county department to have exercised due diligence in its search. What constitutes due diligence is specific to each case.

Although there is not a mandatory checklist of the efforts that must be taken, checklists of possible actions are provided in Appendixes 3A and 3B. The following checklists are meant to be used as a tool to help a county department identify and locate a child's father and are intended to assist the court and the parties in determining what efforts have been made to include the child's father in the abuse, neglect, or dependency proceeding.

---

52. Revised Rules of Prof'l Conduct r. 1.6 (N.C. Bar Ass'n, last amended Oct. 2, 2014).

Appendix 3A

Checklist: Diligent Search to Identify a Father

Purpose: To assist a county department in determining if a man is identified as a child's father through a legal presumption, evidence of paternity, or judicial adjudication. This form may also assist a county department in determining the identity of a putative father or possible biological father.

Using This Form: This form suggests sources of information a county department may look to when exercising due diligence in identifying the father of a child who is the subject of an abuse, neglect, or dependency proceeding. This form is not intended to be an exhaustive list or a mandatory checklist that a county department must complete.

Suggestions for Use: Document the date an action was taken. Record the father's name (if provided) next to the source of information. Document the name of the individual and agency providing the information.

Child's Name: _____

Interviews

___ / ___ / _____ Mother: _____

                                  Name(s) of Father Provided: _____

___ / ___ / _____ Child: _____

                                    Name(s) of Father Provided: _____

___ / ___ / _____ Household Member(s), Name: _____

                                    Name(s) of Father Provided: _____

___ / ___ / _____ Relative(s), Name: _____

                                    Name(s) of Father Provided: _____

___ / ___ / _____ Friend(s), Name: _____

                                    Name(s) of Father Provided: _____

Documents

Birth Certificate	Source of Birth Certificate:	Other Documents:
☐ Original	☐ Parent	☐ Affidavit of Parentage (AOP)
☐ Amended	☐ Vital Records	☐ Marriage Certificate
	☐ Register of Deeds	☐ Court Order Adjudicating Paternity
	☐ Child's Educational Record	☐ Other _____
	Name of Father: _____	

Mother's Marital Status (at Time of Child's Conception through Birth)

___ / ___ / _____ Child's DOB

___ / ___ / _____ Estimated Date of Conception (280 days before DOB)

☐ Never married   ☐ Married ___ / ___ / _____

                            Husband's Name: _____

                            ☐ Divorced ___ / ___ / _____

Child Support Enforcement Agency

___ / ___ / _____   Child Support Enforcement Agency _____

Agency Representative: _____

Father's Name Provided: _____

Court Records

___ / ___ / _____   VCAP (Civil): Case Name: _____

Court and Docket No.: _____

Date of Order: ____ / ____ / _____

Father Named in Order: _____

___ / ___ / _____   ACIS (Criminal): Case Name: _____

Court and Docket No.: _____

Date of Order: ____ / ____ / _____

Father Named in Order: _____

Appendix 3B

Checklist: Diligent Search to Locate a Father

Purpose: This form suggests efforts a county department may take when exercising due diligence in locating the father of a child who is the subject of an abuse, neglect, or dependency proceeding. This form is not intended to be an exhaustive list or a mandatory checklist where each suggestion must be acted upon. The diligence of a search is determined on a case-by-case basis.

Suggestions for Use: Document the date and type of action taken (e.g., letter sent to XYZ address, voicemail left for X at ###-####), the name of the agency or company contacted, and the name of the person interviewed. Record the information provided regarding the father's current or formerly known contact information and/or location.

Child's Name: _____

Father's Name: _____

Contact Child's Father: _____

___ / ___ / _____   Mailed Letter to: _____
_____

___ / ___ / _____   Called Phone Number: _____
☐ No answer   ☐ Left message   ☐ Spoke to: _____

___ / ___ / _____   Sent Email to: _____

Result: _____

Family Interviews

___ / ___ / _____   Mother, Father's Contact Information Provided: _____
_____
_____

___ / ___ / _____   Child, Father's Contact Information Provided: _____
_____
_____

___ / ___ / _____   Household Member or Relative (Name): _____
Information Provided: _____
_____

___ / ___ / _____   Household Member or Relative (Name): _____
Information Provided: _____
_____

Other Interviews

___ / ___ / _____   Employer (Current or Former)
Name of Person Contacted: _____
Information Provided: _____
_____

___ / ___ / _____   Co-Worker (Current or Former) Name: _____
Information Provided: _____
_____

___ / ___ / _____ Child Support Services Agency (Agency Name): _____

Name of Person Contacted: _____

Information Provided: _____

___ / ___ / _____ Landlord (Current or Former) (Name): _____

Information Provided: _____

___ / ___ / _____ Provisional Counsel Appointed to Father (Name): _____

Information Provided: _____

___ / ___ / _____ Department of Public Safety, Division of Adult Corrections (Jail, Incarceration, Probation)

Name of Person and Agency/Facility Contacted: _____

Information Provided: _____

___ / ___ / _____ Utility Company (Electric, Gas, Water) (Company Name): _____

Name of Person Contacted: _____

Information Provided: _____

___ / ___ / _____ Other (Name): _____

Information Provided: _____

Records Search

___ / ___ / _____ DMV Search (Driver's License, Vehicle Registration), State: _____

Information Listed: _____

___ / ___ / _____ Property Tax Search (Real Property, Vehicle), State, County: _____

Information Listed: _____

___ / ___ / _____ Board of Election (Voter Registration), State, County: _____

Information Listed: _____

___ / ___ / _____ N.C. Wildlife Commission or Other State's Equalivent (Hunting/Fishing License): _____

Information Listed: _____

___ / ___ / _____ Professional Licensing Board (Name, State): _____

Information Listed: _____

___ / ___ / _____ Telephone Directory (Directory Assistance, Phone Book, Internet White Pages)

Information Listed: _____

___ / ___ / _____ U.S. Post Office

Information Listed: _____

___ / ___ / _____ Internet Search (Include Social Media): _____

Identify Searches Made: _____

Contact Information Discovered: _____

___ / ___ / _____ Internal Agency Database

Program Contacted: Child Welfare, Child Support, Other _____

Information Listed: _____

___ / ___ / _____ Offender Public Information Search

Information Listed: _____

___ / ___ / _____ N.C. Sex Offender and Public Protections Registry Search

Information Listed: _____

___ / ___ / _____ N.C. Statewide Automated Victim Assistance and Notification (NC SAVAN)

Information Listed: _____

___ / ___ / _____ VCAP (Civil): Case Name: _____

Court and Docket No.: _____ *Date of Record:* ___ / ___ / _____

Information Listed: _____

___ / ___ / _____ ACIS (Criminal): Case Name: _____

Court and Docket No.: _____ *Date of Record:* ___ / ___ / _____

Information Listed: _____

Chapter 4

Determining When Paternity Is at Issue

This chapter discusses the mandatory inquiry that the court in an abuse, neglect, or dependency action must make about whether paternity is an issue. The court must answer the question and make findings of the efforts that have been taken to establish paternity. To do that, the court will need to look to common law and to various North Carolina statutes that address paternity. This chapter explains those laws and the procedures in North Carolina to assist the court and the parties in determining whether paternity is an issue.

Required Court Inquiry

Along with the inquiry to identify and locate a missing parent (see chapter 3), the court must inquire as to whether paternity is an issue in the abuse, neglect, or dependency action.[1] This court inquiry takes place throughout the proceeding. If nonsecure custody was ordered, the court's inquiry starts with the first hearing on the need for continued nonsecure custody and continues with every hearing on nonsecure custody thereafter.[2] The inquiry must also be made at the pre-adjudication hearing, and if the child is adjudicated abused, neglected, or dependent, at the initial dispositional hearing.[3]

_____

1. Chapter 7B, Section 506(h)(1) of the North Carolina General Statutes (hereinafter G.S.); G.S. 7B-901(b). Note that the statutory language refers to whether paternity is "at issue" and "an issue." The term "an issue" is used throughout this chapter. _See also id._ § 7B-800.1(a)(3).

2. G.S. 7B-506(h)(1).

3. G.S. 7B-800.1(a)(3); 7B-901(b).

Paternity is obviously an issue when the father's identity is unknown and no father is named by the county department as a respondent parent in the abuse, neglect, or dependency petition that has been filed with the district court. But that is not the only circumstance when paternity is an issue. Data collected by the Urban Institute indicated that paternity is known for more than 80 percent of foster children.[4] However, knowing the identity of a child's father is not the same as having paternity established. Paternity may be raised as an issue when someone has been identified as the child's father but not adjudicated as such. Possible scenarios include:

1. when only one man is believed to be the child's father but he is not married to the mother and no steps have been taken to establish his paternity;

2. when there is a legally recognized father based on the marital presumption of the child's legitimacy or an executed Affidavit of Parentage but someone else is believed to be the child's biological father; or

3. when a party in the abuse, neglect, or dependency proceeding raises paternity as an issue when that party believes the named respondent father is not the child's father.

A county department may also have raised paternity in its petition, putting the court and parties on notice that it intends to prove the paternity or non-paternity of a respondent as part of the abuse, neglect, or dependency action.

A party may raise the issue of paternity during the court's mandatory inquiry. When paternity is raised as an issue, a good starting point for the court's determination as to whether paternity is an issue is to ask the party why he or she is raising the issue and also ask the county department how it decided whether to name or not name a respondent father. The county department should be prepared to explain both the basis on which it made its decision and the information on which it relied.

---

4. 1 N.C. Div. of Soc. Servs., Child Welfare Services Manual Ch. VIII, § 1412, at 12 (2009) (citing Karin Malm, "Getting Noncustodial Dads Involved in the Lives of Foster Children," *Caring for Children: Facts and Perspectives Brief No. 3* (Nov. 2003)), http://info.dhhs.state.nc.us/olm/manuals/dss/csm-60/man/pdfdocs/CS1412.pdf.

Note that chapters in volume 1 of the North Carolina Division of Social Services Manual that were last amended before 2013 are referred to as the "Family Services Manual," and chapters that were amended in 2013 or later are referred to as the "Child Welfare Services Manual." For consistency in this book, all chapters will hereinafter be referred to as the "Child Welfare Services Manual."

Court Findings

If the court concludes that paternity is not an issue, the court should make findings supporting that conclusion. Examples of findings may be

- the named respondent father's paternity was adjudicated in the court action, captioned X versus X, docket number X, by order signed on X date or
- the marital presumption of the child's legitimacy applies and, although it is a rebuttable presumption, it is not challenged.

If the court determines that paternity is an issue, the court must make findings of the efforts that have been taken to establish paternity.[5] The court may also want to add the reason paternity is an issue in its findings. Examples of findings include the following:

- No efforts have been made.
- The mother and her husband have relied on the rebuttable marital presumption of the child's legitimacy but seek a court order that adjudicates the husband's paternity in order to replace the rebuttable presumption.
- The parties executed an Affidavit of Parentage but there has not been an adjudication of paternity.
- An action addressing paternity is pending.
- There has been an adjudication of paternity but a party in this action has raised paternity and is not collaterally estopped from doing so.

To determine whether paternity is an issue and identify the efforts that have been taken to establish paternity, the court should look to North Carolina common law and statutes that address parentage. The court must also give full faith and credit to a paternity determination that was made in another state.[6]

The Child's Birth Certificate

A court may start its inquiry on the question of whether paternity is an issue by looking at whether a father is named on the child's birth certificate, but the inquiry cannot end there. In North Carolina, there is no presumption that a father who is named on a birth certificate has had his paternity *judicially* determined.[7] A father may be named on a

---

5. G.S. 7B-506(h)(1); 7B-901(b).

6. G.S. 110-132.1.

7. *See* G.S. 130A-101(e), (f); 49-12; 49-13; 130A-118(b)(2), (3); Title 10A of the North Carolina Administrative Code (hereinafter N.C.A.C.), Chapter 41H, § .0910. *But see In re J.K.C.*, 218 N.C. App. 22 (2012) (there is a rebuttable presumption that the father took the required legal steps necessary to establish paternity if he is named on the child's amended birth certificate; note that this holding applies to a termination of parental rights (TPR) action on the ground set forth at G.S. 7B-1111(a)(5) of an unwed father failing to acknowledge or establish

child's birth certificate through a variety of different ways, not all of which resulted from an order adjudicating paternity. As a result, a court may determine that paternity is an issue even when a father is named on a child's birth certificate.

Recorded at Child's Birth

Within ten days of a live birth occurring in North Carolina, a birth certificate must be completed and filed with the local registrar in the county where the birth occurred.[8] The mother is listed on the birth certificate. If she is not married at any time from the child's conception through birth, a father will only be named on the birth certificate if there is a properly executed "Affidavit of Parentage" (hereinafter AOP).[9] An AOP is an admission of paternity that is signed, under oath, by both the mother and father.[10] The father declares that he believes he is the natural father of the child.[11] The mother consents to the man's assertion that he is the father, declares the man is the father, and further declares that she was not married during the time of conception through the child's birth.[12] Both the AOP and birth certificate will be recorded with the local register of deeds and the State Registrar.[13] The AOP is not an adjudication of paternity.[14] If an AOP was executed after December 12, 2005, it does not create a presumption of paternity.[15] Instead, the AOP is an admission of the parties who signed it, and a certified

---

paternity before the TPR action was initiated). S.L. 2013-129, § 35 codified this holding as applied to TPR actions brought pursuant to G.S. 7B-1111(a)(5). *See also* Gunter v. Gunter, 228 N.C. App. 138 (2013) (unpublished) (mother's reliance on holding of *J.K.C.* that husband's name on child's birth certificate *judicially* established paternity was misplaced).

8. G.S. 130A-101(a), (b) (the certificate is completed by the person in charge of the hospital or medical facility where the child is born); 130A-101(c) (if the birth occurred outside of a hospital or medical facility, the certificate is completed by (1) the physician in attendance at or immediately after the birth, (2) any other person in attendance at or immediately after the birth, (3) the father, (4) the mother, or (5) the person in charge of the premises where the birth occurred).

9. G.S. 130A-101(f).

10. *Id.* There are three Affidavit of Parentage forms: DHHS 1660, DSS 4697, and AOC-CV-604. The Administrative Office of the Courts (AOC) form is available at www.nccourts.org/Forms/Documents/266.pdf.

11. G.S. 130A-101(f).

12. *Id.* The affidavit must also include the mother's and father's social security numbers and information explaining the effect of signing the affidavit, including information about parental rights and responsibilities.

13. G.S. 130A-97(5), (6); 130A-99; 130A-101(a), (f); 130A-118(a).

14. *See* G.S. 130A-101(f) (a certified copy is admissible in an action to establish paternity).

15. S.L. 1993-333, § 1 created a presumption of paternity for an AOP pursuant to G.S. 130A-101(f), but the presumption was removed in 2005 by S.L. 2005-389, § 4. Even when the presumption existed, G.S. 130A-101(f) stated that a certified copy of the affidavit was admissible in an action to establish paternity.

copy of the AOP may be admitted as evidence of paternity in a court proceeding where paternity is an issue.[16]

If the mother is married during the time of the child's conception through birth, her husband must be named as the father on the child's birth certificate.[17] An AOP is not required. There are two statutory exceptions to when a husband is named as the child's father on the birth certificate. Another man should be named as the child's father when

1. a court has adjudicated paternity for another man or
2. the mother, her husband, and the putative father each sign an AOP acknowledging that the putative father is the child's father, and there is DNA testing showing that the putative father is the child's biological father.[18]

Once the birth certificate is completed, it will be sent to the local register of deeds and the State Registrar.[19] If a man other than the husband is named as the father, the executed AOP or proof of the court order adjudicating paternity will be sent as well.

Amendment of Birth Certificate after Child's Birth

After a birth certificate is recorded with the State Registrar, it may only be amended by the State Registrar.[20] A birth certificate must be amended if the State Registrar receives

- notification from the clerk of court of a court order addressing parentage that differs from what is on the child's birth certificate,[21]
- satisfactory proof of a court order that determines parentage that differs from what is on the child's birth certificate,[22] or
- a certified copy of the marriage certificate showing that the child's parents were subsequently married when no father was named on the child's birth certificate.[23]

The Court Inquiry

In the abuse, neglect, or dependency proceeding, when the court is determining whether paternity is an issue, the court may inquire as to how a man was named as the child's father on the birth certificate. The court should determine if the birth certificate

---

16. G.S. 130A-101(f).

17. G.S. 130A-101(e).

18. *Id.*

19. G.S. 130A-97(5), (6); 130A-99; 130A-101(a), (f); *see* 130A-118(a).

20. G.S. 130A-118.

21. G.S. 130A-118(b)(2); *see also id.* § 130A-119.

22. G.S. 130A-118(b)(3); G.S. 49-13 and 49-12.1(e) require the clerk of court send a certified copy of a court order of legitimation.

23. G.S. 49-13; 130A-118(b)(1). *See also* 10A N.C.A.C. 41H, § .1102 (completed affidavits by the mother and father, information about the father, and the marriage certificate must be provided to the State Registrar before a new birth certificate may be issued that adds the father's name based on the child's legitimation resulting from the parents' marriage).

has been amended, reflecting that some action was taken to name the father.[24] A court may also ask the county department if it obtained a certified copy of the child's birth certificate and any accompanying documents (such as an AOP, marriage certificate, or court order) from the local register of deeds or State Registrar. If a county department obtained a certified copy of any documents that identify the child's father, it should introduce the documents in evidence at any hearing addressing whether paternity is an issue.

The court may want to hear testimony from one or both of the respondent parents in an attempt to answer questions such as

- Was the man named on the birth certificate because he was the mother's husband at the time of the child's conception or birth?
- Was he named because the mother and father signed an AOP?
- Was he named because the mother or father have been to court for a paternity, legitimation, divorce, custody, child support (civil or criminal), adoption, or previous juvenile proceeding involving the child who is the subject of the abuse, neglect, or dependency proceeding?
- Was he named because the mother and father married one another after the child was born and filed affidavits with the State Registrar requesting an amended birth certificate?
- Is there another reason the father is named on the child's birth certificate?

Upon receiving this evidence, the court will need to apply North Carolina's laws addressing parentage when determining whether paternity is an issue in the abuse, neglect, or dependency proceeding.

Applying the North Carolina Laws That Address Parentage

Parentage by Operation of Law

There are two North Carolina statutes that establish parentage as a matter of law: one covering adoption and the other addressing heterologous artificial insemination. In both these situations, the child is not the biological child of the father,[25] but the respective laws establish the child's parentage.

Adoption creates the parent-child relationship, giving the child the same legal status as that of a legitimate child born to the adoptive parents.[26] Adoption also severs the

---

24. G.S. 130A-118(a), (b); *see In re* J.K.C., 218 N.C. App. 22 (2012).

25. *But see* G.S. 48-1-106(d) (he may be the child's biological father if his spouse adopts the child in a stepparent adoption).

26. G.S. 48-1-106(a), (b); *see also id.* § 29-17(a), (c).

relationship between the biological (or former adoptive) parent and the child.[27] An adoptive father is the child's father under North Carolina law. In this situation, paternity should not be an issue in an abuse, neglect, or dependency proceeding.

A child "born as the result of heterologous artificial insemination shall be considered at law in all respects the same as a naturally conceived legitimate child of the husband and wife requesting and consenting in writing to the use of such technique."[28] In heterologous artificial insemination, the sperm donor is not the woman's husband.[29] Although there is no dispute that the husband is not the child's biological father, the husband is the child's father by operation of law. As a result, his paternity over the child is not an issue in an abuse, neglect, or dependency proceeding.

Child Conceived by Rape and Parent Is Convicted

If a child is conceived by a first- or second-degree forcible rape,[30] statutory rape of a child by an adult,[31] or first-degree statutory rape[32] and the perpetrator is convicted of that criminal act, that perpetrator's rights over the child are limited. Although the criminal defendant is the child's biological parent, he or she is not a party to and has no rights in an abuse, neglect, or dependency action involving that child.[33] He or she is not entitled to receive notice of an adoption petition filed for that child, and his or her consent to the child's adoption is not required.[34] Because a parent who falls under this category has no rights in the abuse, neglect, dependency, or adoption proceedings, a court may determine that paternity is not an issue.

Although this person's parental rights are limited by statute, he or she is still legally recognized as the child's parent. The district court may hear a termination of parental rights action naming the criminal defendant as the respondent even after the court has determined that paternity was not an issue in the abuse, neglect, or dependency proceeding. One of the statutory grounds to terminate a parent's rights to a child is the parent's conviction for a sexually related offense designated in the North Carolina

---

27. G.S. 48-1-106(a), (b). *See also id.* § 29-17(b), (d). *But see id.* § 48-1-106(d) (a stepparent adoption does not affect the relationship between the child and parent who is the spouse; the adoption only severs the child's relationship with the parent who is not the spouse).

28. G.S. 49A-1. Other than this one statute, North Carolina law does not address parentage or a child's legitimacy when a child is born using reproductive technology that involves a sperm donor, egg donor, or gestational carrier. Without additional statutes or case law, questions remain as to what, if any, rights a sperm donor, egg donor, or gestational carrier has to the child conceived through reproductive technology.

29. Taber's Cyclopedic Medical Dictionary (22d ed. 2013); Stedman's Medical Dictionary (28th ed. 2006).

30. G.S. 14-27.21; 14-27.22.

31. G.S. 14-27.23.

32. G.S. 14-27.24.

33. G.S. 7B-401.1(b)(3). *See also id.* §§ 14-27.21(c); 14-27.22(c); 14-27.23(d); 14-27.24(c). Note *id.* § 50-13.1(a) (that parent has no rights in a civil custody action for that child).

34. G.S. 14-27.21(c); 14-27.22(c); 14-27.23(d); 14-27.24(c); 48-2-401(c)(3); 48-3-603(a)(9).

criminal statutes when the crime resulted in the child's conception.[35] The language in the termination of parental rights statute is broader than in the abuse, neglect, or dependency and adoption statutes. The general reference in the termination of parental rights statute to sexually related offenses resulting in a child's conception includes a conviction for the statutory rape of a person age 15 or younger that results in a child's conception.[36] In contrast, the rights of a parent who is convicted of statutory rape of a person age 15 or younger that results in the child's conception are not limited by the abuse, neglect, or dependency and the adoption statutes.[37]

The Marital Presumption

In North Carolina, there is a common law presumption that a husband is the father of a child born to or conceived by his wife during their marriage.[38] Conception is presumed to have occurred ten lunar months, or 280 days, prior to the child's birth.[39] The marital presumption of legitimacy is rebuttable by clear and convincing evidence.[40] Evidence includes testimony of the husband's lack of access to his wife during the period of conception or the husband's impotency; perceived racial differences between the mother, husband, and child; or genetic test results.[41] Because the marital presumption is rebuttable, paternity may be at issue even when a husband is named on the child's birth certificate and is legally recognized as the child's father.

Children Born Out of Wedlock

Legitimation and paternity actions require that the child be "born out of wedlock."[42] "Out of wedlock" has two definitions. First, a child is born out of wedlock when his or her mother is not married during the time of the child's conception through birth.

---

35. G.S. 7B-1111(a)(11).

36. *Id.*; G.S. 14-27.25 (victim is 15 or younger and defendant is at least four years older).

37. G.S. 7B-401.1(b)(3); 48-2-401(c)(3); 48-3-603(a)(9); *In re* J.L., 183 N.C. App. 126 (2007).

38. Eubanks v. Eubanks, 273 N.C. 189 (1968); Jones v. Patience, 121 N.C. App. 434 (1996); State v. White, 300 N.C. 494 (1980); State v. McDowell, 101 N.C. 734 (1888); *see also* G.S. 50-11.1 (if a marriage is ultimately annulled because it is voidable or is a bigamous marriage, a child born during that marriage is a legitimate child of that marriage).

39. Byerly v. Tolbert, 250 N.C. 27 (1959); Lenoir Cty. *ex rel.* Dudley v. Dawson, 60 N.C. App. 122 (1982); *see also* G.S. 48-3-601(2)b.1.

40. Jeffries v. Moore, 148 N.C. App. 364 (2002) (Greene, J., concurring); *In re* Papathanassiou, 195 N.C. App. 278 (2009); *see also* G.S. 49-12.1.

41. *Eubanks*, 273 N.C. 189; Wake Cty. *ex rel.* Manning v. Green, 53 N.C. App. 26 (1981); *Jeffries*, 148 N.C. App. 364; *see* G.S. 8-57.2 ("Presumed father or mother as witnesses where paternity at issue"). *See also* Cole v. Cole, 74 N.C. App. 247 (1985) (evidence of husband's infertility dramatically drops the high probability of paternity blood test results; in this case, the scientific evidence of husband's sterility at the time of the child's conception reduced the probability of the paternity test result from 95.98 percent to zero), *aff'd per curiam*, 314 N.C. 660 (1985).

42. G.S. 49-10; 49-12; 49-14.

Second, "out of wedlock" refers to the relationship of the child's parents with one another. A child is born out of wedlock if his or her mother is married to someone other than his or her biological father at the time of the child's conception or birth.[43]

Legitimation

Legitimation is about the child's status.[44] A child is "declared" or "held to be" legitimate.[45] The child is legally recognized as the child of his or her parents and is entitled to inherit from his or her mother and father intestate.[46] Legitimation differs from paternity[47] because paternity solely addresses the father's status as the child's biological father.[48] Legitimation addresses the child's and father's status and "impose[s] upon the father and mother all of the lawful parental privileges and rights, as well as all of the obligations which parents owe to their lawful issue."[49]

A child who is born out of wedlock may be legitimated through his or her parents' marriage, which occurs after the child's birth,[50] or by court order.[51] Both of these legitimation methods allow the father to establish himself as the child's lawful parent.[52]

Legitimation through Marriage after the Child's Birth

A child born out of wedlock may be legitimated if his or her mother and "reputed father" marry one another at any time after the child is born.[53] No court action is required. The child's birth certificate will be amended to name the father after the State Registrar receives a certified copy of the marriage certificate and completed affidavits from the mother and father acknowledging that the husband is the child's

---

43. Wright v. Gann, 27 N.C. App. 45 (1975); *In re* Legitimation of Locklear, 314 N.C. 412 (1985). Note that at the time these cases were decided, G.S. 49-14(b) required a beyond a reasonable doubt standard to establish paternity. S.L. 1999-333, § 3 amended the standard of proof, effective October 1, 1993, to clear, cogent, and convincing evidence.

44. *See* Carter v. Carter, 232 N.C. 614 (1950).

45. *Id.*; G.S. 49-10; 49-12.

46. *See Carter*, 232 N.C. 614; G.S. 49-11, 49-12; 29-18; 29-19(a) (legitimate child of mother). *See also* G.S. 29-19(b) (makes no reference to a child's legitimation as to father); Greenlee v. Quinn, 255 N.C. 601 (1961) (legitimated child has same rights to inherit from collateral relations of mother and father).

47. G.S. 49-14 ("The establishment of paternity shall not have the effect of legitimation."). Smith v. Barbour, 154 N.C. App. 402 (2002) (legitimation vests greater rights in the parent and child than a paternity order).

48. G.S. 49-14. *But see id.* § 49-15 (allows for custody and support).

49. G.S. 49-11; *see In re* Papathanassiou, 195 N.C. App. 278 (2009).

50. G.S. 49-12.

51. G.S. 49-10; 49-12.1.

52. *In re* Legitimation of Locklear, 314 N.C. 412 (1985).

53. G.S. 49-12 (the term "reputed father" and not "putative father" is used).

natural father.[54] Even if a request to amend the birth certificate is not made, the child will still be recognized as the legitimate child of his or her parents who married after the child's birth.[55]

The statute does not explicitly state whether the subsequent marriage that legitimates the child creates a rebuttable presumption of the child's legitimacy, as when a child is conceived or born during a marriage. The North Carolina Supreme Court has held that "[t]he use of the word 'reputed' rather than 'putative' in [G.S. 49-12] 'was intended merely to dispense with absolute proof of paternity, so that, if the child is "regarded," "deemed," "considered," or "held in thought," by the parents themselves, as their child, either before or after marriage, it is legitimate.' "[56] The court further held that a "reputed father" who reasonably believed he was the child's father and married the child's mother may later raise the issue of whether the child was born of the marriage in a proceeding for the court to decide.[57] Based on this holding, the presumption of legitimacy resulting from the parents' subsequent marriage is rebuttable. Based on case law and the legitimation statute that applies when the mother was married to another man during the child's conception through birth, the burden of proof to rebut the marital presumption of legitimacy is clear and convincing evidence.[58]

Paternity may be an issue when a child is legitimated by his or her parents' marriage. It is important to note that a husband or wife may be estopped from subsequently raising paternity as an issue. A man who knows that he is not the child's biological father but marries the child's mother, holds himself out as the child's father, and requests an amended birth certificate to name him as the father is estopped from later challenging his paternity.[59] Similarly, a mother who has legitimated her child through marriage and requested an amended birth certificate naming her husband as the child's father may not bring a paternity action against another man.[60]

---

54. G.S. 49-13 (note that *Jones v. McDowell*, 53 N.C. App. 434 (1981), held that the language requiring the child's surname to be changed to the father's surname is unconstitutional); 130A-118(b)(1); 10A N.C.A.C. 41H, §§ .1101, .1102. *See* Myers v. Myers, 39 N.C. App. 201 (1978).

55. *See* Batcheldor v. Boyd, 119 N.C. App. 204 (1995).

56. Carter v. Carter, 232 N.C. 614, 617 (1950) (quoting Bowman v. Howard, 182 N.C. 662, ___, 110 S.E. 98, 100 (1921)).

57. *Carter*, 232 N.C. 614. *See* Chambers v. Chambers, 43 N.C. App. 361, 364 (1979) (A husband who marries a child's mother after the child's birth knowing that he is not the child's father and who completes a false affidavit to amend the child's birth certificate to name him as the child's father is collaterally estopped from raising paternity as an issue.).

58. G.S. 49-12.1; Jeffries v. Moore, 148 N.C. App. 364 (2002) (Greene, J., concurring); *In re* Papathanassiou, 195 N.C. App. 278 (2009).

59. *Chambers*, 43 N.C. App. 361 (a man who knows he is not the child's father is not a "reputed father"; he must adopt the child to assume the status of father).

60. *See* Lewis v. Stitt, 86 N.C. App. 103 (1987) (when child is legitimated by marriage, the mother may not subsequently initiate a paternity action against a man who is not her husband).

Legitimation by Court Order

Legitimation is a special proceeding in the superior court that declares a child is legitimate.[61] The clerk of superior court presides over the legitimation proceeding.[62] The clerk must transfer the proceeding to superior court when there is an issue of fact, request for equitable relief, or equitable defense.[63]

A legitimation proceeding is commenced when a putative father files a verified petition seeking the child's legitimation.[64] The putative father must name the mother (if living) and child as necessary parties.[65] A putative father may bring a legitimation action when the mother was married at the time of the child's conception or birth.[66] In that case, the husband is also a necessary party.[67]

A legitimation proceeding must address the factual question of the putative father's paternity, for the only issue that is decided is whether the petitioner is the child's biological father.[68] When the mother was not married during the time of the child's conception through birth, the court may declare the child legitimate "[i]f it appears to the court that the petitioner is the father of the child."[69] Neither the statute nor case law addresses the required burden of proof. It is unclear if the civil standard of preponderance of the evidence or the higher standard used to establish paternity in a civil paternity action[70] or to rebut the marital presumption—clear, cogent, and convincing evidence—applies. A best interests of the child analysis does not apply.[71] When the mother was married to a different man during the time of the child's conception through birth, the statute authorizing legitimation in that context requires that the putative father prove by clear and convincing evidence that he is the child's father.[72]

When a child is legitimated, the clerk of court must send a certified copy of the legitimation order to the State Registrar.[73] The State Registrar must amend the child's birth certificate to name the father.[74] If the mother was married when the child was conceived or born, the husband's name will be removed as the child's father. The court's

61. G.S. 49-10; 49-12.1; *see also In re* Legitimation of Locklear, 314 N.C. 412 (1985).
62. G.S. 1-301.2(a).
63. G.S. 1-301.2(b). *See also Locklear*, 314 N.C. 412.
64. G.S. 49-10; 49-12.1. Note that the statute uses the term "putative father" without defining the term.
65. G.S. 49-10; 49-12.1.
66. G.S. 49-12.1.
67. *Id.*
68. *Locklear*, 314 N.C. 412; *In re* Papathanassiou, 195 N.C. App. 278 (2009).
69. G.S. 49-10.
70. G.S. 49-14(b).
71. *Papathanassiou*, 195 N.C. App. 278.
72. G.S. 49-12.1(b).
73. G.S. 49-13; 49-12.1(e).
74. G.S. 49-13; 130A-118(b)(2), (3); 10A N.C.A.C. 41H, § .1101.

determination that the petitioner and not the husband is the child's biological father terminates the husband's rights to the child.[75]

Paternity Action

A civil paternity action for a child born out of wedlock is heard in the district court.[76] The action may be initiated by the father, the mother, the child, or a personal representative of the mother or child at any time before the child's 18th birthday.[77] A county department or state or county child support services agency may also initiate a paternity action if the child or the mother, because of her medical expenses, is likely to become a public charge.[78] Although a child may initiate a paternity action, a child is not a necessary party when the action is initiated by a different party.[79]

Paternity must be proved by clear, cogent, and convincing evidence.[80] If a paternity action is initiated after the child turns 3 years old or within one year of the father's death and paternity is contested, there must be evidence of blood or genetic marker testing.[81] If the court's adjudication regarding paternity differs from what is reflected on the child's birth certificate, the clerk must send a copy of the order or provide written notice of the contents of the order to the State Registrar.[82] Upon receipt of that information, the State Registrar must amend the child's birth certificate.[83]

Declaratory Judgments

A child's legitimation or a father's paternity or non-paternity of a child may be ordered through a declaratory judgment.[84] Declaratory judgments have been brought in estate proceedings where a child of a decedent who died intestate sought to have his or her right to inherit from the alleged father's estate determined through a declaration that the child was legitimated by the decedent or that paternity was established entitling the child to inherit from the decedent.[85] Declaratory judgments regarding parentage

---

75. *Papathanassiou*, 195 N.C. App. 278.

76. G.S. 49-14; 7A-244.

77. G.S. 49-14 (uses the term "putative father"); 49-16(1) (uses the term "father"; it is unclear if "father" includes both a legal father (i.e., mother's husband) and a putative father; if a putative father initiates a paternity action and there is a legal father, the legal father is a necessary party pursuant to G.S. 1A-1, Rule 19).

78. G.S. 49-16(2); 110-130.

79. Smith v. Bumgarner, 115 N.C. App. 149 (1994).

80. G.S. 49-14(b). Prior to October 1, 1993, the standard of proof was beyond a reasonable doubt. S.L. 1993-333, § 3 amended the standard to clear, cogent, and convincing evidence.

81. G.S. 49-14(d). If the putative father is deceased before the action commences, the action must be initiated within one year of the putative father's death or within the time specified in G.S. 28A-19-3(a) for presentation of claims against his estate. *See* G.S. 49-14(c).

82. G.S. 130A-119; *see also id.* §§ 130A-118(b)(2), (3).

83. G.S. 130A-118(b)(2), (3).

84. G.S. 1-253.

85. Batcheldor v. Boyd, 119 N.C. App. 204 (1995); Mitchell v. Freuler, 297 N.C. 206 (1979).

are not limited to estate proceedings.[86] A declaratory judgment action has also been initiated outside of the context of an estate proceeding to declare that a man was not the child's father.[87]

If there is a declaratory judgment of paternity or non-paternity,[88] the clerk of court should send to the State Registrar satisfactory proof or written notice of the resulting order that contains the different or additional information related to a person's parentage.[89] Upon receiving notification from the clerk of court, the State Registrar must amend the child's birth certificate to reflect the court's determination of parentage.[90]

Court Actions Where Paternity Is an Element of the Claim

A man's paternity of a child may have been determined in a court action when paternity was raised as an issue or was an element of the claim.

Criminal Action for Nonsupport

A parent may be convicted for willfully neglecting or refusing to provide adequate support for his or her child.[91] A conviction requires that the State prove three elements of the crime beyond a reasonable doubt: (1) the defendant is the child's parent, (2) the defendant failed to provide his or her child with adequate support, and (3) the failure was willful.[92] A man cannot be convicted of this crime without an adjudication of his paternity because the "verdict necessitate[s] a finding, express or implied, that defendant [is] the father of the minor children."[93]

If the judgment in the criminal action for nonsupport makes a conclusion about parentage that is different from what is stated on the child's birth certificate, the clerk should send written notification or satisfactory proof of the court's determination of parentage to the State Registrar.[94] The State Registrar must then amend the child's birth certificate to reflect the court's determination.[95]

---

86. G.S. 1-253 ("Courts of record . . . shall have power to declare rights, status, and other legal relations, whether or not further relief is or could be claimed.").

87. *In re* Williamson, 91 N.C. App. 668 (1988) (petitioners in a termination of parental rights action also filed for a declaratory judgment finding that the respondent was not child's father; however, petitioners voluntarily dismissed the declaratory judgment claim).

88. G.S. 1-253 (a declaration may be affirmative or negative).

89. G.S. 130A-119; 130A-118(b)(2), (3). Note that *id.* § 130A-118(b)(3) does not limit who may submit to the State Registrar satisfactory proof of a court order related to parentage; a parent may submit an order with a request for an amended birth certificate. *See also* 10A N.C.A.C. 41H, §§ .0909, .0910.

90. G.S. 130A-118(b)(2), (3).

91. G.S. 14-322; 49-2.

92. State *ex rel.* New Bern Child Support Agency v. Lewis, 311 N.C. 727 (1984).

93. *Id.* at 731.

94. G.S. 130A-119; 130A-118(b)(2), (3). *See* note 89, *supra*.

95. G.S. 130A-118(b)(2), (3).

Divorce and Child Custody

An absolute divorce is an action to dissolve a marriage.[96] A complaint for divorce must state the name and age of any minor child or children born during the marriage or state that no children were born during the marriage.[97] Although children born during a marriage must be named in the divorce complaint, paternity and custody are not necessarily adjudicated along with the divorce. An absolute divorce may be granted without any provisions addressing paternity or custody of the minor children.

A judgment for absolute divorce may find that a child or children were born during the marriage. A divorce order may also state that the husband is the father of a child because of the court's reliance on the marital presumption that a child born during a marriage is the legitimate child of the husband and wife. Findings like these are not necessarily a judicial determination of paternity.[98] Paternity is not a necessary element of the claim for an absolute divorce, which is granted on the ground of living separate and apart for one year or "incurable insanity."[99]

Although paternity is not a necessary element of a divorce, paternity of a child born during the marriage may be raised in the divorce proceeding.[100] If paternity is raised as an issue, a judgment that addresses whether the child is born during the marriage or whether the husband is the child's father is an adjudication of paternity or non-paternity. To determine if paternity was adjudicated in a divorce proceeding, the court in an abuse, neglect, or dependency proceeding should examine

- whether paternity was raised as an issue;
- whether the divorce judgment addressed child custody, including visitation; and
- the evidence that was introduced to prove or disprove paternity.

Child custody may be decided in a divorce proceeding[101] or in a separate civil child custody action.[102] Paternity may be an element of the child custody claim.[103] Evidence of paternity may be introduced in a hearing and may consist of genetic testing or

---

96. G.S. 50-8.

97. *Id.*

98. Guilford Cty. *ex rel.* Gardner v. Davis, 123 N.C. App. 527 (1996) (divorce judgment identified husband as child's father based solely on the marital presumption of legitimacy; divorce judgment did not adjudicate paternity where the issue was not litigated, no evidence of paternity was introduced, and paternity was not necessary to adjudicate the divorce).

99. *Id.; see also* G.S. 50-6; 50-5.1.

100. Sutton v. Sutton, 56 N.C. App. 740 (1982).

101. G.S. 50-11.2; 50-13.5(b)(3), (5), (6).

102. G.S. 50-13.1; *see also id.* § 49-15.

103. Rice v. Rice, 147 N.C. App. 505, 508 (2001) ("[I]t is illogical for the consent order and judgment to operate as *res judicata* for child support and visitation rights, and not for issues of paternity."). Paternity is not an element of a custody action that involves a non-parent. G.S. 50-13.1.

witness testimony. Paternity may also be proved in an uncontested hearing by admissions or stipulations of the parties. In an uncontested hearing, a court may consider as part of the evidence a party's acknowledgment of paternity made in the court pleadings.[104] A court finding and conclusion that the parties are the biological parents of the child(ren) is an adjudication of paternity.[105]

If a divorce judgment addresses child custody or visitation, paternity has been adjudicated by the court.[106] If a settlement agreement addressing custody or visitation is incorporated into a divorce judgment or custody order, paternity has been adjudicated.[107]

When a divorce judgment determines that the husband is not the father of a child born during the marriage, the clerk of court should send written notification or satisfactory proof of the court's determination to the State Registrar. If a civil custody order names a father when no father or a different father is named on the child's birth certificate, the clerk of court should send written notification or satisfactory proof of the court's determination of parentage to the State Registrar. The State Registrar must then amend the child's birth certificate to reflect the court's paternity determination.[108]

Child Support

An action for child support is another civil action that may adjudicate paternity.[109] Child support may be ordered through a variety of proceedings. Although not required, a divorce judgment may have a provision for child support if there are minor children born during the marriage.[110] Parents, a person or agency with custody of a child or bringing an action for custody of the child, or the child through a guardian may initiate a child support action.[111] The State or a county child support services agency may also seek child support.[112] If more than one state or country is involved, a county child support services agency or parent may initiate a child support action under the Uniform Interstate Family Support Act.[113]

104. *Rice,* 147 N.C. App. 505.

105. Helms v. Landry, 363 N.C. 738 (2009) (based on reasons stated in the dissenting opinion in *Helms v. Landry,* 194 N.C. App. 787 (2009) (Jackson, J., dissenting)).

106. *Rice,* 147 N.C. App. 505 (paternity was adjudicated in a divorce when the father acknowledged paternity in the verified complaint for absolute divorce, the mother admitted that the marriage produced three children in her answer and counterclaim, and the separation agreement, which was incorporated into and made part of the divorce judgment, stated that there were three children born of the marriage and addressed custody and child support).

107. *Id.*

108. G.S. 130A-118(b)(2), (3); 130A-119. *See* note 89, *supra.*

109. *See* G.S. 110-132.2; 52C-3-305(b)(1); 52C-4-401(b); 52C-4-402; 52C-7-704(b)(3).

110. G.S. 50-11.2; 50-13.5(b)(3), (5), (6). *See also Rice,* 147 N.C. App. 505.

111. G.S. 50-13.4(a).

112. G.S. 110-130.

113. G.S. 52C-3-301(c) ("[A]n individual petitioner or support enforcement agency may initiate a proceeding . . .").

Absent a statutory exception, the court may only order the child's *parents* to pay child support, such that paternity is an element of a child support action between a mother and father.[114] A child support obligation may be based on the marital presumption of legitimacy, a judicial determination of paternity, or an Affidavit of Parentage (AOP) that has been executed by the mother and father.[115] When a child support services agency relies on an AOP to establish a child support obligation, North Carolina law treats the AOP as an adjudication of paternity for purposes of the child support case only.[116] The AOP does not have the effect of an adjudication of paternity for the abuse, neglect, or dependency action. When paternity is raised as an issue in the abuse, neglect, or dependency proceeding, the court will need to inquire as to how a child support obligation was established and whether paternity was adjudicated by the court in the child support case.

Child Support Services and the Establishment of a Child Support Obligation

North Carolina's child support enforcement program is governed by Article 9 of G.S. Chapter 110.[117] The purpose of the child support services program is to provide for the financial support of dependent children.[118] A child support services agency finds absent parents, establishes paternity for the purpose of obtaining child support, establishes and enforces child support obligations, and, if the child receives public assistance, ensures that the right to support is assigned from the caretaker to the state, creating a debt owed to the state.[119] Child support services are available to parents and custodians of minor children regardless of whether public assistance is received for

---

114. G.S. 50-13.4(b). The court may order a person or agency standing in loco parentis to the child to pay support if that person has voluntarily agreed in writing to assume a support obligation for the child. The court may order the parent of an unemancipated minor parent to pay for his or her grandchild's support until the minor parent turns 18 or is emancipated.

115. G.S. 110-132; 110-132.1; 110-133. *See id.* § 130A-101(f).

116. G.S. 110-132(a).

117. *See* 42 U.S.C. § 652. Each state has a child support enforcement program that is responsible for complying with Title IV-D of the federal Social Security Act. The North Carolina Department of Health and Human Services (DHHS) is the state agency responsible for administering the program, and the Division of Social Services (DSS) supervises the county-operated child support services programs. *See* G.S. 110-141; N.C. Dep't of Health & Human Servs., Child Support Services Policy Manual (hereinafter Child Support Services Policy Manual), http://info.dhhs.state.nc.us/olm/manuals/dss/cse/man/; 42 U.S.C. Ch. 7, Subch. IV, Pt. D.

118. G.S. 110-128; *see also* Child Support Services Policy Manual, Child Support Program Basics, CSS Program Overview, Program Purpose and Legal Authority, http://info.dhhs.state.nc.us/olm/manuals/dss/cse/man/CSEcB.pdf.

119. 42 U.S.C. §§ 654, 671; G.S. 110-128; 110-129.1; *See also* Child Support Services Policy Manual, Child Support Program Basics, Provision of CSS Services, CSS Services Overview, http://info.dhhs.state.nc.us/olm/manuals/dss/cse/man/CSEcB-02.htm#P642_64159.

the child.[120] A child support services agency may establish a child support obligation through a court proceeding or a voluntary support agreement.[121]

In establishing child support through a voluntary support agreement, a child support services agency will identify the "responsible parent" by relying on an executed Affidavit of Parentage (AOP), the marital presumption that the husband is the child's father, or any court-ordered paternity determination.[122] The AOP is legally recognized as a basis for seeking child support without the need to initiate a court proceeding to establish paternity.[123] The AOP used for child support purposes may be the same AOP that was executed at the time of a child's birth.[124] If an AOP was not executed at or near the child's birth, the mother and putative father may sign an AOP as part of the child support case.[125]

The parties may enter into a voluntary child support agreement, which the child support services agency files with the court for approval by a judge.[126] If paternity for purposes of child support is based on an executed AOP, the child support services agency will file the AOP with the voluntary support agreement.[127] When the voluntary support agreement is approved by the district court judge, the agreement is enforceable and subject to modification as if it were a child support order entered by the court.[128] The court's approval of a voluntary support agreement is not the same as a civil action involving a live controversy that must be decided by the court. A voluntary support agreement is filed with the district court without a petition or complaint to initiate a civil action. There is no summons or service on a party. No parties appear before the court, and no court hearing is held. The court is merely approving an agreement; it

---

120. 45 C.F.R. § 302.33(a)(1); G.S. 110-130.1.

121. G.S. 110-130; 110-132 through -134.

122. *See* G.S. 110-129(3) (the definition of "responsible parent" is "the natural or adoptive parent of a dependent child who has the legal duty to support said child and includes the father of a child born out-of-wedlock and the parents of a dependent child who is the custodial or noncustodial parent of the dependent child requiring support"); *see also id.* § 110-132; 110-133.

123. 45 C.F.R. § 302.70(a)(5)(vii); G.S. 110-132.

124. G.S. 110-132(a), 130A-101(f). There are three state forms: DHHS Form 1660, DSS Form 4697, and AOC-CV 604, "Affidavit of Parentage," that is available at www.nccourts.org/Forms/Documents/266.pdf.

125. G.S. 110-132. *See id.* § 130A-101(f).

126. G.S. 110-133; 110-134.

127. G.S. 110-132(a), (a3); 110-133 (both statutes address an executed agreement of support; note that if a written support agreement involves a responsible parent for a child that is born of a marriage, an AOP will not be executed by the legal father, whose status automatically results from the presumption that the child is the legitimate child of the mother and her husband); *id.* § 110-134.

128. G.S. 110-132(a3); 110-133. *See* 45 C.F.R. § 302.70(a)(2). *See also* Form AOC-CV-607, Voluntary Support Agreement and Approval by Court," www.nccourts.org/Forms/Documents/267.pdf.

is not deciding a controversy. For child support purposes only, the AOP has the legal effect of a judgment of paternity.[129]

Although an AOP executed in North Carolina is not treated as an adjudication of paternity for actions other than for child support, other states' laws may treat an AOP as a conclusive presumption of paternity with application to any proceeding that has paternity as an element of the claim.[130] In those cases, a North Carolina court must give full faith and credit to another state's paternity determination.[131] A party in an abuse, neglect, or dependency proceeding who is asserting that paternity was adjudicated in another state by virtue of that state's laws about the AOP should be prepared to inform the court of the applicable state's law.

Although a voluntary support agreement is not an adjudication of paternity, a civil action for child support initiated by a child support services agency may include a paternity adjudication. There are several different ways paternity may be adjudicated in a child support action.

First, paternity may be adjudicated when a mother or putative father requests that the court rescind the AOP (1) before sixty days elapses from the date on which the AOP was executed or (2) before a court enters an order adjudicating paternity or establishing a child support obligation, whichever is earlier.[132] If a request to rescind the AOP is filed with the court, all parties must be served in accordance with Rule 4 of the North Carolina Rules of Civil Procedure.[133] If there is a hearing, the court may order the rescission and determine the putative father's paternity or non-paternity of the child.[134] If the court's paternity determination differs from who is named as the father on the child's birth certificate, the clerk must send a copy of that order to the State Registrar.[135] The State Registrar must amend the child's birth certificate to reflect the

---

129. G.S. 110-132(a). Prior to October 1, 1997, an AOP that was filed with and approved by a judge of the district court had the same force and effect as a judgment of that court. S.L. 1997-433, § 4.7 amended G.S. 110-132(a) by repealing that language, adding the right to rescind an AOP, and classifying the AOP as "an admission of paternity." S.L. 1999-293, § 1 further amended G.S. 110-132(a) by adding language that the acknowledgment was an admission of paternity with "the same legal effect as a judgment of paternity *for the purpose of establishing a child support obligation*" (emphasis added). See also the section entitled "Paternity: Voluntary Methods of Establishing Paternity" and the subsection entitled "Voluntary Paternity Establishment Procedures" in the Child Support Services Policy Manual ("When paternity is established voluntarily, no court hearing is held and no court order is issued"), http://info.dhhs.state.nc.us/olm/manuals/dss/cse/man/CSEcI-03.htm#P287_25090.

130. *See* 45 C.F.R. § 302.70(a)(5)(vi).

131. G.S. 110-132.1.

132. G.S. 110-132(a).

133. *Id. See also* Form AOC-CV-916M, Motion and Notice of Hearing to Rescind Affidavit of Parentage, www.nccourts.org/Forms/Documents/342.pdf.

134. G.S. 110-132(a).

135. *Id.*

court's determination.[136] If the putative father fails to prosecute the issue of paternity or defaults at the rescission hearing, the court must issue an order finding that he is the child's biological father as a matter of law.[137] The child's birth certificate should be amended by the State Registrar after it receives notice from the court clerk of the order.

Second, paternity may be adjudicated in a child support action when a mother or putative father seeks to have the AOP being relied upon for child support purposes set aside because of fraud, duress, mutual mistake, or excusable neglect.[138] If a motion to set aside the AOP properly pleads fraud, duress, mutual mistake, or excusable neglect, the court must order genetic marker testing and hold a hearing to determine paternity.[139] In that hearing, the court may adjudicate the putative father's paternity or non-paternity. The AOP may only be set aside if the court finds both that (1) the putative father is not the child's biological father and (2) the AOP was executed as a result of fraud, duress, mutual mistake, or excusable neglect.[140]

Third, if an AOP has not been executed, a child support services agency may initiate a paternity and child support action.[141] The child support services agency may seek genetic marker testing for the purposes of establishing paternity. The agency may subpoena the mother, child, putative father, and, if the mother is married, her husband for genetic marker testing.[142] A party may contest the test results and seek additional genetic testing.[143] Or the agency may request that the court order the mother, alleged

---

136. *Id.*; G.S. 130A-118(b).

137. G.S. 110-132(a). A mother who files a motion to rescind the AOP may want to dismiss her motion if the putative father fails to appear for the hearing. Under this law, if the putative father does not appear and the action moves forward, the court must order that the putative father is the biological father. The court finding of paternity is contrary to the relief the mother, who is the movant, is seeking. If the putative father files the motion and fails to prosecute, as opposed to dismissing his motion, he will be found at law to be the biological father.

138. G.S. 110-132(a1), (a2).

139. G.S. 110-132(a2); 8-50.1(b1). *See also* Form AOC-CV-670, Motion and Notice of Hearing to Set Aside Order of Paternity/Affidavit of Parentage, www.nccourts.org/Forms/Documents/1340.pdf.

140. G.S. 110-132(a1), (a2). *See also* Form AOC-CV-674, Order Granting or Denying Setting Aside Affidavit of Parentage or Prior Order of Paternity, www.nccourts.org/Forms/Documents/1344.pdf. G.S. 50-13.13 provides another procedure for a father who is ordered to pay child support to seek relief from that child support order through a determination of non-paternity.

141. G.S. 49-14; 49-16; 50-13.4; 110-130. The section entitled "Paternity: Judicial Methods of Establishing Paternity" and the subsection entitled "Civil Paternity Action Procedures" in the Child Support Services Policy Manual states that the child support services agency should initiate a civil action to establish paternity when the mother and alleged father have not voluntarily established paternity. *See* http://info.dhhs.state.nc.us/olm/manuals/dss/cse/man/CSEcI-04.htm#TopOfPage. *See also* G.S. Chapter 52C.

142. G.S. 110-132.2. A person who is served with the subpoena may contest it by requesting a court hearing within fifteen days of being served.

143. G.S. 110-132.2(a).

father-defendant, and child to submit to genetic marker testing.[144] When the parties have submitted to genetic marker testing (either by subpoena or court order), the court must conduct a hearing to adjudicate paternity (see chapter 5). Paternity is established by clear, cogent, and convincing evidence.[145] When the court determines the putative father's paternity or non-paternity, the clerk should notify the State Registrar of the resulting order when the determination of parentage differs from what is listed on the child's birth certificate.[146] The State Registrar must amend the child's birth certificate.[147]

Depending on the process used, the establishment of a child support obligation does not necessarily mean that paternity has been adjudicated. If a party in the abuse, neglect, or dependency proceeding raises paternity as an issue, the court should inquire about the process that was used to create the child support obligation and determine if paternity was adjudicated. For example, a voluntary support agreement that was signed by the mother and her husband at the time of the child's conception or birth and was approved by the court is not a court order with a judicial determination of paternity. An AOP that was filed with the court in the child support case is an adjudication of paternity for child support purposes only and is an admission of paternity for purposes of the abuse, neglect, or dependency action.[148] A certified copy of the AOP may be introduced as evidence in a proceeding where paternity is an issue.[149]

Collateral Estoppel

Even when there has been a court adjudication of paternity, paternity may still be an issue in an abuse, neglect, or dependency action depending on who raises it. There are multiple parties in an abuse, neglect, or dependency proceeding: the county department, the child, the respondent mother, the respondent father, and, if applicable, the child's guardian, custodian, or caretaker.[150] Although any one of these parties may raise paternity as an issue, some of them may be barred from doing so. The court will have to determine if collateral estoppel applies to the party raising the issue. The court's collateral estoppel analysis will depend on whether the party seeking to use the prior paternity adjudication had a full and fair opportunity to litigate paternity in that earlier proceeding.

---

144. G.S. 8-50.1(b1).
145. G.S. 49-14(b).
146. G.S. 130A-118(b)(2), (3); 130A-119. *See* Form AOC-CV-672, Notice of Non-Paternity Determination, www.nccourts.org/Forms/Documents/1342.pdf.
147. G.S. 130A-118(b)(2), (3); 130A-119.
148. G.S. 110-132(a).
149. G.S. 110-132(a); 130A-101(f).
150. G.S. 7B-401.1.

The Elements of Collateral Estoppel

Collateral estoppel, or issue preclusion, bars a party from relitigating issues that were actually determined in a previous proceeding.[151] The purpose of collateral estoppel is twofold: "(1) that each person have his day in court to completely adjudicate the merits of his claim for relief, and (2) that the courts must demand an end to litigation when a court of competent jurisdiction has ruled on the merits of his right."[152]

Collateral estoppel applies when

1. the issue in question is identical to an issue actually litigated and necessary to the prior judgment;
2. the prior action resulted in a final judgment on the merits; and
3. the parties in the pending action are the same as, or in privity with, the parties to the prior action.[153]

The third element is not always required (see the section entitled "Nonmutual Collateral Estoppel," below).

The application of collateral estoppel is based on whether all three elements are met and not on whether the order in the previous action was correct.[154] Collateral estoppel applies even when the prior judgment was based on an erroneous determination of law or fact.[155]

The First Element

In determining if the first requirement for collateral estoppel has been satisfied, the court must apply a four-prong test made up of the following questions:

- Is the issue the same one that was involved in the prior action?
- Was the issue raised and actually litigated in the prior action?
- Was the issue material and relevant to the disposition of the prior action?
- Was the determination of the issue in the prior action necessary and essential to the resulting judgment?[156]

Issues are considered identical if they are subject to the same burden of proof.[157] Collateral estoppel requires that the previous and pending actions be subject to the

---

151. Tar Landing Villas Owners' Ass'n v. Town of Atl. Beach, 64 N.C. App. 239 (1983).
152. *Id.* at 243 (quoting Blake v. Norman, 37 N.C. App. 617, 624 (1978)).
153. McInnis v. Hall, 318 N.C. 421 (1986).
154. Johnson v. Smith, 97 N.C. App. 450 (1990).
155. *McInnis*, 318 N.C. 421.
156. State v. Summers, 351 N.C. 620, 623 (2000).
157. State v. Saffrit, 154 N.C. App. 727 (2002).

same burden of proof.[158] Collateral estoppel does not apply when the first action was based on a lower standard of proof than the second action; for example, when preponderance of the evidence is the standard in the first action and clear and convincing evidence applies in the second action.[159] Similarly, collateral estoppel does not apply when the *failure to prove* an issue in the first action was based on a higher standard of proof (e.g., beyond a reasonable doubt) than the standard applied in the second action (e.g., preponderance of the evidence).[160] But appellate courts have held that collateral estoppel precludes a plaintiff from relitigating an issue in a civil suit that was previously determined in a prior criminal proceeding,[161] even though the standard in the criminal case is a higher burden of proof from the standard in the civil case.

An issue may be considered to have been actually litigated even though there is not a specific finding about the issue in the court order.[162] In determining what issues were actually decided in the earlier judgment, the court in the pending action may look beyond the court order in the first action and examine the pleadings and the evidence. "[I]f the rendering court made no express findings on issues raised by the pleadings or the evidence, the court may infer that in the prior action a determination appropriate to the judgment rendered was made as to each issue that was so raised . . . ."[163] The party asserting collateral estoppel may need to introduce the court order and a sufficient record of the proceeding for the court in the pending action to determine what issues were litigated.[164]

---

158. *Id. In re* K.A., 233 N.C. App. 119, 127 (2014); State *ex rel.* New Bern Child Support Agency v. Lewis, 311 N.C. 727 (1984) (Note that at the time this case was decided the standard of proof for a civil paternity action was beyond a reasonable doubt.).

159. *K.A.*, 233 N.C. App. 119.

160. Hussey v. Cheek, 31 N.C. App. 148 (1976); *see also Saffrit*, 154 N.C. App. 727 (in the first action, the defendant was found not to be a violent habitual felon based upon the standard of beyond a reasonable doubt; in the second action, which was a sentencing hearing, the standard was preponderance of the evidence; because the standards were not the same, the State was not collaterally estopped from seeking the defendant's status as a violent habitual offender in second action); McHan v. C.I.R., 558 F.3d 326, 332 (4th Cir. 2009).

161. Burton v. City of Durham, 118 N.C. App. 676 (1995) (citing Allen v. McCurry, 449 U.S. 90, 103–05 (1980)).

162. King v. Grindstaff, 284 N.C. 348 (1973).

163. *Id.* at 360 (citation omitted); Southerland v. Atl. Coast Line R.R., 148 N.C. 442 (1908); *see also* Miller Bldg. Corp. v. NBBJ N.C., Inc., 129 N.C. App. 97 (1998).

164. *Miller Bldg. Corp.*, 129 N.C. App. 97 (1998).

The Second Element

A judgment is either a final or interlocutory determination of the rights of the parties to the action.[165] A final judgment generally ends the litigation on the merits and resolves the entire substantive controversy.[166] A judgment on the merits may be considered final when a collateral issue of attorneys' fees remains for a court to decide.[167] An entry of a final judgment on the merits entitles a party to appeal as of right.[168] Collateral estoppel will apply to a judgment entered on the merits and from which a timely appeal was not taken or, if an appeal was taken, the appeal has been resolved.

The Third Element

Under traditional collateral estoppel, the parties in the prior and pending actions must be the same or in privity. North Carolina courts have consistently held "[t]here is no definition of the word 'privity' which can be applied in all cases."[169] Privity requires a case-by-case analysis to determine if a person's interest has been legally represented at the trial or if the two people have "a mutual or successive relationship to the same rights of property."[170] Privity requires that the nonparty had control over the previous action so that his or her legal interests were represented.[171] Privity is not based on two people being "interested in the same question or in proving or disproving the same state of facts, or because the question litigated was one which might affect such other person's liability as a judicial precedent in a subsequent action."[172] In determining if the parties are the same or in privity, the court in the pending action must look beyond the named party in the prior action and "consider the legal questions raised as they may affect the real party or parties in interest."[173]

Using Collateral Estoppel

Collateral estoppel is used against the party who lost on the issue in the first action.[174] Collateral estoppel may be used offensively or defensively. When used offensively, the plaintiff in the current action seeks to prevent the defendant from relitigating the issue

---

165. G.S. 1A-1, Rule 54.

166. Johnson v. Lucas, 168 N.C. App. 515 (2005), *aff'd per curiam*, 360 N.C. 53 (2005); Veazey v. City of Durham, 231 N.C. 357 (1950).

167. Duncan v. Duncan, 366 N.C. 544 (2013).

168. G.S. 1-277(a); *Duncan*, 366 N.C. 544.

169. Masters v. Dunstan, 256 N.C. 520, 524 (1962); Settle *ex rel.* Sullivan v. Beasley, 309 N.C. 616, 619 (1983) (citation omitted); State *ex rel.* Tucker v. Frinzi, 344 N.C. 411, 416–17 (1996).

170. *Frinzi*, 344 N.C. at 416–17 (citation omitted).

171. Hill *ex rel.* Hill v. West, 189 N.C. App. 189 (2008).

172. *Frinzi*, 344 N.C. at 417 (citations omitted).

173. State v. Summers, 351 N.C. 620, 623–24 (2000) (citation omitted).

174. Parklane Hosiery Inc. v. Shore, 429 U.S. 322 (1979).

the defendant lost in the first action.[175] Used defensively, the defendant in the current action seeks to stop the plaintiff from relitigating the same issue that the plaintiff lost in the earlier action.[176]

The burden of proving the elements of collateral estoppel is on the party who is asserting it to bar another party from relitigating an issue.[177] A party who contests the application of collateral estoppel against him or her has the burden of proving that he or she did not have a full and fair opportunity to litigate the issue in the previous action.[178]

Nonmutual Collateral Estoppel

North Carolina also recognizes the use of nonmutual collateral estoppel.[179] This means that both parties in the current action do not have to have been parties in or been in privity with the parties in the previous action.[180] Other than the requirement for the parties in each action to be the same or in privity with one another, the elements of collateral estoppel apply. Nonmutual collateral estoppel may be used offensively or defensively.

Nonmutual Defensive Collateral Estoppel

Nonmutual defensive collateral estoppel is used by the defendant in the pending action against the plaintiff. The defendant is seeking to prevent the plaintiff from relitigating an issue that was decided in the previous action.[181] The defendant in the current case was not a party in the previous action, but the plaintiff was. The defendant may rely on the judgment from the previous action when asserting the defense of nonmutual collateral estoppel. The defendant is relying on the "former judgment as conclusively establishing in his favor an issue which he must prove as an element of his defense."[182] The plaintiff must have "had a full and fair opportunity to litigate" the issue in the previous action.[183] It is irrelevant whether the plaintiff in the pending action was the plaintiff or defendant in the prior action, so long as the plaintiff was a party in the prior action with a full and fair opportunity to litigate the issue.[184]

---

175. *Id.*

176. *Id.*

177. Powers v. Tatum, 196 N.C. App. 639 (2009); Bluebird Corp. v. Aubin, 188 N.C. App. 671 (2008).

178. Miller Bldg. Corp. v. NBBJ N.C., Inc., 129 N.C. App. 97, 100 (1998).

179. Rymer v. Estate of Sorrells, 127 N.C. App. 266 (1997); *In re K.A.*, 233 N.C. App. 119 (2014).

180. McInnis v. Hall, 318 N.C. 421 (1986); *Rymer*, 127 N.C. App. 266.

181. *McInnis*, 318 N.C. 421.

182. Johnson v. Smith, 97 N.C. App. 450, 453 (1990) (citation omitted).

183. *McInnis*, 318 N.C. at 432–34.

184. Burton v. City of Durham, 118 N.C. App. 676 (1995) (plaintiff in civil rights action against city was collaterally estopped by prior criminal action brought by the State against

Nonmutual Offensive Collateral Estoppel

Nonmutual offensive collateral estoppel is when the plaintiff in the pending action seeks to prevent the defendant from relitigating an issue that the defendant unsuccessfully litigated in a prior action.[185] The plaintiff in the present action was not a party in or in privity with a party in the prior action. The use of nonmutual offensive collateral estoppel is limited because it does not necessarily promote judicial efficiency and its application may be unfair to a defendant.[186] Nonmutual offensive collateral estoppel may encourage a potential plaintiff to adopt a wait and see approach.[187] Is there a lawsuit that will involve the same issue but a different plaintiff against the same defendant? If so, the potential plaintiff has an incentive to wait and see what the outcome of that case is. If the defendant prevails, the potential plaintiff will not be bound by the judgment, but if the defendant loses, the potential plaintiff may initiate his or her suit and raise nonmutual collateral estoppel against the defendant.[188]

A trial court is given broad discretion when determining if nonmutual offensive collateral estoppel promotes judicial economy or is inequitable as applied to the defendant.[189] The court may consider whether

- the plaintiff could have easily joined in the previous action,
- the defendant had an incentive to vigorously defend all the issues in the prior action, or
- the defendant has different procedural opportunities in the pending action that could lead to a different result.[190]

Applying Traditional or Nonmutual Collateral Estoppel

Although nonmutual collateral estoppel has been recognized by North Carolina, the appellate courts "have defined collateral estoppel variously, applying the privity element in some cases and refraining to do so in others."[191] Decisions addressing the application of collateral estoppel to paternity have held that "the issue of paternity must necessarily have been determined previously."[192] Regarding the mutuality or nonmutuality of the parties, some appellate opinions have held "the parties to that prior action

him where he was convicted); *McInnis*, 318 N.C. 421 (plaintiff was collaterally estopped from seeking judgment against defendant to augment damages award plaintiff obtained when it prevailed against different defendant in prior action based on same breach of contract claim).

185. *Rymer*, 127 N.C. App. 266.
186. *Id.*
187. *Id.*
188. *Id.*
189. Tar Landing Villas Owners' Ass'n v. Town of Atl. Beach, 64 N.C. App. 239 (1983).
190. *Rymer*, 127 N.C. App. at 270.
191. *In re* K.A., 233 N.C. App. 119, 126 (2014).
192. Devane *ex rel.* Robinson v. Chancellor, 120 N.C. App. 636, 637 (1995) (citation omitted).

must be identical or privies to the parties in the instant case."[193] Other opinions have held that mutuality of the parties is not always necessary for collateral estoppel to apply in different causes of action that establish parentage.[194] To address these different holdings, a court may want to first analyze the application of traditional collateral estoppel, which requires mutuality between the parties in the current and former action. If the court finds that there is no mutuality of the parties, the court may then determine whether nonmutual collateral estoppel applies. The adoption of nonmutual collateral estoppel does not appear to prohibit the application of traditional collateral estoppel when the elements regarding mutuality of parties exist.

The Questions before the Juvenile Court

An abuse, neglect, or dependency proceeding is not a typical lawsuit with a plaintiff versus a defendant. The action is brought in the name of the child and involves multiple parties. The number of parties and their designated roles as petitioner, child, and respondent causes the application of collateral estoppel to be less straightforward than in a case where there is one plaintiff and one defendant. Despite this difference, the analysis for the court is the same. A court should look at the definitions of both traditional collateral estoppel and nonmutual collateral estoppel. In determining if collateral estoppel applies because of a previous adjudication of paternity, the court must ask and answer the following questions:

- Was there a final judgment on the merits in a previous action?
- Was paternity raised and actually litigated in that action?
- Was paternity material and relevant to the disposition of that action?
- Was the determination of paternity necessary and essential to the resulting judgment?
- What was the burden of proof for paternity in the prior action?
- Is the party asserting collateral estoppel and the party against whom collateral estoppel is asserted the same as or in privity with the party or parties in the prior action?
- If there is no mutuality of parties, did the party against whom collateral estoppel is asserted have a full and fair opportunity to litigate paternity in the prior action?
- If nonmutual offensive collateral estoppel is being raised, is it equitable to collaterally estop the respondent from challenging the paternity determination in the prior action?

---

193. *Id.* (citation omitted).
194. Guilford Cty. *ex rel.* Gardner v. Davis, 123 N.C. App. 527 (1996).

Collateral Estoppel as Applied to the Child

The child is a party in the abuse, neglect, or dependency proceeding and is represented by a court-appointed guardian ad litem and attorney advocate.[195] The role of the attorney advocate is "to assure protection of the juvenile's legal rights throughout the proceeding."[196] As a party in the proceeding, the child may raise paternity as an issue.

A child is likely to be collaterally estopped if he or she was a party in a prior proceeding where paternity was actually litigated and necessary to the final judgment. A child is a necessary party to a legitimation proceeding and is bound by the judgment.[197] A child has standing to initiate a paternity action and a child support action.[198] If a paternity or child support action is initiated by the child's mother, putative father, or a county agency, the child may be named as a party but is not a necessary party.[199] A child may also bring a declaratory judgment action to decide his or her paternity or legitimation.[200] The party seeking to collaterally estop the child from litigating paternity should introduce evidence showing that the child (1) was a party in the earlier proceeding, (2) was in privity with a party, or (3) had a full and fair opportunity to litigate paternity in the prior proceeding. If the child was not a party or not in privity with a party, a court may want to consider whether the child was notified of the earlier proceeding and whether the child's interests were represented in that proceeding by a guardian ad litem appointed under Rule 17 of the North Carolina Rules of Civil Procedure.[201] Knowing if the child was aware of or had a way to participate in the earlier proceeding may assist the court in its determination of whether the child had a full and fair opportunity to litigate paternity in the prior action.

The court of appeals has held that a child is not in privity with a county child support services agency that initiated a paternity and child support action in the child's mother's name after she assigned her rights to child support to the county.[202] The court of appeals determined that in such circumstances the child support agency is the real

---

195. G.S 7B-401.1(f); 7B-601(a) (a guardian ad litem (GAL) for the child must be appointed when abuse or neglect is alleged, but the court has discretion in appointing a GAL for a child if dependency is the only ground alleged; an attorney advocate is appointed when the GAL is not an attorney).

196. G.S. 7B-601(a).

197. G.S. 49-10; 49-12.1.

198. G.S. 49-16(1); 50-13.4(a).

199. Smith v. Bumgarner, 115 N.C. App. 149 (1994).

200. Mitchell v. Freuler, 297 N.C. 206 (1979) (paternity); Batcheldor v. Boyd, 119 N.C. App. 204 (1995) (legitimation).

201. G.S. 1A-1, Rule 17.

202. Settle ex rel. Sullivan v. Beasley, 309 N.C. 616, 623 (1983) (Collateral estoppel did not bar the child from proceeding with his paternity action against the same defendant in the prior proceeding, even though that defendant was found not to be the child's father in the first action. The court reasoned the child was entitled to an opportunity to relitigate paternity because "[t]he impact of the first action upon [the child] is devastating.")

party in interest, as the action is brought for the economic benefit of the county that has an assignment of the mother's rights to child support as a condition for her receipt of public assistance.[203] Because a child has a right to an "accurate determination of paternity"[204] and "to know who is his father,"[205] "privity does not exist to bar the child's subsequent suit."[206] If a mother who has not received public assistance sought child support services from a county agency,[207] the court will need to address whether the child was in privity with the mother or whether nonmutual collateral estoppel applies to the child.

A child is not a party in a child custody, divorce, or criminal nonsupport action. In applying the traditional definition of collateral estoppel, the court must determine if the child was in privity with a party in the prior proceeding. The determination of privity should consider more than the parent-child relationship. The fact that a child's parent is a party is irrelevant to the child's right to litigate his or her own cause of action.[208] The court should determine whether the child's legal interests were represented in the prior action. Without standing in the previous action, it is unlikely that the child's interests were legally represented. For nonmutual collateral estoppel, the court must determine if the child had a full and fair opportunity to litigate the issue of paternity. Such an opportunity is unlikely, given that the child lacks standing to be a party in a divorce, child custody, or criminal nonsupport proceeding.

Prior Civil Proceeding between Mother and "Father"

Paternity, including non-paternity, may have been litigated between the mother and putative or legal father in a variety of different proceedings. If there is a final judgment where paternity was raised or was a necessary element of the claim decided by the order, and the issue was litigated, the mother and father will be collaterally estopped from raising paternity as an issue in the abuse, neglect, or dependency proceeding.

Even though the mother and father (or the man who was found not to be the father) are barred from raising paternity, another party in the abuse, neglect, or dependency action may not be barred. The court must decide whether the party raising paternity was in privity with the mother or father (or man found not to be the father) or had the opportunity to fully and fairly litigate the issue in the prior action.

For example, suppose an abuse, neglect, or dependency petition is filed and names the mother and her ex-husband as respondent parents and her live-in boyfriend as a respondent caretaker. There is a divorce judgment that concludes the now ex-husband

---

203. *Settle*, 309 N.C. 616.
204. *Id.* at 620–21.
205. *Id.* at 621.
206. *Id.* at 620.
207. G.S. 110-130.1.
208. Thompson v. Hamrick, 23 N.C. App. 550 (1974); Hill *ex rel.* Hill v. West, 189 N.C. App. 189 (2008).

and wife are the biological parents of the child born during the marriage and addresses custody and child support. But the boyfriend believes that he is the child's biological father and raises paternity as an issue in the abuse, neglect, or dependency action. The respondent father raises nonmutual defensive collateral estoppel to bar the boyfriend from raising paternity. In this scenario, the boyfriend was not a party to the divorce. He was not in privity with the wife or the husband, and his legal interests were not represented even though he had an interest in the child's paternity. The boyfriend did not have a full and fair opportunity to litigate paternity in the divorce proceeding. Neither traditional nor nonmutual defensive collateral estoppel applies to the boyfriend. He may raise paternity as an issue in the abuse, neglect, or dependency action. Suppose that instead of the boyfriend, the mother raises paternity as an issue. She argues that she made a mistake in the divorce judgment and is now claiming that her boyfriend is the child's father. The respondent father may raise defensive collateral estoppel to bar the mother from relitigating paternity in the abuse, neglect, or dependency action, as she was a party in the prior action.

Prior Proceeding Involving the State or a County
Civil Child Support

The North Carolina appellate courts have held that when a state or county child support services agency initiates an action to establish paternity and child support because rights of support have been assigned to the state or county, the parent in whose name the case was prosecuted is not in privity with the child support services agency.[209] The child support services agency is the real party in interest because it is protecting its economic interest by obtaining a child support obligation that has been assigned to it by the mother as a requirement for her receipt of public assistance.[210] If a mother who has not received public assistance sought child support services from a county agency,[211] the court will need to address whether she was in privity with the child support services agency or whether nonmutual collateral estoppel applies to her.

If the child support proceeding was initiated by a county child support services agency and the same county's child welfare department initiates the abuse, neglect, or dependency proceeding, they are the same parties: the county. Collateral estoppel would apply to the county department and other parties to the child support case. If the county is not the same, traditional collateral estoppel will not apply and a party seeking to assert collateral estoppel will need to prove the elements of nonmutual collateral estoppel.

---

209. State *ex rel.* Tucker v. Frinzi, 344 N.C. 411 (1996); Devane *ex rel.* Robinson v. Chancellor, 120 N.C. App. 636 (1995); *Settle*, 309 N.C. 616.

210. *Settle*, 309 N.C. 616.

211. G.S. 110-130.1.

For example, suppose that there was a prior paternity and child support action brought in the mother's name by the child support services agency in county one. The defendant was determined not to be the child's father. A different county (county two) later files an abuse, neglect, or dependency action and names the defendant from the child support action that was brought by county one as a caretaker respondent. The mother raises paternity as an issue in the abuse, neglect, or dependency action and alleges that the caretaker respondent is the child's father. The caretaker respondent might assert nonmutual defensive collateral estoppel against the mother. The court will need to determine if the mother had a full and fair opportunity to litigate her interests in the prior child support action that was initiated by county one. Was she represented by her own attorney? Did she work closely with county one's child support services agency and testify at the hearing to establish the defendant's paternity? Was genetic testing ordered and did the mother cooperate with that testing? If county two also raises the caretaker respondent's paternity as an issue in the abuse, neglect, or dependency action, the court will need to determine if nonmutual collateral estoppel applies to county two. Did county two have a full and fair opportunity to litigate the defendant's paternity in the child support action initiated by county one's child support services agency?

Similarly, if county one's child support services agency obtained a child support order against a father and county two files an abuse, neglect, or dependency action naming the father as a respondent, can county two assert nonmutual offensive collateral estoppel against the respondent father if he denies paternity? The court will have to determine if paternity was actually litigated and if there is a final judgment on the merits from county one's child support case. The court will need evidence of what procedure was used to establish child support and will need to determine what the basis of the paternity adjudication was for the child support obligation. Was an Affidavit of Parentage filed with the court or was there an adjudication of paternity? Was there a court order or a court approval of a filed voluntary support agreement? If the court in the abuse, neglect, or dependency action determines that there was an adjudication of paternity in a final judgment on the merits in the child support action, the court will need to apply the elements of nonmutual offensive collateral estoppel and consider the fairness to the defendant. The court may consider the procedural differences between the two actions and the impact of those differences on the named respondent father who is denying paternity. For example, an indigent defendant in a child support case that includes paternity as an element of the claim is not entitled to a court-appointed attorney. That same indigent defendant who is named as a respondent father is entitled to a court-appointed attorney in an abuse, neglect, or dependency proceeding where paternity may also be decided. Ultimately, the court will be given broad discretion in its decision about the fairness of applying nonmutual offensive collateral estoppel against the respondent father.

Criminal Nonsupport

Collateral estoppel may not apply when the prior action was a criminal nonsupport action. The burden of proof for each element in the criminal proceeding is beyond a reasonable doubt, which is a higher standard than the burden of proof to establish paternity in a civil action.[212] An acquittal based on the State's failure to prove beyond a reasonable doubt that the defendant is the child's father will not collaterally estop a party in the abuse, neglect, or dependency action from asserting that the defendant in the criminal action is the child's father.[213] The burden of proof in the criminal proceeding is higher than the burden in an abuse, neglect, or dependency proceeding. Similarly, a conviction will not bar a party in the abuse, neglect, or dependency action from raising paternity as an issue, unless the party raising the issue was a party in the criminal action.[214]

The State, a county department, or the mother may initiate a misdemeanor criminal action for nonsupport.[215] With the exception of the defendant and the mother or the same county if one of them initiated the criminal action, the parties in the abuse, neglect, or dependency action were not parties in the criminal action. The other parties in the abuse, neglect, or dependency proceeding are not likely to be in privity with the parties in the criminal action since the State's or county's interest in the criminal action is to protect itself from having the child become a public charge.[216] And only the initiating party (the State, county department, or mother who initiated the criminal action) has control over the prosecution of the case.[217] As a result, it is unlikely that a party in the abuse, neglect, or dependency action who was not a party in the criminal action had a full and fair opportunity to litigate the issue of paternity warranting the application of nonmutual collateral estoppel against him or her.

---

212. G.S. 49-14 and 49-12.1 require proof by clear and convincing evidence. Rebutting the marital presumption or statutory presumptions of genetic test results ordered pursuant to G.S. 8-50.1(b1) requires clear and convincing evidence. *See* Eubanks v. Eubanks, 273 N.C. 189 (1968). The statutes and court opinions do not address whether the standard to establish paternity in other proceedings is based on the civil standard of preponderance of the evidence or the higher standard of clear and convincing evidence.

213. Hussey v. Cheek, 31 N.C. App. 148 (1976); *see also* State v. Saffrit, 154 N.C. App. 727 (2002).

214. Burton v. City of Durham, 118 N.C. App. 676 (1995).

215. G.S. 14-322; 49-5 (note that a county department's standing is limited to when the child is likely to become a public charge).

216. County of Rutherford *ex rel.* Child Support Enforcement Agency v. Whitener, 100 N.C. App. 70 (1990) (county had no control over prior criminal action and nothing in record indicated that county was represented in criminal trial); Devane *ex rel.* Robinson v. Chancellor, 120 N.C. App. 636 (1995) (defensive collateral estoppel did not apply when the defendant failed to prove that the plaintiffs (mother and children) were in privity with the state, which did not prevail in a criminal nonsupport action against defendant, or with the county child support services agency, which dismissed with prejudice its civil action against the defendant to establish paternity and child support); Tidwell v. Booker, 290 N.C. 98 (1976).

217. *Tidwell*, 290 N.C. 98.

Summary

Determining that paternity is an issue may be as simple as finding that a father is not named on the child's birth certificate. Or determining whether paternity is an issue may be as complex as requiring the court to identify and apply the relevant North Carolina laws on parentage and decide whether collateral estoppel applies to the party raising paternity as an issue in the abuse, neglect, or dependency proceeding. Paternity does not need to be unknown or contested for it to be an issue. The parties may agree upon who the father is but want to replace a rebuttable presumption or an admission of paternity with a judicial determination that binds the father, child, mother, and county (via its various agencies) to the judgment.

To assist the court in its determination of whether paternity is an issue, a worksheet identifying the ways a father is named on a birth certificate and the different court actions and procedures that establish parentage or a child support obligation is set out in Appendix 4A. Appendix 4B is a user-friendly table that explains the different elements of traditional and nonmutual collateral estoppel.

Appendix 4A

Worksheet: Determining When Paternity Is an Issue in the Abuse, Neglect, or Dependency Proceeding

Purpose: This worksheet is designed to assist the court in its determination of whether paternity is an issue. By using this worksheet, the court will be able to determine if and how a child's father has been named. The court will be able to identify if the father's status is a result of a marital presumption of legitimacy, an admission of the parties, or a court adjudication of paternity. If there was a court adjudication, the court may find it useful to list the parties that were involved in the prior action in the event that the court also must decide whether collateral estoppel applies to the party in the abuse, neglect, or dependency proceeding who is raising paternity or non-paternity as an issue. Although this worksheet is designed with the court determination in mind, the parties may find it useful when deciding whether to raise paternity as an issue in the abuse, neglect, or dependency proceeding.

Child's Name: _____

Birth Certificate

☐ Father *Is Not* Named on Original Birth Certificate

☐ Father *Is* Named on Original Birth Certificate: _____

Basis for Name on Birth Certificate

☐ Marital Presumption (Rebuttable by Clear, Cogent, and Convincing Evidence)

☐ AOP Executed within 10 Days of Child's Birth:

Mother: _____ *Date Signed:* ___ / ___ / _____

Father: _____ *Date Signed:* ___ / ___ / _____

[Note: If Executed before 12/12/2005: Presumption of Paternity Applies.]

Certified Copy May Be Admitted as Evidence of Paternity (Admission by Signatories)

☐ Court Order

Amended Birth Certificate

Date of Amendment: ___ / ___ / _____

Basis of Amendment: _____

Name of Father: _____

Name of Father Removed (if Applicable): _____

[Note: It is possible that a legitimation by marriage or court order declaring the child's legitimacy or adjudicating paternity or non-paternity occurred without an accompanying amendment to the child's birth certificate. The husband and wife may not have filed a request to amend the child's birth certificate with an accompanying affidavit and a certified copy of the marriage certificate with the State Registrar. The clerk of court may not have notified or sent a certified copy of a court order determining different parentage to the State Registrar.]

Legitimation

☐ Legitimation by Marriage, Proof: _____   Date of Marriage: ____ / ____ / _____

☐ Court Order of Legitimation, Case Name: _____

Court and Docket Number: _____   Date of Order: ____ / ____ / _____

Parties:

Putative Father: _____

Mother: _____

Child: _____

Child's Rule 17 GAL: _____

Husband (if Applicable): _____

☐ Child Is Legitimated   ☐ Child Is NOT Legitimated

Judicial Determinations Addressing Paternity

☐ Court Order of Paternity, Case Name: _____

Court and Docket Number: _____   Date of Order: ____ / ____ / _____

☐ Order of Paternity Set Aside   Date ____ / ____ / _____

Parties:

Putative Father: _____

Mother: _____

Child (if Applicable): _____

Child's Rule 17 GAL (if Applicable): _____

Child Services Agency (if Applicable): _____

Husband (if Applicable): _____

☐ Paternity Adjudicated   ☐ Non-Paternity Adjudicated

☐ Criminal Nonsupport Action, Case Name: _____

Court and Docket Number: _____

Parties:

Prosecuting Party: _____

Named Defendant: _____

☐ Convicted   ☐ Acquitted   Date: ____ / ____ / _____

☐ Declaratory Judgment, Case Name: _____

Court and Docket Number: _____   Date of Order: ____ / ____ / _____

Parties:

Plaintiff: _____

Defendant: _____

Other: _____

☐ Declared the Father   ☐ Declared NOT the Father

☐ Divorce, Case Name: _____

Court and Docket Number: _____   Date of Order: ____ / ____ / _____

Parties:

Plaintiff: _____

Defendant: _____

Paternity Decided   ☐ Yes   ☐ No

☐ Incorporated Separation Agreement Includes Child Support or Custody

☐ Provision for Child Custody or Support in the Divorce Judgment

Finding Husband   ☐ Is the Father   ☐ Is NOT the Father

Evidence of That Finding: _____

☐ Child Custody, Case Name: _____

Court and Docket Number: _____ Date of Order: ____ / ____ / _____

Parties:

Plaintiff: _____

Defendant: _____

Intervenor (if Applicable): _____

GAL for Child (if Applicable): _____

Finding of Fact Determining Paternity ☐ Yes ☐ No

Child Support

☐ Court Order Establishing Child Support, Case Name: _____

Court and Docket Number: _____ Date of Order: ____ / ____ / _____

Parties:

Mother: _____

Father: _____

Child (if Applicable): _____

Child's Guardian (if Applicable): _____

Child Support Services Agency (if Applicable): _____

☐ Child Support Order Terminated after Order of Non-Paternity, G.S. 50-13.13   Date: ____ / ____ / _____

☐ Affidavit of Parentage (AOP) for Child Support Purposes

[Note: Adjudication of paternity is for child support purposes only; AOP is evidence of paternity in non–child support action.]

Mother: _____ Date Signed: ____ / ____ / _____

Father: _____ Date Signed: ____ / ____ / _____

☐ AOP Rescinded

[Note: Must be rescinded within 60 days of execution or before an entry of an order establishing paternity or child support, whichever occurs first.]

☐ Court Order on Rescission of AOP, Case Name: _____

Court and Docket Number: _____

☐ Granted   ☐ Denied   Date: ____ / ____ / _____

Parties:

Mother: _____

Father: _____

Child Support Services Agency: _____

☐ AOP Set Aside by Court Order, Case Name: _____

Court and Docket Number: _____

☐ Granted   ☐ Denied   Date: ____ / ____ / _____

Parties:

Mother: _____ ☐ Moving Party

Father: _____ ☐ Moving Party

Child Support Services Agency: _____

☐ Voluntary Support Agreement (VSA)

Parties:

Mother: _____ Date Signed: ____ / ____ / _____

Father: _____ Date Signed: ____ / ____ / _____

Child Support Services Agency: _____

Date Filed ____ / ____ / _____   Date Approved ____ / ____ / _____   Court: _____

Basis of VSA: ☐ AOP   ☐ Marital Presumption   ☐ Court Order of Paternity   ☐ Other: _____

Appendix 4B

Figure: Applying Collateral Estoppel

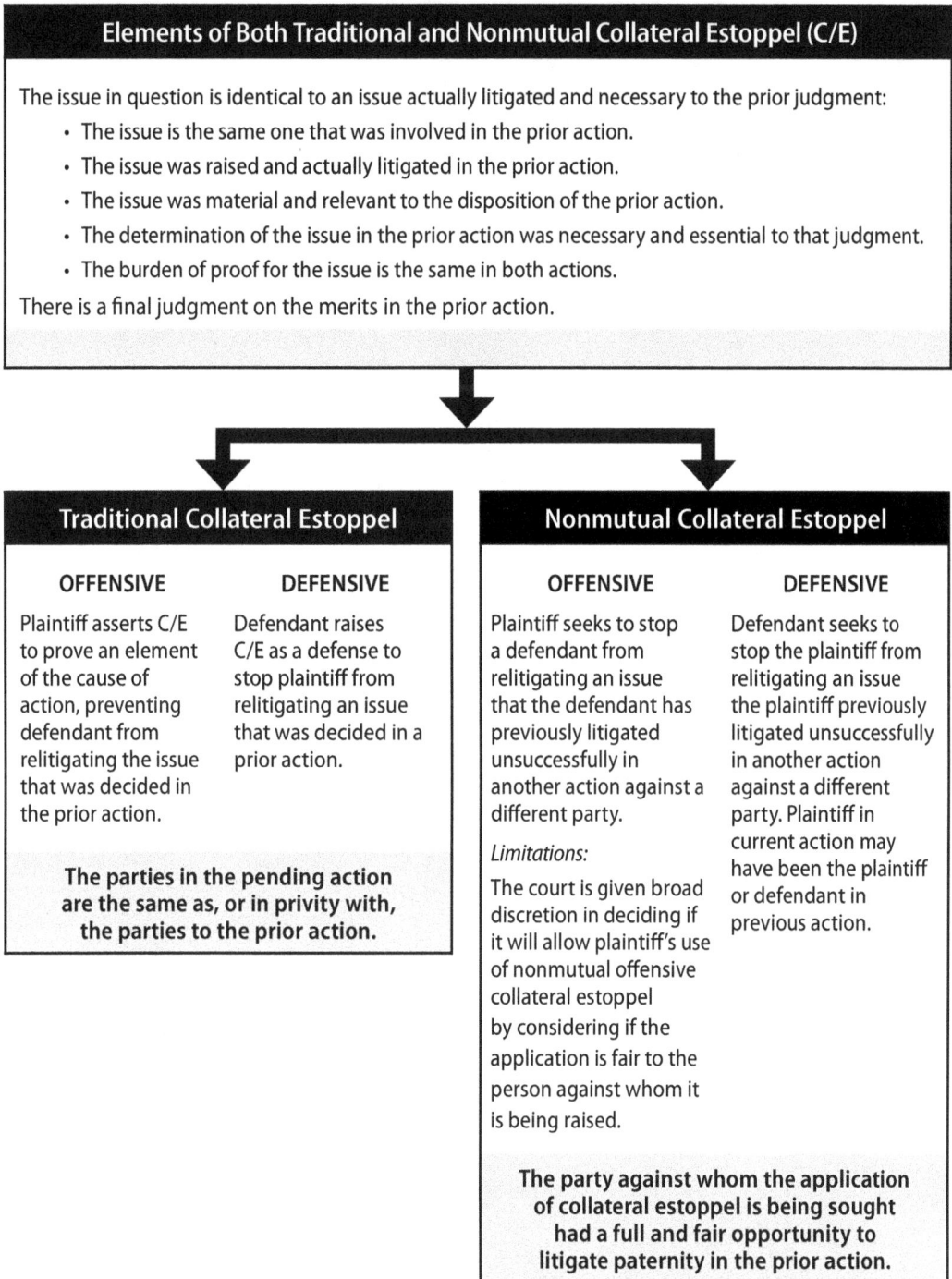

Elements of Both Traditional and Nonmutual Collateral Estoppel (C/E)

The issue in question is identical to an issue actually litigated and necessary to the prior judgment:
- The issue is the same one that was involved in the prior action.
- The issue was raised and actually litigated in the prior action.
- The issue was material and relevant to the disposition of the prior action.
- The determination of the issue in the prior action was necessary and essential to that judgment.
- The burden of proof for the issue is the same in both actions.

There is a final judgment on the merits in the prior action.

Traditional Collateral Estoppel

OFFENSIVE

Plaintiff asserts C/E to prove an element of the cause of action, preventing defendant from relitigating the issue that was decided in the prior action.

DEFENSIVE

Defendant raises C/E as a defense to stop plaintiff from relitigating an issue that was decided in a prior action.

The parties in the pending action are the same as, or in privity with, the parties to the prior action.

Nonmutual Collateral Estoppel

OFFENSIVE

Plaintiff seeks to stop a defendant from relitigating an issue that the defendant has previously litigated unsuccessfully in another action against a different party.

Limitations:

The court is given broad discretion in deciding if it will allow plaintiff's use of nonmutual offensive collateral estoppel by considering if the application is fair to the person against whom it is being raised.

DEFENSIVE

Defendant seeks to stop the plaintiff from relitigating an issue the plaintiff previously litigated unsuccessfully in another action against a different party. Plaintiff in current action may have been the plaintiff or defendant in previous action.

The party against whom the application of collateral estoppel is being sought had a full and fair opportunity to litigate paternity in the prior action.

Chapter 5

Establishing Paternity When It Is an Issue

Findings and Orders About Efforts to Establish Paternity

When the court in the abuse, neglect, or dependency action determines that paternity is an issue, the court must make findings as to what efforts have been taken to establish paternity. Findings of efforts made to establish paternity may range from

- no efforts have been made;
- the parents married or executed an Affidavit of Parentage after the child's birth but have not initiated a court action;
- there is pending court action that will determine paternity; or
- there is a final judgment that established paternity, but it is not binding on the party raising paternity in the abuse, neglect, or dependency action.

The court has the authority to order a party to make specific efforts to establish paternity.[1] The mother, putative father, child, and county department all have standing to initiate a paternity action in district court.[2] The putative father also has standing to commence a legitimation proceeding in superior court.[3] When the court has personal jurisdiction over the mother, child, putative father, and/or county department, the court may order one of those parties to initiate a separate paternity action in district court.[4] The court may also order the putative father to initiate a legitimation proceeding rather than a paternity proceeding.[5]

Before ordering a party to initiate a separate paternity or legitimation proceeding, the court may want to consider whether it is in the child's best interests to remove the determination of paternity from the abuse, neglect, or dependency action. Decisions regarding the child's placement and visitation in the abuse, neglect, or dependency action are directly impacted by the time required to litigate a separate paternity or legitimation action. Any delays in the separate proceeding would also delay the abuse, neglect, or dependency proceeding and impact the child's permanency. Another issue the court may want to consider is judicial efficiency. Not only is a second court action involved, but a guardian ad litem must be appointed under Rule 17 of the North Carolina Rules of Civil Procedure for the child in any separate action that names the child as a party.[6] In addition, financial considerations regarding the payment of filing fees and/or the costs of genetic marker testing for an indigent parent or child who is ordered to initiate the separate action may arise.[7]

If the court orders a party to initiate a separate action or if a separate action involving the parties in the abuse, neglect, or dependency action was pending when the abuse, neglect, or dependency petition was filed with the district court, paternity should no longer be an issue in the abuse, neglect, or dependency proceeding once there is an adjudication of paternity in the separate action. See chapter 4 for a discus-

---

1. Chapter 7B, Section 506(h)(1) of the North Carolina General Statutes (hereinafter G.S.); G.S. 7B-901(b).

2. G.S. 49-16. Note that G.S. 49-16(1) uses the term "father" but G.S. 49-14(c), (d), (f), and (h) use the term "putative father."

3. G.S. 49-10; 49-12.1.

4. *See* G.S. 7B-506(h)(1); 7B-901(b).

5. G.S. 49-10; 49-12.1 (only the putative father has standing to initiate a legitimation action).

6. G.S. 1A-1, Rule 17 (a minor must sue or be sued by a general or testamentary guardian or a guardian ad litem (GAL) appointed pursuant to G.S. 1A-1, Rule 17(b)). The child's GAL in the abuse, neglect, or dependency proceeding is appointed pursuant to G.S. 7B-602 and not G.S.1A-1, Rule 17. The G.S. 7B-601 GAL has standing to represent the child in proceedings brought under Subchapter I of G.S. Chapter 7B.

7. *See* G.S. 7A-305 (costs in civil actions); 7A-306 (costs in special proceedings; legitimation is a special proceeding); 8-50.1(b1) (court requires person requesting genetic marker testing to pay for the tests, but in its discretion the court may tax the expenses of the tests as costs).

sion of collateral estoppel. Similarly, an adjudication of non-paternity in the separate action impacts the abuse, neglect, or dependency action. When non-paternity of one man has been judicially determined and another man has not been determined to be the child's father, paternity will still be an issue in the abuse, neglect, or dependency action. Evidence of the adjudication of paternity or non-paternity should be admitted at a hearing in the abuse, neglect, or dependency action so that the court may find that paternity is no longer an issue or that a named respondent father is not a parent. See chapter 6 for a discussion of removing and adding parties based on an adjudication of paternity or non-paternity.

When there is a separate proceeding that adjudicated paternity or non-paternity, a party in that proceeding should confirm that the clerk of court notified the State Registrar of the adjudication or that the mother or father should send a certified copy of the court order to the State Registrar with a request to amend the child's birth certificate.[8] A certified copy of the amended birth certificate may be admitted as evidence in the abuse, neglect, or dependency action. The county department should obtain a copy of the amended birth certificate and place it in the child's case plan.[9] Other parties may also want to obtain a copy of the amended birth certificate.

Deciding to Adjudicate Paternity in the Abuse, Neglect, or Dependency Action

Rather than order a party to initiate a separate proceeding, the court may decide to adjudicate paternity in the abuse, neglect, or dependency action. Establishing paternity in the abuse, neglect, or dependency proceeding is judicially efficient. Not only is a second court action not required, but it is likely that most if not all of the necessary parties for a paternity adjudication were already named and served as parties in the abuse, neglect, or dependency proceeding.[10] In all abuse or neglect and in some dependency actions, the child will already be represented by a guardian ad litem (GAL) appointed under the Juvenile Code,[11] obviating the need for the appointment of a GAL under Rule 17 of the North Carolina Rules of Civil Procedure[12] to represent the child in a separate

---

8. G.S. 130A-118(b)(2), (3); 130A-119; see 10A N.C.A.C. 41H, §§ .0909, .0910.

9. 42 U.S.C. § 675(1) (defining "case plan," which must be in writing and is designed to ensure that the child receives safe and proper care, addresses services that are provided to the child and parents, and facilitates the child's permanent placement; a case plan must contain certain documents); see 42 U.S.C. § 675(5)(I)(2) (a child aging out of foster care must be provided an official or certified copy of his or her birth certificate); G.S. 7B-912(b).

10. G.S. 7B-401.1; 7B-406 (the child is not issued a summons); 7B-407.

11. G.S. Chapter 7B is referred to as the "Juvenile Code."

12. G.S. 1A-1, Rule 17.

paternity action.[13] The hearing to determine paternity may be scheduled as part of a required hearing in the abuse, neglect, or dependency proceeding, be it a nonsecure custody, pre-adjudication, adjudication, or any dispositional hearing.

Indigent respondent parents have a statutory right to appointed counsel in the abuse, neglect, or dependency action.[14] This statutory right does not apply to paternity, legitimation, child support,[15] child custody, divorce, or declaratory judgment proceedings. Deciding paternity in the abuse, neglect, or dependency action enables indigent parents to be represented by counsel.

The establishment of paternity "dramatically affect[s]" a child's "mental health, outlook, attitude, and personality."[16] Establishing paternity also impacts a child's interests in inheritance, support, and dependency benefits; knowing who has a right to claim custody; and having an accurate family medical history.[17] A paternity adjudication impacts a putative father's property interests, liberty interests, and family relationships.[18] Determining a child's parentage directly impacts the abuse, neglect, or dependency action in terms of who has the right to participate in the court action, receive reunification services, and visit with the child, as well as who is obligated to pay for the child's support. All of these factors speak to the purposes of the Juvenile Code: protect the constitutional rights of parents and children, provide services that respect family autonomy and the juvenile's need for safety and permanency, prevent the unnecessary separation of children from their parents, and ensure that the best interests of the juvenile are paramount.[19]

---

13. G.S. 7B-601(a) (a GAL for the child must be appointed in actions alleging abuse or neglect; the court has discretion in deciding whether to appoint a GAL for a child when only dependency is alleged; note that when the GAL is not an attorney, an attorney advocate will also be appointed for the child). *See In re* J.H.K., 365 N.C. 171 (2011), *and In re* S.T.B., Jr., ___ N.C. App. ___, 761 S.E.2d 734 (2014) (the GAL program represents the child and involves up to three participants who function as a team: the volunteer GAL, an attorney advocate (if the volunteer is not an attorney), and a GAL program staff member).

14. G.S. 7B-602.

15. *But see* McBride v. McBride, 334 N.C. 124 (1993) (after child support has been established, due process requires that an indigent respondent be appointed court-appointed counsel in a contempt proceeding for nonpayment of child support when incarceration is a remedy the court may impose).

16. Settle *ex rel.* Sullivan v. Beasley, 309 N.C. 616, 620, 621 (1983).

17. *Id.* at 621.

18. Leach v. Alford, 63 N.C. App. 118, 124 (1983).

19. G.S. 7B-100.

Ordering Genetic Marker Testing

The abuse, neglect, or dependency action is a civil proceeding.[20] Pursuant to Chapter 8, Section 50.1(b1) of the North Carolina General Statutes (hereinafter G.S.), a court is required to order genetic marker testing when, in a civil action, the question of parentage arises and a party moves for genetic marker testing. If any of the parties in the abuse, neglect, or dependency proceeding who are not collaterally estopped from raising paternity as an issue (see chapter 4 for a discussion of collateral estoppel) move for genetic marker testing, the court must order the mother, child, and "alleged father-defendant" to submit to testing by a duly certified physician or expert.[21] If more than one respondent party is alleged to be the child's father, the court should order each of the alleged father-respondents to submit to genetic marker testing. This includes a respondent who is the child's legal father based on the marital presumption of the child's legitimacy (see chapter 4 for an explanation of the marital presumption).[22]

If a court determines that a party is not an alleged father-respondent but wants that party to submit to testing, the court may use Rule 35 of the North Carolina Rules of Civil Procedure[23] to order that the party submit to testing.[24] Rule 35 authorizes the court to order a party to submit to a physical examination when a physical condition, including blood group, is in controversy and a motion for a physical examination, based on good cause, has been filed with the court.[25] The comments to this Rule explain that

---

20. State v. Adams, 345 N.C. 745 (1997).

21. G.S. 8-50.1(b1). *See* State *ex rel.* New Bern Child Support Agency v. Lewis, 311 N.C. 727 (1984) (defendant was collaterally estopped from raising paternity and requesting blood grouping tests); *see also In re* J.S.L., 218 N.C. App. 610 (2012) (applying G.S. 8-50.1(b1) to a termination of parental rights action where the respondent denied paternity and moved for DNA testing in his answer). Note that the term "defendant" is not used in an abuse, neglect, or dependency proceeding. A "respondent" is defined by Black's Law Dictionary (10th ed. 2014) as a "party against whom a motion or petition is filed."

22. *See* Rockingham Cty. Dep't of Soc. Servs. *ex rel.* Shaffer v. Shaffer, 126 N.C. App. 197, 199 (1997) (the decision states that the mother, husband, putative father, and child "submitted" to blood testing; the issue decided addressed the application of the evidentiary standards for tests completed pursuant to G.S. 8-50.1(b1) (emphasis added), which requires that the court *"order the [parties] to submit to . . . test[ing]"*); *see also* Jeffries v. Moore, 148 N.C. App. 364 (2002) (limits the holding in *Johnson v. Johnson*, 343 N.C. 114 (1996), to the former language of G.S. 8-50.1(b)); *see also Jeffries*, 148 N.C. App. at 371 (Greene, J. concurring) (emphasis added) (footnote omitted) (the term "alleged father-defendant" used in G.S. 8-50.1(b1) "does not appear to authorize an order compelling the husband of a mother of a child born during wedlock to submit to a blood or genetic marker test, *unless he is a defendant in a parentage case who is alleged to be the father of the child*").

23. G.S. 1A-1, Rule 35.

24. *In re Williams*, 149 N.C. App. 951 (2002), references the application of Rule 35 in a juvenile proceeding, specifically, a termination of parental rights action.

25. G.S. 1A-1, Rule 35(a). *See also Jeffries*, 148 N.C. App. at 371 n.3 (Greene, J., concurring); Brondum v. Cox, 292 N.C. 192 (1977).

the use of the language, "including the blood group" gives the court the right to require a blood test in an action in which blood relationships are in controversy.[26]

The court must have personal jurisdiction over any person it orders to submit to genetic marker testing. If only one putative father is named as a respondent party, he is the only putative father who can be ordered by the court to submit to genetic marker testing. If the test results show that it is unlikely that he is the child's father, the abuse, neglect, or dependency petition will need to be amended[27] to name a different putative father as a respondent party if the court wants to order a different respondent to submit to genetic marker testing. If the petition is amended, the newly added respondent will need to be served with a summons and a copy of the amended petition, unless he waives any defenses related to personal jurisdiction and service of process.[28]

Adjudicating Paternity or Non-Paternity Requires a Hearing

Paternity and non-paternity cannot be adjudicated by the court without a hearing and the introduction of evidence.[29] The Juvenile Code is silent about the timing or requirements for a hearing on paternity. Due process requires that the parties receive notice of the hearing. The court may conduct a stand-alone hearing on the issue of paternity or notify the parties that paternity will be an issue that is part of a required hearing in the abuse, neglect, or dependency action. A hearing, regardless of whether it is contested, requires the introduction of evidence.[30]

Evidence of Paternity/Non-Paternity

Witness testimony is likely to be the most common evidence that is introduced in a hearing deciding paternity. The testimony may consist of statements that the mother and alleged father had sexual intercourse around the time of the child's conception. If the testimony of the mother and alleged father contradict one another, the court will need to determine the credibility of the witnesses and the weight to give their

---

26. G.S. 1A-1, Rule 35(a) Official Commentary.

27. G.S. 7B-800 authorizes amending an abuse, neglect, and dependency petition. G.S. 1A-1, Rule 15 does not apply.

28. *See* G.S. 7B-200(b); 7B-407; 7B-800; *In re* K.J.L., 363 N.C. 343, 346 (2009) ("Even without a summons, a court may properly obtain personal jurisdiction over a party who consents or makes a general appearance, for example, by filing an answer or appearing at a hearing without objecting to personal jurisdiction.").

29. *In re* L.D.B., 168 N.C. App. 206 (2005) (there must be competent evidence to support the court's findings of fact and conclusions of law; the court's observation of genetic test results before the hearing is not evidence; without evidence a court cannot make proper findings of fact or conclusions of law).

30. *Id.; In re* I.D., ___ N.C. App. ___, 769 S.E.2d 846 (2015).

respective testimony.[31] If the mother and alleged father executed an Affidavit of Parentage (AOP), a certified copy of the AOP may be introduced as evidence.[32] The AOP may be used to support or impeach a witness's testimony. If a party has not moved for genetic marker testing, the court may adjudicate paternity without genetic marker testing having been completed. In actions where genetic marker testing is completed, the test results should be introduced as evidence. The court must consider the test results as one item of evidence along with all the other evidence that was introduced at the hearing.[33] The court has discretion to determine the weight it will apply to all the evidence that is admitted.[34]

Genetic Marker Testing

Genetic marker testing may have been conducted through a variety of ways, which include

- the voluntary participation of the parties,
- a subpoena issued by a child support services agency,[35] or
- a court order.

For a court determination of paternity, it is not sufficient to inform the court of the test results. The results must be admitted in evidence for the court to consider them and make necessary findings.[36]

---

31. Nash Cty. Dep't of Soc. Servs. *ex rel.* Williams v. Beamon, 126 N.C. App. 536 (1997) (mother testified that she had sexual relations with defendant and that he was the only man she had intercourse with during the period of the child's conception; defendant testified that he never met the mother and did not have sexual intercourse with her; the court gave weight to defendant's testimony and decided in his favor); *In re* Oghenekevebe, 123 N.C. App. 434 (1996).

32. G.S. 130A-101(f); 110-132(a).

33. *See* State v. Fowler, 277 N.C. 305, 310 (1970) ("Since the statutes do not make the test which establishes nonpaternity conclusive of that issue but merely provide that the results of such test 'when offered by . . . a duly qualified person' shall be admitted in evidence, it seems clear that the legislative intent was that the jury should consider the test results, whatever they might show, along with all the other evidence in determining the issue of paternity."); *Beamon*, 126 N.C. App. 536.

34. *Beamon*, 126 N.C. App. 536. Note that if the results of genetic marker testing ordered pursuant to G.S. 8-50.1(b1) are admitted in evidence and are not challenged, G.S. 8-50.1(b1) sets forth presumptions that the court applies to those results.

35. G.S. 110-132.2 authorizes a child support services agency to subpoena without court order the mother, child, and putative father to appear for genetic marker testing.

36. *In re* L.D.B., 168 N.C. App. 206 (2005).

Admitting Genetic Marker Test Results

Different evidentiary rules apply to the test results depending upon how the testing was initiated. If the genetic marker tests were ordered pursuant to G.S. 8-50.1(b1), the statute addresses the admissibility of the results in a hearing. The chain of custody of the DNA specimens is established through verified documentary evidence.[37] The test results may be admitted without foundation testimony if no objections were filed with the court.[38] If a party intends to object to the testing procedure or to the test results, the party must file a written objection with the court and serve copies on the parties at least ten days before the hearing where the results will be admitted.[39] The basis for the objection must be included in the written statement.[40] The objecting party is authorized to subpoena the testing expert who conducted the test to testify at the hearing.[41]

Test results based on the parties voluntarily submitting to genetic marker testing, complying with a child support services agency's subpoena, or complying with a court order for testing under Rule 35 of North Carolina Rules of Civil Procedure[42] are not governed by the provisions of G.S. 8-50.1(b1).[43] The evidentiary provision that authorizes the use of verified documentary evidence to prove the chain of custody of the DNA specimens and the authenticity of the test results does not apply. As a result, the party seeking to admit as evidence test results that were not based on an order of the court pursuant to G.S. 8-50.1(b1) will need to lay a foundation "by way of expert testimony explaining the way the test is conducted, attesting its scientific reliability, and vouching for its correct administration."[44] A witness must also be competent to testify to the proper chain of custody, transportation, and safekeeping of the samples allegedly taken from the relevant individuals.[45] Foundation evidence must address the entire chain of custody, starting with the taking of the sample from the individual and ending with the custodian who analyzed the samples.[46] Chain of custody evidence may be in the form of a sworn affidavit or witness testimony.[47] If a proper foundation is not established, the test results should not be admitted in evidence and may not be considered by the court.

---

37. G.S. 8-50.1(b1).

38. *Id.*

39. *Id.*

40. *Id.*

41. *Id.; see also id.* § 1A-1, Rule 35.

42. G.S. 1A-1, Rule 45.

43. Columbus Cty. *ex rel.* Brooks v. Davis, 163 N.C. App. 64 (2004).

44. Lombroia v. Peek, 107 N.C. App. 745, 749 (1992) (citation omitted).

45. *Lombroia*, 107 N.C. App. at 749.

46. *Davis*, 163 N.C. App. 64 (proper foundation was not established when there was no evidence from the custodian who took the samples and no affidavit or testimony from the person who performed the test about the untampered state of the samples when he received them).

47. *Id.*

Presumptions Applied to Genetic Marker Test Results

When genetic marker testing has been ordered pursuant to G.S. 8-50.1(b1), statutory presumptions apply to the results. If the test results indicate that the probability of parentage is less than 85 percent, there is a rebuttable presumption of non-paternity.[48] If the test results show that the probability of parentage is 97 percent or higher, there is a rebuttable presumption of paternity.[49] These two statutory presumptions may be rebutted by clear, cogent, and convincing evidence.[50]

No Presumptions Applied to Genetic Marker Test Results

There is no statutory presumption of parentage if the test results ordered pursuant to G.S. 8-50.1(b1) show a probability of parentage between 85 and 97 percent or if the experts disagree.[51] The statutory presumptions of paternity or non-paternity are limited to testing conducted pursuant to a court order entered under G.S. 8-50.1(b1). There are no presumptions for genetic marker test results when the testing was conducted pursuant to a court order under Rule 35 of the North Carolina Rules of Civil Procedure,[52] a child support services agency subpoena, or the parties' own initiative.

What Is a Rebuttable Presumption

The marital presumption of legitimacy and the statutory presumptions regarding genetic test results ordered pursuant to G.S. 8-50.1(b1) are rebuttable presumptions.[53] A rebuttable presumption infers a fact (e.g., paternity) and may be used to establish the prima facie case.[54]

When the presumption is challenged by rebutting evidence, "[s]upporting evidence [of the fact the presumption infers] must be introduced, without giving any evidential weight to the presumption itself."[55] This means that the presumption interpreting the genetic marker test result that the alleged father who submitted to the testing is or is not the father is neither evidence nor a conclusion of paternity. Instead, the evidence a court must consider is the test result itself, without the presumption being applied. For example, evidence of genetic marker test results and witness testimony contradicting those results may be introduced, and each may constitute clear, cogent, and convincing evidence of parentage. When deciding paternity, the court does not look to the statutory presumption but instead considers all the evidence (the results and the testimony) and decides the appropriate weight to place on the different evidence that

---

48. G.S. 8-50.1(b1)(1).
49. G.S. 8-50.1(b1)(4).
50. G.S. 8-50.1(b1)(1), (4).
51. G.S. 8-50.1(b1)(2), (3).
52. G.S. 1A-1, Rule 35(a).
53. G.S. 49-12.1; 8-50.1(b1)(1), (4). *In re* Papathanassiou, 195 N.C. App. 278 (2009).
54. *See In re* L.D.B., 168 N.C. App. 206, 211 (2005).
55. *L.D.B.*, 168 N.C. App. at 211 (citation omitted); G.S. 8C-301.

was introduced.[56] A court may decide to place greater weight on witness testimony and find that a statutory presumption of paternity based on genetic marker test results has been rebutted by witness testimony.[57]

Standard of Proof

The Juvenile Code does not state what standard of proof is required to establish paternity in an abuse, neglect, or dependency action. The marital presumption of legitimacy must be rebutted by clear and convincing evidence.[58] As a result, the court in an abuse, neglect, or dependency case must use the standard of clear and convincing evidence when determining the paternity or non-paternity of a legal father based on marriage. This standard should apply when the paternity determination only names the mother's husband as the respondent; for example, when the husband's paternity is not contested but paternity is an issue because a party is seeking to supplement the rebuttable presumption of legitimacy with a court adjudication of paternity. The clear and convincing standard should also apply when the petition names as respondents both the mother's husband and a putative father such that the court is determining which of the two men is the child's biological father.

When there is no marital presumption to rebut, the standard the court should apply is not specified. The court in the abuse, neglect, or dependency action may look to the standard that applies to a civil action for paternity, which is clear, cogent, and convincing evidence.[59] This is also the same standard that is required to adjudicate abuse, neglect, or dependency.[60] Or the court may use the standard that applies to ordinary civil actions: preponderance of the evidence.[61] In reading the various laws addressing paternity and legitimation in harmony with one another,[62] it is reasonable for a court to conclude that the applicable standard of proof for a paternity determination is clear

---

56. *L.D.B.,* 168 N.C. App. 206.

57. *Id.* (test result showed zero probability of paternity, but putative father should have had opportunity to admit evidence to rebut presumption); Nash Cty. Dep't of Soc. Servs. *ex rel.* Williams v. Beamon, 126 N.C. App. 536 (1997) (defendant's testimony that he did not know or have sexual relations with the child's mother was clear, cogent, and convincing evidence sufficient to rebut the presumption created by the 99.96 percent probability of paternity test results introduced in evidence along with mother's testimony that she had a one-night stand with defendant). *See also* Cole v. Cole, 74 N.C. App. 247 (1985) (expert testimony of husband's infertility dramatically drops the high probability of paternity blood test results from a probability of paternity of 95.98 percent to zero), *aff'd per curiam,* 314 N.C. 660 (1985).

58. *See* G.S. 49-12.1; *In re* Papathanassiou, 195 N.C. App. 278 (2009).

59. *See* G.S. 49-14(b).

60. G.S. 7B-805; 7B-807(a). Note that "clear and convincing evidence" is the same as "clear, cogent, and convincing evidence." *In re* Montgomery, 311 N.C. 101 (1984).

61. Wyatt v. Queen City Coach Co., 229 N.C. 340 (1948).

62. *See* Victory Cab Co. v. City of Charlotte, 234 N.C. 572 (1951) (a cardinal rule of statutory construction is to reconcile the laws and adopt the construction of a statute that harmonizes with other statutory provisions); G.S. 49-12.1; 49-14.

and convincing evidence. Using this higher standard may also allow for the application of collateral estoppel in a subsequent civil paternity action, if one is brought (see chapter 4 for a discussion of collateral estoppel). Regardless of which standard the court chooses, the court should place the parties on notice of the standard that it will apply prior to the commencement of the hearing that will determine paternity.

The Paternity or Non-Paternity Order

Contents of the Order

After the hearing, the court should enter an order determining paternity and/or non-paternity. A court order that references the genetic marker test results without determining paternity is not an adjudication of paternity.[63]

The court order should explicitly state the following:

- the court's conclusion of paternity or non-paternity,
- the standard that was used (e.g., clear, cogent, and convincing evidence), and
- the court's findings of fact.

The findings of fact must be based on competent evidence in the record. The court may want to reference in its order what evidence it relied upon (e.g., a specific witness's testimony, the Affidavit of Parentage, genetic test results) when making its finding of fact. The court may also want to include findings about a witness's credibility when there is conflicting evidence.

An order of non-paternity is as important as an order determining paternity. The order determines who is a necessary party in the action, who is entitled to court-appointed counsel (see chapter 1), who must be considered for placement (see chapter 2), who receives reunification services and visitation, and who must be considered for the child's permanent plan (see chapter 6). The order also determines whose rights must be terminated or who must execute a relinquishment or consent for the child's adoption if adoption is the child's permanent plan (see chapter 7).[64] A respondent father

---

63. *In re* D.K., 227 N.C. App. 649 (2013) (unpublished) (In a termination of parental rights proceeding, respondent's paternity had not been judicially established in the underlying dependency action when there was evidence that, in November 2010, a court order referred to respondent as father but also found that it would be in the child's best interests that paternity be established. Evidence also showed that a paternity test was performed in December 2010 that indicated a 99.99 percent probability that respondent was the father, but there was no evidence that the court's review orders in the underlying dependency action addressed the paternity test or made any factual findings regarding respondent's paternity.).

64. G.S. 48-2-401(c)(3); 48-3-603(a)(2); *see also In re* J.S.L., 218 N.C. App. 610, 611 (2012) (in mother's action to terminate respondent father's rights, if respondent had been excluded as the child's father, the court would have been required to dismiss the petition against respondent).

who is later adjudicated not to be the child's father has no legal rights to the child.[65] Because he has been adjudicated not to be the child's parent, he should be removed as a party from the abuse, neglect, or dependency proceeding unless he meets the statutory criteria for party status as the child's guardian, custodian, or caretaker.[66] To avoid confusion, the court should enter an order either removing him as a party to the abuse, neglect, or dependency action or explicitly identifying his party status as the child's guardian, custodian, or caretaker.

The Order Is Withheld from Public Inspection

Court records of an abuse, neglect, or dependency proceeding are withheld from public inspection.[67] Limited statutory exceptions apply to the parties in the abuse, neglect, or dependency proceeding and to their right to examine and obtain copies of written parts of the court records.[68] Nonparties must obtain a court order to access the court records of an abuse, neglect, or dependency action.[69] Because an order of paternity and/or non-paternity has implications both within and outside of the abuse, neglect, or dependency proceeding, the court may want to enter an order in the abuse, neglect, or dependency proceeding that only addresses the child's parentage. This way, if a motion to examine the order that determined a man's paternity or non-paternity to the child is filed with the court,[70] the information from the abuse, neglect, or dependency court record that the court authorizes to be disclosed may be limited to the order that only contains a determination of paternity or non-paternity.

Creating an Order That Is Available for Public Inspection

The court has the authority to order that a record in the abuse, neglect, or dependency court file be examined.[71] As a result, a court may want to consider adopting a practice of entering a second order that is essentially a duplicate of the paternity or non-paternity order for the sole purpose of making it available for public inspection.

---

65. *In re* Papathanassiou, 195 N.C. App. 278, 284 (2009) ("A determination that a petitioner in a legitimation action, and not the husband, is the biological father of the child terminates the husband's rights to the child, conferring them onto petitioner."); Lombroia v. Peek, 107 N.C. App. 745, 751 (1992) ("Mr. Lombroia's rights and responsibilities with regard to the minor child were finally determined when the Florida court found that he was not the father of the child.").

66. G.S. 7B-401.1(b), (c), (d), (e), (g). See chapter 1.

67. G.S. 7B-2901(a).

68. *Id.*

69. *Id.*

70. *Id.*

71. *Id.*

The court could order the clerk to create a new civil file for the duplicate order and assign it with the next available civil file (CVD) number.[72] By ordering the clerk to create a CVD file, the court would be issuing an order that authorizes the examination of the juvenile court order that determined paternity or non-paternity as part of the abuse, neglect, or dependency proceeding.[73] In creating this duplicate order, the court could remove any information about the abuse, neglect, or dependency action, including the docket number that identifies the action as a juvenile case.[74] This duplicate order should identify the parties who were part of the proceeding, the standard of proof that was used to prove or disprove paternity, and the court's determination of paternity or non-paternity. The original order that was entered in the abuse, neglect, or dependency action would continue to be part of that court record and would be withheld from public inspection.

By maintaining a CVD file that contains an order of paternity or non-paternity, an individual or an agency who is involved in a subsequent abuse, neglect, dependency; paternity; legitimation; child support; child custody; estate; or other proceeding where paternity may be raised as an issue would be more easily able to determine whether paternity had been previously adjudicated and, if so, who the parties were to that action. Without a CVD file, a party in a later court action would need to obtain an order that authorizes the examination of orders that were entered in the abuse, neglect, or dependency action to determine whether there had been a court adjudication of paternity or non-paternity.[75] With a record of the paternity order available for public inspection, the need to obtain a court order to examine whether paternity had been adjudicated in the abuse, neglect, or dependency proceeding would be obviated.

Amended Birth Certificate

When the court in the abuse, neglect, or dependency proceeding enters an order that determines parentage that differs from what is stated on the child's birth certificate, the clerk of court is required to notify the State Registrar of the contents of that order so

---

72. CVD is the case file number code that identifies the action as a civil action in district court. *See* State of North Carolina, Administrative Office of the Courts, Records of the Clerks of Superior Court, Rules of Recordkeeping (hereinafter Rules of Recordkeeping), Ch. XII, "Juvenile Records," Rule 12.19 (adopted December 1, 2015, this new rule allows the clerk to create a CVD file for a stand-alone order of parentage when the court issues such an order in a juvenile proceeding); *see also id.* Ch. III, "Civil District and Civil Superior," Rule 3.1B12(b) (effective November 20, 2015, this rule authorizes the clerk to create a CVD file for a stand-alone order of parentage entered in a juvenile proceeding and to send a certified copy of the order to the State Registrar).

73. G.S. 7B-2901(a).

74. Rules of Recordkeeping, Ch. XII, "Juvenile Records," Rule 12.3 (the court designates "J" for "juvenile" when creating a file number for a juvenile proceeding initiated pursuant to G.S. Chapter 7B).

75. G.S. 7B-2901(a).

that the child's birth certificate will be amended.[76] If a duplicate CVD order has been entered, the clerk should send a certified copy of that order to the State Registrar.[77] If the order only exists in the juvenile court record, the clerk must first obtain authorization from the court to either disclose the contents of the order or send a certified copy of the order to the State Registrar.[78]

If the clerk fails to notify the State Registrar of the court order determining paternity or non-paternity, a parent may request that the child's birth certificate be amended. Because a parent who is a party in the abuse, neglect, or dependency proceeding is entitled to copies of written parts of the record without a court order, it appears that the parent may attach a certified copy of the court order that determined paternity or non-paternity to his or her request for an amended birth certificate, so long as the court has not also ordered that further dissemination is prohibited.[79]

As discussed in chapter 4, an amended birth certificate is not sufficient to prove that paternity has been judicially determined. Access to the court order that adjudicated paternity will be necessary to determine whether paternity has been judicially established.

Summary

Once the court has determined that paternity is an issue, it must decide how the issue will be resolved. A variety of factors support the adjudication of paternity being made in the abuse, neglect, or dependency proceeding. The court must hold a hearing where evidence supporting and/or refuting the alleged father's paternity must be introduced. Upon considering the evidence that was admitted, the court will ultimately adjudicate the respondent's paternity or non-paternity. The court's determination must be recorded in a court order that is entered in the action that adjudicated the issue of paternity. If the court's determination differs from what is reflected on the child's birth certificate, the State Registrar should be notified and/or sent a certified copy of the order adjudicating paternity or non-paternity so that the child's birth certificate will be amended to reflect the court's determination of parentage.

---

76. G.S. 130A-118(b)(2); 130A-119.

77. G.S. 130A-119; Rules of Recordkeeping, Ch. III, "Civil District and Civil Superior," Rule 3.1B12(b).

78. *See* G.S. 7B-2901(a); Rules of Recordkeeping, Ch. XII, "Juvenile Records," Rule 12.5 ("abuse, neglect and dependency cases are not open to public inspection.").

79. G.S. 7B-2901(a)(4).

Chapter 6

The Effect of a Paternity Adjudication

A judicial determination of paternity or non-paternity impacts the familial relationship between the child and father and the rights and interests that accompany that relationship. A judicial determination of paternity also directly impacts the abuse, neglect, or dependency proceeding, both procedurally and substantively. This chapter discusses the effect of a paternity adjudication on the abuse, neglect, or dependency proceeding. The impact of the paternity adjudication will vary depending on what stage in the abuse, neglect, or dependency proceeding paternity is established: pre-adjudication, adjudication, initial disposition, post-adjudication review hearings, or permanency planning hearings.

The Stages of an Abuse, Neglect, or Dependency Proceeding

The *pre-adjudication stage* refers to any court hearing that is held before the adjudicatory hearing. This includes a pre-adjudication hearing,[1] and if the child was placed in nonsecure custody, the hearing(s) on the need for continued nonsecure custody.[2]

The *adjudication stage* involves the adjudicatory hearing where the court will either conclude that the child is abused, neglected, and/or dependent or not.[3] If the court does not adjudicate the child as abused, neglected, and/or dependent, the court must dismiss the action with prejudice.[4] The adjudicatory hearing must be held within sixty days of when the petition alleging abuse, neglect, or dependency was filed with the court, unless the court grants a continuance based on good or extraordinary cause.[5]

The *initial disposition phase* involves the first disposition hearing that occurs after the child is adjudicated as abused, neglected, and/or dependent. This hearing must be held after the adjudicatory hearing and conclude within thirty days of when the adjudicatory hearing ended.[6] The purpose of the disposition hearing is to create an appropriate plan, via the court order, that is designed to meet the child's needs.[7] The disposition order is based on the court's determination of what is in the child's best interest and will address the child's placement and visitation; decision-making authority over the child; services to be provided to the child and/or parent, guardian, custodian, or caretaker (including whether reasonable efforts to reunify the child with the parent are not required); and, if applicable, provisions for the parent and/or county to pay for certain services or for a reasonable portion of the child's care.[8]

The *post-adjudication review hearing* is the next stage in the proceeding and starts with the second dispositional hearing that is held by the court after the child is adjudicated. A review hearing must be scheduled within ninety days of an initial disposition order that has removed custody from the child's parent, guardian, or custodian.[9] When a child is not in the parent's custody, review hearings must continue to be held at least

---

1. Chapter 7B, Section 800.1 of the North Carolina General Statutes (hereinafter G.S.).

2. G.S. 7B-506(a), (e). See chapter 2 for a discussion of nonsecure custody.

3. G.S. 7B-801; 7B-802; 7B-805; 7B-807. The county department must prove the allegations in the petition by clear and convincing evidence, and the allegations must satisfy the required elements of abuse, neglect, or dependency as defined in *id.* §§ 7B-101(1), (9), (15).

4. G.S. 7B-807(a).

5. G.S. 7B-801(c); 7B-803.

6. G.S. 7B-901(a).

7. G.S. 7B-900; 7B-901; 7B-905.

8. G.S. 7B-901; 7B-903; 7B-903.1 (referencing 7B-505.1 for medical-decision making); 7B-904; 7B-905.1.

9. G.S. 7B-905(b); 7B-906.1(a). Note that it appears a review hearing is not required if the previous disposition order awarded custody of the child to the child's parent or to the person who was the child's guardian or custodian at the time the child was first removed by the county department. Although the statute does not appear to require a review hearing in this situation, there is nothing that prohibits the court from conducting a review hearing.

every six months until there is a permanency planning hearing.[10] The new disposition order may be the same as or may modify the previous disposition order, which is either the initial disposition order or a prior review order.[11]

The last stage of the abuse, neglect, or dependency action, other than the termination of the court's jurisdiction, is *permanency planning*. The court must hold a "permanency planning hearing" within twelve months of the initial order that removed custody of the child from the parent, guardian, or custodian.[12] However, a permanency planning hearing must occur sooner if the court orders at initial disposition that the county department is not required to make reasonable efforts for reunification with a parent.[13] In that case, the permanency planning hearing must be held within thirty days of the initial disposition order that eliminated reasonable efforts for reunification.[14] After the first permanency planning hearing, additional permanency planning hearings must be held within six-month intervals.[15] These regularly scheduled permanency planning hearings are not required if the child is placed in his or her parent's custody or the court waives further hearings after making written findings of specific statutory criteria.[16]

At the permanency planning hearing, the court determines the child's permanent plans and reviews the progress made in finalizing the plans.[17] At the conclusion of each permanency planning hearing, the court must enter a permanency planning order, which is a disposition order that sets forth "the best permanent plans to achieve a safe, permanent home for the juvenile within a reasonable period of time."[18] There are six possible permanent plans: reunification, adoption, guardianship, custody, Another Planned Permanent Living Arrangement (APPLA), or reinstatement of a parent's rights

---

10. G.S. 7B-906.1(a), (k). Note that subsection (n) of this statute authorizes the court to waive review hearings if all of the criteria of the subsection are found by clear, cogent, and convincing evidence, but one of the required criteria refers to a "permanent custodian or guardian," which contemplates a permanency planning hearing and not a review hearing.

11. G.S. 7B-906.1(i).

12. G.S. 7B-906.1(a). Note that this first order may be the initial nonsecure custody order entered pursuant to G.S. 7B-502 through -505.

13. G.S. 7B-901(c), (d). *See id.* §§ 7B-101(18), (18b) ("reasonable efforts" and "return home or reunification" defined). Note that the language of G.S. 7B-901(c) is limited to the actions of a parent and does not include the actions of the guardian or custodian from whose care the child was removed.

14. G.S. 7B-901(d).

15. G.S. 7B-906.1(a).

16. G.S. 7B-906.1(k), (n); *In re P.A.,* ___ N.C. App. ___, 772 S.E.2d 240 (2015) (G.S. 7B-906.1(n) authorizes the court to waive review hearings if the court makes written findings by clear, cogent, and convincing evidence of each of the five enumerated criteria; failure to make all five required findings is reversible error).

17. G.S. 7B-906.1(a).

18. G.S. 7B-906.1(g).

if those rights were previously terminated.[19] A child must have at least two concurrent permanent plans, and each permanency planning order must designate the primary and secondary permanent plans and the efforts that a county department must make toward finalizing each of the designated plans.[20]

Adding and Removing Parties in the Abuse, Neglect, or Dependency Action

If paternity is established for a father who has not been named as a respondent in the abuse, neglect, or dependency proceeding, he must be added as a necessary party to the proceeding.[21] His status as the child's adjudicated father should be clearly reflected in a court order in the abuse, neglect, or dependency proceeding. Unless he waived service of process, he must be served with a summons and a copy of the abuse, neglect, or dependency petition.[22] As a respondent parent, he will be entitled to court-appointed counsel if he is indigent.[23]

If his paternity is established in the pre-adjudicatory stage of the proceeding, the petition should be amended to name the now adjudicated father as a respondent father.[24] The Juvenile Code[25] does not address whether a petition should be amended after a child's adjudication or whether a necessary party may be added to the proceeding without the need to amend the petition once the action has progressed to dispositional stages. The safest course of action for a county department is to amend the petition for the sole purpose of complying with the procedural requirement that the petition contain the name and last known address of each party, which now must include the child's recently adjudicated father.[26] The court has the discretion to permit

---

19. G.S. 7B-906.2(a). *See id.* §§ 7B-101(18b) (reunification); 7B-600 (guardianship); 7B-912(b) (APPLA); 7B-1114 (reinstatement of parental rights); G.S. Chapter 48 (adoption); Chapter 50 (custody).

20. G.S. 7B-906.2(a), (b).

21. G.S. 7B-401.1(b); 1A-1, Rule 19. *See In re* M.L.N., ___ N.C. App. ___, 779 S.E.2d 527 (2015) (unpublished) (Rule 19 applies in a juvenile proceeding, and parent is a necessary party).

22. G.S. 7B-406; 7B-407. *See id.* § 7B-200(b) (he may waive service of process). See chapter 1 for a discussion of naming parties in the abuse, neglect, or dependency action; see chapter 2 for a discussion of service of the summons and personal jurisdiction over a respondent.

23. G.S. 7B-602.

24. G.S. 7B-401.1(b). *See id.* § 7B-800 (amendment of petition).

25. G.S. Chapter 7B is referred to as the "Juvenile Code."

26. G.S. 7B-402(a). Note that the language in G.S. 7B-1105(b), which authorizes the issuance of a summons to an unknown parent whose identity has been determined in a preliminary hearing in a termination of parental rights action, does not exist in the procedural statutes addressing abuse, neglect, or dependency proceedings; instead, G.S. 7B-800 authorizes the amendment of an abuse, neglect, or dependency petition.

the amendment of a petition and to determine the manner in which the petition must be served on the parties.[27]

The county department may have named a respondent father (or fathers) because of his status as the child's legal father or the belief that he is the child's putative father. It is possible that more than one respondent father was named in the action. For example, the county department may have named two putative fathers or a legal father and a putative father and raised paternity as an issue it seeks to have the court address. In that case, the court order will have determined the paternity or non-paternity of the named respondent father. If two respondent fathers are named, the court order should determine the non-paternity of one of the named respondents when adjudicating the paternity of the other named respondent or determine the non-paternity of both named respondent fathers.

When a court enters an order determining that a respondent parent is not the child's father, his status as legal father or putative father no longer exists. He has no legal rights to the child.[28] Because he has been adjudicated not to be the child's parent, he should be removed as a respondent parent from the abuse, neglect, or dependency proceeding. He no longer has standing to remain as a party unless the court determines that he meets the statutory criteria for party status as the child's guardian, custodian, or caretaker.[29] To avoid confusion, the court should issue an order either removing him as a party to the abuse, neglect, or dependency action or explicitly identifying his party status as the child's guardian, custodian, or caretaker.

If he remains as a non-parent respondent, he no longer meets the statutory requirement for court-appointed counsel for parents.[30] Although not a parent, if the court determines that he continues to have a constitutionally protected interest that will be impacted by the abuse, neglect, or dependency action such that due process requires the appointment of an attorney, the North Carolina Office of Indigent Defense Services (IDS) will pay for the continuation of the attorney's appointment.[31] If the non-parent respondent has an interest in the action that does not trigger constitutional due process protections, his court-appointed attorney will need to seek leave from

---

27. G.S. 7B-800.

28. *In re* Papathanassiou, 195 N.C. App. 278, 284 (2009) ("A determination that a petitioner in a legitimation action, and not the husband, is the biological father of the child terminates the husband's rights to the child, conferring them onto petitioner."); Lombroia v. Peek, 107 N.C. App. 745, 751 (1992) ("Mr. Lombroia's rights and responsibilities with regard to the minor child were finally determined when the Florida court found that he was not the father of the child").

29. G.S. 7B-401.1.

30. G.S. 7B-602.

31. N.C. Office of Indigent Defense Servs., Appointment of Counsel for Non-Parent Respondents in Abuse, Neglect, and Dependency Proceedings (2008), www.ncids.org/Rules%20&%20Procedures/Policies%20By%20Case%20Type/AND-TPR/AppointmentsCounselNon-parentRespondents.pdf.

the court to withdraw from representing the respondent who no longer qualifies for court-appointed counsel or may decide to continue to represent the client without payment by IDS.[32]

The Impact on an Adjudication of Dependency

Dependency Defined

Dependency requires that a child need assistance or placement because

1. the child has no parent, guardian, or custodian responsible for his or her care or supervision or
2. both of the child's parents (and the child's guardian or custodian, if applicable) are
   - unable to provide for the child's care or supervision and
   - lack an appropriate alternative child care arrangement.[33]

Post-Petition Evidence of Paternity

A child is adjudicated abused, neglected, and/or dependent when the county department proves by clear and convincing evidence the conditions alleged in the petition, and those conditions constitute abuse, neglect, and/or dependency.[34] Because the adjudication is based on what was alleged in the petition, evidence at the adjudicatory hearing is limited to the time period up to the date the petition is filed; post-petition facts are not relevant.[35] There is an exception for actions involving dependency and a putative father's failure to establish paternity. When a petition alleges as part of the grounds for the child's dependency that the putative father did not establish paternity, evidence that the putative father established paternity after the petition was filed may be introduced at the adjudicatory hearing.[36] Post-petition evidence is limited to the adjudication of paternity.[37] When the petition also alleges facts that show the putative

32. Smith v. Bryant, 264 N.C. 208 (1965) (attorney-client relationship may be dissolved at any time in good faith; to withdraw, an attorney must have justifiable cause, provide reasonable notice to the client, and obtain permission from the court; nonpayment of fees justifies withdrawal); *see also In re* D.E.G., 228 N.C. App. 381 (2013) (leave to withdraw required in juvenile proceeding).

33. G.S. 7B-101(9); *In re* H.H., ___ N.C. App. ___, 767 S.E.2d 347 (2014); *In re* V.B., ___ N.C. App. ___, 768 S.E.2d 867 (2015) (although the definition expressly mentions "parent" in the singular, the court must look at whether the child has "a parent" who is able to provide care and supervision, requiring the court to look to both parents).

34. G.S. 7B-802; 7B-805; 7B-807(a). *See id.* §§ 7B-101(1), (9), (15) for definitions of "abuse," "dependency," and "neglect."

35. *In re* A.B., 179 N.C. App. 605 (2006).

36. *V.B.,* ___ N.C. App. ___, 768 S.E.2d 867.

37. *Id.*

father is unable to provide care and supervision and lacks appropriate alternative child care for the child, the evidence on those facts would be limited to pre-petition evidence.

Although the North Carolina Court of Appeals has not been presented with this issue, it is reasonable to conclude that the court may determine paternity or non-paternity as part of the adjudicatory hearing for dependency. The question of whether paternity is an issue should have been addressed at the pre-adjudication hearing, and if nonsecure custody had been ordered, at each of the hearings on the need for continued nonsecure custody.[38] As discussed in chapter 5, when paternity is an issue, the court may adjudicate paternity in the abuse, neglect, or dependency action. Part of a dependency determination requires the court to determine if the child has a parent, guardian, or custodian.[39] A paternity determination would prove the child has a parent, specifically a father. If there is only one named respondent father and he is determined not to be the child's father, the county department will have proved at the adjudicatory hearing that the child does not have a father. But the non-paternity determination by itself is not sufficient to prove the child's dependency. The county department will need to prove that the child is without a mother, guardian, or custodian as well. Similarly, a court order of paternity is not an absolute defense to an adjudication of dependency, for the father may have been alleged and proved to be unable to provide proper care and supervision for his child and to lack an appropriate alternative child care arrangement.[40]

Findings for Both Parents Required

Neither the failure to establish paternity nor a court order of non-paternity is, standing alone, sufficient to prove that a child is dependent because the circumstances regarding the child's mother have not also been considered. The county department must allege and prove each element of the definition of dependency for each parent.[41]

The requirement that allegations be made and proof be introduced about each parent makes dependency different from abuse and neglect. The court of appeals discussed the distinction between abuse, neglect, and dependency in *In re H.H.*[42] In that case involving two children, the adjudication that one of the children was abused because the child was bruised as a result of her mother's use of corporal punishment was affirmed. The children's adjudication of neglect was also affirmed based on their not receiving proper care, supervision, and guidance from a parent. Specifically, the children's mother called 911 to say she could not care for her children. She then called the children's father to take them and drove the children to a parking lot, where she

38. G.S. 7B-506(h)(1); 7B-800.1(a)(3).
39. G.S. 7B-101(9) ("caretaker" is not included in the definition of dependency).
40. *See id.*
41. *V.B.,* ___ N.C. App. ___, 768 S.E.2d 867.
42. *In re* H.H., ___ N.C. App. ___, 767 S.E.2d 347 (2014).

left them standing outside her car until their father arrived. When their father pulled into the parking lot, the mother told them that they would never see her again and drove away. After the mother later tried to remove the children from their father's care, the county department filed a petition alleging abuse, neglect, and dependency and obtained an order for nonsecure custody that placed the children with their father. The adjudication of dependency was reversed by the court of appeals because "the juveniles simply cannot be adjudicated dependent" when evidence and findings of fact indicated that they were living with a parent who was willing and able to provide for their care and supervision.[43] The conditions causing abuse and neglect were created by one parent, but dependency requires the condition to be created by both parents.

Because a child is not dependent when that child either lives with a parent or has an appropriate alternative child care placement arranged by a parent, paternity is relevant when a court is determining if a child is dependent. A child will not meet the criteria for dependency if the child is living with his or her putative father who is providing for the child's care or supervision and his paternity is established at the adjudicatory hearing. Similarly, a child may be placed in nonsecure custody outside of the putative father's home even though the putative father is able to care for the child or has suggested appropriate alternative child care for the child. If a county department or court did not act on the available placement options offered by the putative father because paternity had not been established, it is unlikely the county department can prove by clear and convincing evidence that the child is dependent if paternity is determined at the adjudicatory hearing. With paternity adjudicated, the evidence before the court would show that the child had a parent who could provide care and supervision or an appropriate alternative child care arrangement for his child.

Required Protective Services

Protective services are arranged for and provided by a county department and are designed to protect children and preserve and stabilize a family's life.[44] Services may include a family assessment, casework, and counseling for parents to help them improve their parenting.[45] In providing services, mothers and fathers must be equally considered, as there is no presumption that a mother is the better parent or has superior rights to a child.[46]

---

43. *Id.* at 352.
44. G.S. 7B-300.
45. *Id.*
46. G.S. 50-13.2(a); Rosero v. Blake, 357 N.C. 193 (2003) (a father who acknowledged paternity and whose conduct is consistent with his right to care and control of his child who was born out of wedlock has an equal right to custody as the mother).

In developing a child's case plan,[47] a county department must determine how each parent can be appropriately involved in the child's life. The county department is not the sole decision-maker regarding a parent's level of involvement with his or her child. The court in the abuse, neglect, or dependency case provides oversight over all the parties. After hearing from the county department, the child's guardian ad litem, and/or each parent, a court may order a county department to make specific services available to the child and/or each parent.[48] The court may also order a parent to participate in certain services, such as parenting classes or other services that would remedy the conditions that contributed to the child's adjudication or to the court's removal of the child's custody from the child's parent, guardian, custodian, or caretaker.[49] Unless the court makes written findings that the parent forfeited his or her rights to visitation or that visitation is not in the child's best interest, the court must order visitation with each parent if the child has been placed outside of the parent's home.[50] The county department's case plan for the child and the court orders should address each parent, asking questions such as the following:

- What are the services, including visitation, which must be provided to each parent?
- What are the expectations for each parent?
- What are the obligations of each parent?
- What is the parent's progress in alleviating the conditions that led to the child's adjudication or removal?[51]

Reunification with the Father

Absent specific statutory exceptions, a county department is required to make reasonable efforts to preserve and reunify families.[52] The Juvenile Code defines "return home or reunification" as including the "[p]lacement of the juvenile in the home of *either*

---

47. 42 U.S.C. § 675(1) (defines "case plan," which must be in writing and is designed to ensure that the child receives safe and proper care, addresses services that are provided to the child and parents, and facilitates the child's permanent placement).

48. G.S. 7B-903(d), (e); 7B-904.

49. G.S. 7B-904.

50. G.S. 7B-905.1. *See In re* T.R.T., 225 N.C. App. 567 (2013); *In re* K.C., 199 N.C. App. 557 (2009).

51. G.S. 7B-906.1(d).

52. 42 U.S.C. § 671(a)(15) (to qualify for federal funding for adoption and foster care assistance under Title IV-E of the Social Security Act, a state is required to develop, and also to obtain from the U.S. Department of Health and Human Services approval of, a state plan that contains specific requirements set forth by federal law. One of the several requirements is the provision of reasonable efforts that are designed to reunify a child with his or her parent. Reasonable efforts are not required when: (1) a parent has subjected the child

parent.[53] The definition of reunification recognizes the purpose of the Juvenile Code for the "return of juveniles to their homes consistent with preventing the unnecessary or inappropriate separation of juveniles from their parents."[54] A county department must provide reunification services to a father when his paternity has been established, unless the court makes one of the written findings specified in the Juvenile Code that authorizes the court to order that reasonable efforts for reunification are not required.[55]

A child's length of time in a placement before paternity has been established will not relieve the county department of its obligation to make reasonable efforts to reunify the child with his or her father or allow the court to proceed with a plan that fails to consider the child's reunification with his or her father.[56] The establishment of paternity is a changed condition the court must recognize.[57]

Reasonable Efforts to Reunify Are Not Required

The Juvenile Code limits the court's discretion to order that a county department is not required to provide reasonable efforts for reunification. A court *must* order that no reasonable efforts to reunify are required when the court makes written findings of one of the following:[58]

- The parent committed or allowed for an aggravating circumstance against the child. An aggravating circumstance includes sexual abuse, chronic physical or emotional abuse, torture, abandonment, chronic or toxic exposure to alcohol or controlled substances that caused an addiction by or impairment in the

---

to aggravating circumstances; (2) a parent has committed or aided, abetted, attempted, conspired, or solicited to commit murder or voluntary manslaughter of his/her child; (3) a parent has committed felony assault resulting in serious bodily injury to the child who is the subject of the proceeding or another child of the parent; or (4) a parent has had his or her parental rights to a sibling of the child who is the subject of the protective action involuntarily terminated). Pursuant to 42 U.S.C. §§ 5106a(b)(2)(B)(xvi)(V), (VI), reasonable efforts are also not required when a parent (1) has been found to have sexually abused the child who is the subject of the proceeding or another child of the parent or (2) is required to register with a sex offender registry. *See also* 42 U.S.C. § 671(a)(15)(D); G.S. 7B-100; 7B-901(c) (note that subsection (1) identifies aggravated circumstances in North Carolina); 7B-906.2(b).

53. G.S. 7B-101(18b) (emphasis added). Note the definition also includes the child's placement in the home of a custodian or guardian from whose home the child was removed by court order. This definition was added by S.L. 2013-129. The statute abrogates the holding in *In re J.M.D.*, 210 N.C. App. 420 (2011), which limited "return home" to the home of the parent from whom the child was removed.

54. G.S. 7B-100(4). *See In re* Eckard, 148 N.C. App. 541 (2002).

55. G.S. 7B-901(c); 7B-906.2(b)); *see also id.* § 7B-101(18) ("reasonable efforts" defined); 7B-906.1(d), (e), (g); 7B-906.2(c), (d); *In re A.E.C.*, ___ N.C. App. ___, 768 S.E.2d 166 (2015).

56. *Eckard*, 148 N.C. App. 541; *A.E.C.*, ___ N.C. App. ___, 768 S.E.2d 166.

57. *In re V.B.*, ___ N.C. App. ___, 768 S.E.2d 867 (2015); *Eckard*, 148 N.C. App. 541.

58. G.S. 7B-901(c) states that "the court *shall* direct that reasonable efforts for reunification . . . *shall* not be required *if* the court makes written findings of fact pertaining to any of the following" enumerated factors (emphasis added).

child, or another action that increased the enormity or injurious consequences of the child's abuse or neglect.[59]

- The parent's rights to another child were involuntarily terminated.[60]
- The parent committed murder or voluntary manslaughter of another child of the parent.[61]
- The parent sexually abused; committed felony assault resulting in serious bodily injury; or aided, abetted, attempted, conspired, or solicited to commit murder or voluntary manslaughter of this child or any other child of the parent.[62]
- The parent is required to register as a sex offender.[63]

In addition, at a permanency planning hearing, the court may order that the county department is relieved of reunification efforts with a parent if the court finds that

- reunification efforts would clearly be unsuccessful or
- reunification efforts would clearly be inconsistent with the child's health and safety.[64]

There are some cases where a father's paternity will not be established until very late in the proceeding, well after a child has been adjudicated abused, neglected, or dependent and a permanency planning order has been entered that does not include a concurrent plan of reunification with the child's father. A father's involvement at a later stage in the action is sometimes referred to as a "late appearance."[65] Even with a late appearance, unless the court finds a statutory factor authorizing an order that reasonable efforts for reunification are not required, the court should order reunification with the father as a concurrent permanent plan for the child.[66] There are two statutory factors that may authorize the court to relieve the county department of reasonable efforts to reunify the child with his or her father based on a father's late appearance in the case.

The first factor is when the court finds that the father has committed the aggravating factor of abandoning the child.[67] Abandonment requires findings, supported by

---

59. G.S. 7B-901(c)(1).

60. G.S. 7B-901(c)(2). *See* 42 U.S.C. § 671(a)(15)(D)(iii).

61. G.S. 7B-901(c)(3). *See* 42 U.S.C. §§ 671(a)(15)(D)(ii)(I), (II); 42 U.S.C. § 5106a(b)(2)(B)(xvi)(II).

62. G.S. 7B-901(c)(3). *See* 42 U.S.C. §§ 671(a)(15)(D)(ii)(III), (IV); 42 U.S.C. §§ 5106a(b)(2)(B)(xvi)(III), (IV), (V).

63. G.S. 7B-901(c)(3). *See* 42 U.S.C. § 5106a(b)(2)(B)(xvi)(VI).

64. G.S. 7B-906.2(b).

65. *See In re* Eckard, 148 N.C. App. 541 (2002); *In re* A.E.C., ___ N.C. App. ___, 768 S.E.2d 166 (2015).

66. G.S. 7B-906.2(b), (c). *See id.* §§ 7B-906.1(d), (e).

67. G.S. 7B-901(c)(1)d.

competent evidence in the record, of the father's "willful determination to forego all parental duties and relinquish all parental claims to the child."[68] The father's willfulness necessitates his knowledge of the child's existence. It would be difficult to prove that a father who was unaware of his child's birth because of a mother's actions to hide the pregnancy and birth from the father willfully abandoned his child. However, a man who was notified of the pregnancy and/or birth but who failed to take any actions to assert his role as a father may be found to have abandoned his child.

The second factor is when a court finds that reunification efforts clearly would be inconsistent with the child's health and safety.[69] A determination that reunification is clearly inconsistent with a child's health and safety requires the court to make written findings that support that ultimate fact. The sole finding that it is not in the child's best interest to remove him or her from the home in which he or she has bonded with the caregivers will not support the ultimate finding that results in an order relieving the county department of making reasonable efforts to reunify the child with his or her father.[70]

The statutory factors to eliminate reunification as a permanent plan do not specifically include the father's failure to acknowledge or establish paternity or to provide reasonable and consistent support for the mother and child. This differs from the grounds to terminate parental rights or for determining whether a father's consent to the child's adoption is required.[71] The abuse, neglect, or dependency action has different statutory requirements that include, rather than exclude, fathers. In an abuse, neglect, or dependency proceeding, the court must inquire about identifying and locating parents and establishing paternity, consider placement of the juvenile with his or her parent, and order reunification efforts so as to prevent the unnecessary separation of children from their parents.[72] A court should limit its analysis of whether reunification efforts may be eliminated to the explicit statutory factors[73] stated in the Juvenile Code and should not apply the reasoning of appellate opinions that discuss the failure of a father to acknowledge paternity or provide support as required by the termination of parental rights and consent for adoption statutes. For a full discussion of those opinions as they apply to adoption and termination of parental rights proceedings, see chapter 7.

---

68. *In re* A.K.D., 227 N.C. App. 58, 60 (2013) (quoting *In re* Adoption of Searle, 82 N.C. App. 273, 275 (1986)).

69. G.S. 7B-906.2(b).

70. *Eckard*, 148 N.C. App. 541.

71. *See* G.S. 7B-1111(a)(5); 48-3-601(2)b.4. See chapter 7 for a full discussion of these statutes.

72. G.S. 7B-100(4); 7B-503(a); 7B-506(h)(1); 7B-800.1(a)(2), (3), (4); 7B-901(b); 7B-906.2(b). *See also In re* A.C.V., 203 N.C. App. 473 (2010).

73. G.S. 7B-901(c); 7B-906.2(b).

Reasonable Efforts to Reunify Are Required

Without the necessary written findings and an order that reasonable efforts for reunification with the father are not required, the court must consider reunification with
the father after paternity has been established, even if permanent plans have previously
been established for the child.[74] The child's case plan and accompanying court order
will be fact-specific based on the circumstances that exist in each case. Reasonable
efforts may range from an introductory meeting between the child and the father he
or she has never met or had knowledge of, to immediate placement with the father,
and everything in between.

Placement with the Father

If the child was not removed from his or her father's care, a court must consider the
child's placement with the father.[75] The purposes of the Juvenile Code include recog-
nizing a parent's constitutional rights and the right to family autonomy and preventing the unnecessary or inappropriate separation of children from their parents.[76] If
there is no evidence that the father is unfit or that he has acted inconsistently with
his parental rights, his rights to care, custody, and control of the child are superior to
any third party's rights to the child. The court does not apply the best interests of the
child analysis between the father and any third party.[77]

The Juvenile Code prioritizes placement with a parent for nonsecure custody.[78] After
a child's adjudication, the court must prioritize reunification with each parent unless
the court makes written findings that reasonable efforts for reunification with a parent are not required.[79] Reunification may involve an order of custody to a parent.[80]
Although a court may be hesitant to order custody to a father who has recently been
adjudicated as such, the father may have had a relationship with the child prior to the
judicial determination of paternity. If a father did not have a relationship with the child,
a short-term transition plan may be ordered to assist the child in moving from his or
her current placement to his or her father's home. However, if the court is entering a
permanency planning order, unless the father consents to a transition plan the court
should first find by clear and convincing evidence that the father acted inconsistently

---

74. *Eckard*, 148 N.C. App. 541; *In re* A.E.C., ___ N.C. App. ___, 768 S.E.2d 166 (2015).

75. For placement options throughout the various stages of the proceeding, see
G.S. 7B-503(a); 7B-505(b) (nonsecure custody); 7B-903(a)(2)b. (dispositional order);
7B-906.1(a), (d), (e), (i) (review and permanency planning hearings); 7B-906.2 (concurrent
permanency planning).

76. G.S. 7B-100; *See In re* R.R.N., 368 N.C. 167 (2015); *Eckard*, 148 N.C. App. 541.

77. Petersen v. Rogers, 337 N.C. 397 (1994); Price v. Howard, 346 N.C. 68 (1997); *In re* B.G.,
197 N.C. App. 570 (2009).

78. G.S. 7B-503(a). See chapter 2 for a discussion of priority of placements in nonsecure
custody.

79. G.S. 7B-901(c); 7B-906.1(d), (e); 7B-906.2(b).

80. G.S. 7B-901; 7B-903(a)(2), 7B-903(a)(2), (4).

with his parental rights or is unfit before applying a best interests of the child analysis and ordering a transition plan that awards partial or joint custody of the child with a third party (including a county department).[81] Because of a parent's constitutional rights to care, custody, and control of the child, if the father has not acted inconsistently with his parental rights, a transition plan should not be ordered without the father's consent. Although a child's immediate move from the current placement to the father's home may not be ideal, it may be no more abrupt or disruptive than the child's initial removal and placement in a foster home. Unlike placement in a foster home, placement with the father is placement towards a permanent resolution for the child.

Custody to the father may be ordered as a disposition in the ongoing abuse, neglect, or dependency action or as a final disposition that results in the court ordering that its jurisdiction over the abuse, neglect, or dependency proceeding be terminated.[82] If custody to the father is ordered as part of a disposition plan, the court is relieved of its obligation to conduct periodic review and permanency planning hearings.[83] Although review and permanency planning hearings are not required, the court must conduct a review hearing if a motion for review is filed by a party.[84] The Juvenile Code also allows the court to order a final disposition by entering a civil custody order pursuant to Chapter 50 of the North Carolina General Statutes (hereinafter G.S.) and ordering the termination of the court's jurisdiction in the abuse, neglect, or dependency action.[85] This option is available only if the court makes written findings that state intervention on behalf of the child in the abuse, neglect, or dependency proceeding is not necessary.[86] When custody is ordered to a parent, there is no time requirement that must be satisfied before the court may enter the civil custody order and terminate its jurisdiction in the abuse, neglect, or dependency proceeding.[87]

---

81. *See* the cases listed in note 77, *supra*; *In re* P.A., ___ N.C. App. ___, 772 S.E.2d 240, 249 (2015) (regarding a remand of a permanency planning hearing, "the trial court should more clearly address whether respondent [mother] is unfit as a parent or if her conduct has been inconsistent with her constitutionally protected status as a parent, should the trial court again consider granting custody or guardianship to a nonparent.").

82. G.S. 7B-903(a)(4); 7B-911.

83. G.S. 7B-906.1(a); 7B-906.1(k).

84. G.S. 7B-906.1(n).

85. G.S. 7B-911.

86. G.S. 7B-911(c)(2)a.; *In re* J.D.R., ___ N.C. App. ___, 768 S.E.2d 172 (2015).

87. G.S. 7B-911(c)(2). (Note that when the order awards custody to a non-parent, the order must also include a written finding that at least six months have passed since the court determined that the child's placement with the person who is being awarded custody is the child's permanent plan.)

Father Lives Outside of North Carolina: The Interstate Compact on the Placement of Children (ICPC)

If a father lives outside of North Carolina, the court will need to determine if the Interstate Compact on the Placement of Children (ICPC) applies to the child's placement with his or her father. The ICPC is a legally binding agreement between all fifty states, the District of Columbia, and the U.S. Virgin Islands that requires member states to cooperate with one another when children are placed in foster care or a prospective adoption placement across state lines.[88] The purpose of the ICPC is to protect children by having the two involved states (receiving and sending) work together to place the child in a safe environment.[89] The ICPC requires a home study[90] and approval of the placement by the receiving state as soon as practical but no later than 180 days after receiving the request for a home study.[91] In certain limited circumstances, an expedited home study and approval process may apply to a placement.[92] If the proposed placement is approved and the child is placed in the receiving state, the receiving state supervises the child's placement.[93] The sending state retains jurisdiction over and responsibility for the child who is placed in the receiving state.[94] Placements that are covered by the ICPC should not occur unless prerequisites set out in the ICPC have been met.[95]

Before a child is placed with his or her out-of-state parent (for purposes of this book, father), the court must determine whether the child is being placed in foster care, triggering the ICPC. In essence, the court must determine if placement with the child's father is a placement in foster care.

In 2004, the North Carolina Court of Appeals held that the provisions of the ICPC did not apply at a permanency planning hearing when the court awarded custody to

---

88. G.S. 7B-3800, Article I. *See also Welcome to the AAICPC Website* (homepage), Am. Pub. Human Servs. Ass'n (APHSA): Ass'n of Adm'rs of the Interstate Compact on the Placement of Children (AAICPC), www.aphsa.org/content/AAICPC/en/home.html (last visited Nov. 25, 2015).

89. G.S. 7B-3800.

90. G.S. 7B-3800, Article III; ICPC Regulation No. 1, § 6(a), *available at* www.aphsa.org/content/dam/AAICPC/PDF%20DOC/Home%20page/ICPCRegulationNo1Amended.pdf; ICPC Regulation No. 2, § 7, *available at* www.aphsa.org/content/dam/AAICPC/PDF%20DOC/Home%20page/ICPCRegulation2-Sept2011.pdf; ICPC Regulation No. 3, § 4.30(g), *available at* www.aphsa.org/content/dam/AAICPC/PDF%20DOC/Home%20page/ICPC-Regulation3-Sept2011.pdf; *see also* 42 U.S.C. § 671(a)(26) (home study must be completed within sixty days of receipt of request and conditional approval may be granted).

91. ICPC Regulation No. 1, § 7(a); ICPC Regulation No. 2, § 8(a).

92. ICPC Regulation No. 7, *available at* www.aphsa.org/content/dam/AAICPC/PDF%20DOC/Home%20page/ICPC-Regulation7-Sept2011.pdf.

93. ICPC Regulation No. 1, §§ 8, 12; ICPC Regulation No. 11, *available at* www.aphsa.org/content/dam/AAICPC/PDF%20DOC/Home%20page/ICPCRegulationNo11adoptedat2010.pdf.

94. G.S. 7B-3800, Article V.

95. G.S. 7B-3800, Article III(a); Article IV.

an out-of-state mother.[96] The court examined the applicable language of the ICPC statute, "'[n]o sending agency shall send, bring, or cause to be sent or brought into any other party state any child for placement in *foster care* or as a *preliminary to a possible adoption* unless the sending agency shall comply with each and every requirement set forth in this Article.'"[97] The court held that the language of the statute was "clear and unambiguous."[98] The ICPC did not apply because the trial court had not placed the children "in foster care or as a preliminary [placement] to adoption."[99]

In 2011, after this decision was published, substantial amendments were made to the ICPC regulations,[100] but the language of the statute has remained the same. The regulatory definition of "foster care" was amended to include a parent who provides twenty-four-hour-a-day care to his or child "by reason of a court-ordered placement (and not by virtue of the parent-child relationship)."[101] This definition requires a state to comply with the ICPC when placement in an abuse, neglect, or dependency proceeding is made with an out-of-state parent. The regulations exempt compliance with the ICPC when placement is made with an out-of-state parent when all of the following apply:

- the parent is not the parent from whom the child was removed;
- the court has no evidence that the parent is unfit;
- the court does not seek any evidence from the receiving state regarding the parent's fitness; and
- the court relinquishes jurisdiction over the child immediately upon placement with the parent.[102]

In North Carolina, the court cannot order custody to a father and terminate its jurisdiction in the abuse, neglect, or dependency proceeding prior to the adjudicatory hearing.[103] Because the AAICPC regulations require the court to terminate its jurisdiction upon placement of the child with his or her parent, the regulatory exemption for the application of the ICPC to a placement with an out-of-state parent will never apply to a nonsecure custody order entered in the abuse, neglect, or dependency proceeding. The regulation's requirement that the court's jurisdiction terminate is only applicable after the child's adjudication, where upon completion of an initial disposition, review, or permanency planning hearing, the court orders custody of the child to the out-

96. *In re* Rholetter, 162 N.C. App. 653 (2004).
97. *Id.* at 663–64 (quoting G.S. 7B-3800) (emphasis added by court).
98. *Id.* at 664.
99. *Id.*
100. G.S. 7B-3800, Article VII. Each jurisdiction has an officer, and together they have the power to promulgate rules and regulations. The member officers form the AAICPC.
101. ICPC Regulation No. 3, § 4.26.
102. ICPC Regulation No. 2, § 3(a); ICPC Regulation No. 3, § 3(a).
103. *In re* O.S., 175 N.C. App. 745 (2006).

of-state father by entering both a civil custody order[104] and an order terminating its jurisdiction in the abuse, neglect, or dependency action pursuant to G.S. 7B-911.

Since the ICPC regulations were amended, the applicability of the ICPC to placements with out-of-state parents has not been addressed by the North Carolina appellate courts. But the issue has been addressed by other state courts. The decisions are split.

The Connecticut Supreme Court held that the ICPC's statutory language, "placement in foster care or as a preliminary to a possible adoption," does not include placement with a noncustodial parent because "[c]hildren in the care of their own parents are not in 'foster care' in any ordinary sense of that phrase, and parents are not required to adopt their own children."[105] The reasoning by the Connecticut Supreme Court is the same reasoning applied by the North Carolina Court of Appeals in 2004. The Connecticut Supreme Court further stated that "it is reasonable to conclude that the drafters [of the statute] determined that the statute should not be applied to out-of-state parents in light of the constitutionally based presumptions that parents generally are fit and that their decisions are in the child's best interests."[106] Regarding the amended regulations, the court stated that even if the ICPC regulations have the force of law, they are invalid to the extent that they impermissibly expand the scope of the compact itself.[107] The Washington Court of Appeals also found that the ICPC does not apply to parental placements because "[t]he plain, ordinary meaning of the term [foster care] is the placement of a child in a substitute home, one other than that of the child's parents."[108] The Washington court further found the ICPC regulation defining foster care impermissibly expanded the scope of the ICPC.[109] Similarly, but without reference to the regulations, a California court of appeals held that "[c]ompliance with the ICPC is not required for placement with an out-of-state parent."[110]

The Arizona Court of Appeals reached the opposite conclusion, finding that the court was a "sending agency" and that compliance with the ICPC regulations was required for placements with relatives and parents if none of the enumerated exceptions applied.[111] The Arizona court reasoned that the ICPC should be "interpreted liberally because the primary purpose of the ICPC is to protect children by making certain they are placed in a safe environment."[112] The Florida District Court of Appeals also found that the ICPC applies to an out-of-state parent.[113] The Florida court held

---

104. A civil custody order is governed by G.S. 50-13.1; 50-13.2; 50-13.5; 50-13.7.
105. *In re* Emoni W., 48 A.3d 1, 7–8 (Conn. 2012).
106. *Id.* at 8.
107. *Id.* at 10.
108. *In re* Dependency of D.F.-M., 236 P.3d 961, 965 (Wash. Ct. App. 2010).
109. *Id.* at 966.
110. *In re* Patrick S. III, 160 Cal. Rptr. 3d 832, 840 (2013).
111. Ariz. Dep't of Econ. Sec. v. Stanford, 323 P.3d 760 (Ariz. Ct. App. 2014).
112. *Id.* at 764–65 (citation omitted).
113. Dep't of Children & Families v. C.T., 144 So. 3d 684, 686 (Fla. Dist. Ct. App. 2014).

that when the court has jurisdiction and placement responsibility for the child because the parent-child relationship has been interrupted, the court is acting as the sending agency, and the parent is in the same position as a foster parent.

The court hearing the abuse, neglect, or dependency action must ultimately decide whether the applicable ICPC regulations are valid and must be complied with before ordering the child's placement with his or her father who lives outside of North Carolina. The issue hinges on the definition of "foster care." The definition in the ICPC regulations is not the only definition a court may consider. The applicable federal regulation defines foster care as "24-hour substitute care for children placed away from their parents or guardians and for whom the title IV-E agency has placement and care responsibility."[114] North Carolina defines foster care as "the continuing provision of the essentials of daily living on a 24-hour basis for dependent, neglected, abused, abandoned, destitute, orphaned, undisciplined or delinquent children or other children who, due to similar problems of behavior or family conditions, are living apart from their parents, relatives, or guardians in a family foster home or residential child-care facility."[115]

If the court decides that a child's placement with his or her father is not foster care and compliance with the ICPC is not required, a county department may ask the receiving state to conduct a "courtesy check" of the father's home.[116] A courtesy check is independent of the ICPC process and does not involve a full home study.[117] Whether to conduct a courtesy check is in the discretion of the receiving state. When a child is placed with a parent who lives out of state and the placement is made without complying with the ICPC, the receiving state has no responsibility for supervising or monitoring the placement.[118] The county department in North Carolina would be responsible for monitoring the placement.

Visitation between the Father and Child

If a court does not order the child's placement with his or her father, the court must order an appropriate visitation plan between the child and father unless the court finds that the father forfeited his rights to visitation or that visitation is not in the child's best

---

114. 45 C.F.R. § 1355.20(a). The reference in the regulation to "title IV-E" is to Title IV-E of the Social Security Act.

115. G.S. 131D-10.2(9). *See also In re* E.L.E., ___ N.C. App. ___, 778 S.E.2d 445 (2015) (The definition of "family foster home" found at G.S. 131D-10.2(8) includes the placement of a child in a private residence where the child is unrelated by blood, marriage, guardian, or adoption to the adult household members. In this case, the child was not placed in a family foster home because the child was in the home of a maternal great aunt and uncle.).

116. ICPC Regulation No. 2, § 3(b); ICPC Regulation No. 3, § 3(b).

117. ICPC Regulation No. 2, § 3(b); ICPC Regulation No. 3, § 3(b); ICPC Regulation No. 3, § 4.19.

118. ICPC Regulation No. 2, § 2(c).

interests.[119] If the father resides outside of North Carolina, the court does not have to consider the ICPC when ordering visitation in the father's home state so long as the visits have an end date and are no longer than thirty days or the length of the child's school vacation.[120]

A court must consider the child's best interests, health, and safety when developing the visitation plan.[121] The court order must specify the minimum frequency and length of the visits as well as the level of supervision that is required for the visits.[122] In determining the appropriate visitation plan, a court may consider whether the child and father have a pre-existing relationship and, if so, the court may assess the strength of that relationship. If the child and father are strangers, a court may determine that the initial visits should occur in a therapeutic setting.[123] The court may not delegate decisions that change the frequency, duration, or level of supervision for the visits to the counselor or any other third party, including the county department.[124] Instead, the counselor, county department social worker, and others may testify at a hearing about how the relationship between the child and father is progressing. Ultimately, the court must make any decision that changes the frequency, duration, or level of supervision for the visits between the child and father. However, when the court has ordered guardianship or custody of the child to an individual, the court may authorize additional visitation as agreed to between a respondent (e.g., the father) and the guardian or custodian.[125]

Other Services

If a court has personal jurisdiction over a respondent father, the court may order him to engage in services or take specific actions that are authorized by statute.[126] The court is explicitly authorized to order a father to participate in his child's treatment and/or in parenting classes if the classes are available in the judicial district where the father lives.[127] The court is also authorized to order the father to take certain steps, such as counseling, that are designed to remedy the conditions that contributed to the child's adjudication or the court's removal of the child from his or her parent, guardian, custodian, or caretaker.[128] If treatment is ordered, the court is authorized to approve

119. G.S. 7B-905.1; *In re* T.R.T., 225 N.C. App. 567 (2013); *In re* K.C., 199 N.C. App. 557 (2009).

120. ICPC Regulation No. 9, *available at* www.aphsa.org/content/AAICPC/en/ICPCRegulations.html.

121. G.S. 7B-905.1(b).

122. *Id.*

123. G.S. 7B-904(b).

124. *In re* J.D.R., ___ N.C. App. ___, 768 S.E.2d 172 (2015). *See* G.S. 7B-905.1(b).

125. G.S. 7B-905.1(c). *See id.* §§ 7B-600 (guardian); 7B-101(8) (custodian defined).

126. G.S. 7B-904; 7B-406(c).

127. G.S. 7B-904(b), (d1)(1).

128. G.S. 7B-904(c), (d1)(3).

a treatment plan, order the father to comply with the treatment plan, and condition the child's placement with or legal custody to the father on his compliance with the treatment plan.[129] Remedial actions will be specific to the case and to the conditions surrounding the child at the time of a child's removal or the reason for the child's adjudication. A court does not have broad authority to order a respondent father to take any action the court finds to be in the child's best interest.[130] As a result, the court may want to make written findings that identify the nexus between the actions it is ordering the father to complete and the conditions that led to the child's adjudication or removal from his or her home. Upon a finding that the father has the financial ability to do so, the court may also order him to pay (1) the cost of the child's and/or his own treatment and/or (2) a reasonable sum for the child's care, which may be a child support order that is based on the child support guidelines.[131]

Permanency Planning

Once the abuse, neglect, or dependency proceeding has progressed to the permanency planning stage, the court must order concurrent permanent plans for the child, with a minimum of a designated primary and secondary permanent plan.[132] Possible permanent plans are reunification, adoption; guardianship, custody with a non-parent, Another Planned Permanent Living Arrangement for a 16- or 17-year-old child, or, when a parent's rights have been terminated, the reinstatement of parental rights.[133] An adjudication of paternity directly impacts the child's permanent plans.

The Juvenile Code prioritizes reunification as a permanent plan by requiring that the court order reunification as a primary or secondary plan unless the court has made written findings that reasonable efforts for reunification are not required.[134] Reunification involves the child's placement with either parent regardless of whether the child

---

129. G.S. 7B-904(c).

130. *In re* H.H., ___ N.C. App. ___, 767 S.E.2d 347 (2014) (court lacked authority under G.S. 7B-904 to order mother to maintain stable housing and employment because there were no allegations in the abuse, neglect, and dependency petition or findings made by the court that these were the issues that led to the children's removal from their mother's custody or adjudication as abused and neglected).

131. G.S. 7B-903(d); 7B-904(a), (c), (d). *See id.* §§ 50-13.4(c), (c1) (establishment of child support guidelines); N.C. ADMIN. OFFICE OF THE COURTS, *Child Support Resources*, Child Support Guidelines, www.nccourts.org/courts/crs/childsupport.asp.

132. G.S. 7B-906.2.

133. G.S. 7B-906.2(a). *See id.* §§ 7B-101(18b) (reunification); 7B-600 (guardianship); 7B-912(c) (Another Planned Permanent Living Arrangement/APPLA); 7B-1114 (reinstatement of parental rights); 7B-903(a)(4) (custody); 7B-911 (custody and termination of jurisdiction in abuse, neglect, or dependency proceeding); G.S. Chapter 50 (child custody); Chapter 48 (adoption).

134. G.S. 7B-906.2(b).

was removed from that parent's home.[135] The definition of "either" in this context likely means "each" or "both."[136] As a result, the child's concurrent permanent plans must include reunification with both the child's mother and father unless the court made written findings that one of the statutory factors authorizing the court to eliminate reasonable efforts for reunification applies to one or both of the child's parents.[137]

The Juvenile Code does not specify how the court must craft the permanent plans. It appears that the court has discretion to order "reunification with a parent" as the child's permanent plan and include within that plan specific reasonable efforts that are directed toward the mother and specific reasonable efforts that are directed toward the father. If the court chooses to order "reunification with a parent" as one of the permanent plans, the court must also order a second permanent plan, such as custody or guardianship with a relative, and designate which of the permanent plans is primary and which is secondary.[138] Or the court may order "reunification with the mother" as one permanent plan and "reunification with the father" as another permanent plan. In that case, the court must designate which plan is the primary permanent plan and which plan is the secondary permanent plan.[139] In identifying and ordering a child's concurrent permanent plans, the court does not appear to be limited to two permanent plans and may identify additional permanent plans that it finds are in the child's best interests.[140] It is unclear how the court should designate a third permanent plan; the statute does not state whether there can be more than one primary or secondary plan or whether a third permanent plan should be identified as a tertiary plan. In ordering a

---

135. G.S. 7B-101(18b). Note the definition of "return home or reunification" also includes the child's placement in the home of a custodian or guardian from whose home the child was removed by court order; if applicable, the court should also include reunification with a guardian or custodian as a concurrent permanent plan unless it makes the findings that are necessary to eliminate reunification as a permanent plan pursuant to G.S. 7B-906.2(b).

136. *Either*, MERRIAM-WEBSTER DICTIONARY ("being the one and the other of two . . . each"), www.merriam-webster.com/dictionary/either; *either*, CAMBRIDGE DICTIONARIES ONLINE ("one or the other of two . . . can also use either to mean both"), http://dictionary.cambridge.org/us/dictionary/english/either. *See* G.S. 7B-100 ("This subchapter shall be interpreted and construed so as to implement the following purposes and policies: (1) [t]o . . . protect the constitutional rights of . . . parents; (2) [t]o develop a disposition . . . that reflects consideration of . . . the strengths and weaknesses of the family; . . . (4) [t]o provide . . . for the return of juveniles to their homes consistent with preventing the unnecessary or inappropriate separation of juveniles from their parents . . . ").

137. 7B-906.2(b). *See id.* § 7B-901(c). Note that G.S. 7B-1001(a)(3) authorizes a parent to appeal an initial disposition order that eliminates reasonable efforts for reunification, and G.S. 7B-1001(a)(5) allows a parent to appeal a permanency planning order that eliminates reunification with him or her as a permanent plan.

138. G.S. 7B-906.2(a), (b).

139. G.S. 7B-906.2(b).

140. G.S. 7B-906.2(a) states that "the court shall adopt one or more of the following permanent plans . . . " Note that the reference to "one" is believed to be in error, given that two plans must be identified in each permanency planning order. *See id.* § 7B-906.2(b).

child's permanent plans, a court should look to a child's best interests when determining how to craft each permanent plan, identify each plan as primary or secondary, and decide if more than two concurrent permanent plans are appropriate for the child.[141]

Other than reunification, the Juvenile Code does not give priority to one permanent plan over another.[142] For non-reunification plans, the Juvenile Code does give placement preference to the child's relatives over nonrelatives, regardless of whether that placement will result in a permanent plan of adoption by or guardianship or custody to the relative.[143]

Once paternity is adjudicated, the court should look to paternal as well as maternal relatives as possible placement options for the child's permanent plans. In determining if a court will place a child with a relative who is willing and able to provide a "safe home,"[144] the court must consider the child's best interests. The Juvenile Code requires a court to order the child's placement with a relative who is willing and able to provide a safe home for the child *unless* the court finds the placement would be contrary to the child's best interests.[145] The need to consider the child's best interests gives the court discretion when deciding whether a child should be placed with a relative. Best interests of the child factors are not specified in the abuse, neglect, or dependency statutes. There are six best interests of the child factors that are identified in the termination of parental rights statute[146] that may provide guidance for a court when deciding a child's concurrent permanent plans. The relevant best interests factors identified in the termination of parental rights statute are the child's age, the likelihood of the child's adoption, the bond between the child and parent, the quality of the relationship between the child and caregiver in the proposed permanent placement(s), and any other relevant consideration.[147]

A relevant consideration may be the length of time a child has been in a specific placement. The court may determine that moving a child from a pre-adoptive placement where the child has bonded with the caregivers is not in the child's best interests. This may be a relevant factor for a court regardless of whether the relative was

---

141. *See* G.S. 7B-906.2(a).

142. *But see* G.S. 7B-912(c) (Another Planned Permanent Living Arrangement/APPLA may not be ordered as the primary permanent plan unless the court finds that the child is 16 or 17 years old; diligent efforts were made to place the child permanently with a parent or relative, or in a guardianship or adoptive placement; reunification, custody to a relative, guardianship, or adoption are not in the child's best interests; and APPLA is the best permanency plan for the child). *See* 42 U.S.C. § 675a(a).

143. G.S. 7B-903(a1); 7B-906.1(e).

144. G.S. 7B-101(19) ("safe home" is "a home in which the juvenile is not at substantial risk of physical or emotional abuse or neglect").

145. G.S. 7B-903(a1); *In re* L.L., 172 N.C. App. 689 (2005).

146. G.S. 7B-1110(a)(1) through (6).

147. G.S. 7B-1110(a)(1), (2), (4), (5), (6).

recently identified or was aware of the child's placement early on in the case but did not express a willingness to be a placement for the child until very late in the case. Unlike a parent, a relative does not have constitutional rights to care, custody, and control of the child,[148] and the court is not required to order reasonable efforts for reunification with a relative. In addition to the stability of a child's placement, the permanency of the proposed plan may be a relevant consideration for the court. For example, a court may find that adoption is a more permanent plan than guardianship. A court may also consider how long a child has been in care, the anticipated time that will be necessary to achieve a proposed permanent plan, and whether the time involved will delay achieving permanency for the child such that it is not in the child's best interests to pursue a new permanent plan as a primary plan. The Juvenile Code repeatedly states that the child needs a safe and permanent home within a reasonable period of time.[149] Although a reasonable period of time is not defined in the Juvenile Code, a permanency planning order that places a child outside of a parent's home must include relevant statutory findings, many of which reference the next six months from when the permanency planning hearing was held.[150] Although a court may determine that it is not in the child's best interests to place the child with a relative such that the placement is not the child's primary permanent plan, a court may still order custody or guardianship to or adoption by the relative as the child's secondary permanent plan in the event that the designated primary permanent plan is not achieved.

In addition to affecting a child's permanent plans regarding reunification with a parent and custody, guardianship, or adoption by a paternal relative, an adjudication of paternity directly impacts a permanent plan of adoption regardless of who the adoption petitioner is. An adjudication of paternity may limit who is entitled to notice of an adoption proceeding and whose consent, relinquishment, or termination of parental rights is required in order to achieve the child's permanent plan of adoption. See chapter 7 for a discussion of a child's adoption as the primary permanent plan.

---

148. Eakett v. Eakett, 157 N.C. App. 550, 554 (2003) ("The grandparent is a third party to the parent-child relationship. Accordingly, the grandparent's rights to the care, custody and control of the child are not constitutionally protected while the parent's rights are protected.").

149. G.S. 7B-100(5); 7B-101(18); 7B-906.1(d)(3); 7B-906.1(g); 7B-906.2(b), (c), (d)(1).

150. G.S. 7B-906.1(e)(1) through (4).

Summary

The adjudication of paternity or non-paternity impacts every stage of the abuse, neglect, or dependency proceeding, starting with who is named as a respondent father and ending with the child's permanent plan. Because a paternity adjudication directly impacts a child's permanency, including a dependency adjudication and whether the proceeding continues to disposition or is dismissed, paternity should be addressed as soon as possible in the action. The options for the child's permanent plans increase when paternity is established because of the opportunity to place the child with his or her father or with paternal relatives. Achieving permanency for a child may be delayed when steps to determine paternity are not made initially and continuously throughout the proceeding.

Chapter 7

A Child's Primary Permanent Plan of Adoption: The Process and the Role of Fathers

As discussed in chapter 6, there are six possible permanent plans for a child who has been adjudicated abused, neglected, or dependent and removed from a parent, guardian, or custodian.[1] One plan is the child's adoption.[2] Although the district court in the abuse, neglect, or dependency proceeding determines and enters the permanency planning order,[3] the child's adoption requires a separate court action. It is the only permanent plan that cannot be achieved in the abuse, neglect, or dependency proceeding. Paternity issues arise in a child's adoption, and an adjudication of paternity or non-paternity in the abuse, neglect, or dependency action impacts the adoption proceeding. This chapter discusses

- the judicial process of adoption before the clerk of superior court;
- the selection of and placement with prospective adoptive parents;
- the rights of a father and possible biological father to notice of the filing of an adoption petition;
- when a father's or possible biological father's consent to the child's adoption or relinquishment or termination of parental rights over the child is required; and
- the impact of a judicial determination of paternity or non-paternity on notice, consent, relinquishment, and termination of parental rights requirements related to a child's father and possible biological father.

This chapter is not a comprehensive analysis of North Carolina's adoption laws. The discussion contained herein is limited to the adoption process and statutes as they relate to a child who is the subject of an abuse, neglect, or dependency action and who has a primary permanent plan of adoption. This chapter pays particular attention to required procedures related to the rights of the child's father or possible biological father.

What Is an Adoption?

An adoption is a complete substitution of the child's family and, by operation of law, creates a parent-child relationship between the petitioner and adoptee.[4] A final adoption decree legally severs the relationship between a child and his or her biological

---

1. Chapter 7B, Section 906.2(a) of the North Carolina General Statutes (hereinafter G.S.).
2. G.S. 7B-906.2(a)(2).
3. G.S. 7B-906.1; 7B-906.2(a). See chapter 6 for a discussion of permanency planning.
4. G.S. 48-1-101(2); 48-1-106(a), (b). *But see id.* § 48-1-106(d) (adoption by a stepparent does not sever the rights of the parent who is the stepparent's spouse). Note that if a child is adopted by a relative or stepparent, the child's biological grandparent, who has a substantial relationship with the child, may enforce a visitation order that was entered before the adoption or seek a court order for visitation with the child after the adoption. *Id.* §§ 50-13.2(b1); 50-13.2A; 50-13.5(j); 48-1-106(f); 48-4-105.

parents, including a child's rights to inherit through intestate succession from his or her natural parent.[5]

An Adoption and an Abuse, Neglect, or Dependency Proceeding Are Related but Separate Actions

An adoption is a special proceeding initiated before the clerk of superior court when a signed and verified petition for adoption is filed by the petitioner.[6] The petitioner is the prospective adoptive parent[7] and is not necessarily a party in the abuse, neglect, or dependency proceeding.[8] The adoption petition may be filed after the child has been placed with the prospective parent in accordance with the requirements of the applicable North Carolina adoption statutes.[9] The clerk of superior court may waive the placement requirement for cause.[10]

The clerk has jurisdiction to hear the adoption proceeding, unless an issue of fact, claim for equitable relief, or equitable defense is raised before the clerk.[11] In that case, the clerk must transfer the action to the district court.[12] Upon transfer, the district court may either determine the entire action or decide the issue that resulted in the transfer and remand the remainder of the adoption proceeding back to the clerk.[13] An adoption proceeding that is transferred to the district court is a separate action

---

5. G.S. 48-1-106(c); 48-1-107; *see also id.* § 7B-1112. *But see id.* § 48-1-106(d) (stepparent adoption does not sever the rights of the parent who is the stepparent's spouse).

6. G.S. 48-2-100(a). *See id.* § 48-2-304(a) (each petitioner must sign and verify the petition).

7. G.S. 48-2-301. If the petitioner is married, G.S. 48-2-301(b) requires that the petitioner's spouse join the petition to adopt the child, unless the spouse is incompetent or the court waives the requirement for good cause. *In re* Adoption of Kasim, 58 N.C. App. 36 (1982) (the statute requiring a spouse to join the petition supports the policy that a child should be brought into a family where both spouses want the child). The petitioner does not have to be married. G.S. 48-2-301(c).

8. *See* G.S. 7B-401.1 (parties).

9. G.S. 48-2-301(a) ("A prospective adoptive parent may file a petition . . . only if a minor has been placed with the prospective adoptive parent pursuant to Part 2 of Article 3 of this Chapter . . ."). *See id.* § 48-3-201 (an agency, a guardian, a parent with legal and physical custody of the child, or both parents when (1) they are married or (2) one has legal custody and the other has physical custody but neither parent has both are authorized by statute to place a child for adoption). *See also id.* §§ 48-3-202 (parent or guardian makes a direct placement of the child with a prospective adoptive parent); 48-3-203 (an agency makes the child's placement with the prospective adoptive parent).

10. G.S. 48-2-301(a).

11. G.S. 48-2-100(a); 48-2-601(a1).

12. G.S. 48-2-601(a1); 1-301.2(b).

13. G.S. 1-301.2(c).

from the abuse, neglect, or dependency proceeding. If the clerk does not transfer the proceeding, the district court does not have jurisdiction to hear the adoption.[14]

While the adoption action is pending, the district court continues to have jurisdiction over the abuse, neglect, or dependency proceeding.[15] The district court continues to hear periodic review and permanency planning hearings, unless the district court waives its jurisdiction for good cause.[16] The final decree of adoption terminates the district court's jurisdiction in the abuse, neglect, or dependency proceeding[17] and, therefore, is the final disposition of the abuse, neglect, or dependency action.

Selecting Prospective Adoptive Parents

The child's prospective adoptive parents must be selected before the adoption proceeding is commenced, since the prospective parents file the adoption petition.[18] For a child who has been adjudicated abused, neglected, or dependent and who has a permanent plan of adoption, the county department selects the child's prospective adoptive parents.[19] The selection is made by a county department's "adoption committee."[20]

In selecting the prospective adoptive parents, the Juvenile Code[21] requires the county department to consider the child's current placement provider when that person wants

---

14. G.S. 48-2-100(a) ("Adoption shall be by a special proceeding before the clerk of superior court."); 1-301.2(d); 7B-1101. Note that G.S. 48-2-607(b) grants the district court jurisdiction to hear an appeal of a final decree of adoption. *See also* G.S. 1-301.2(e) (appeal to district court for a hearing de novo).

15. G.S. 48-2-102(b).

16. *Id.*; *see also* G.S. 7B-906.1; 7B-1000. See chapter 6 for a discussion of review and permanency planning hearings.

17. G.S. 48-2-102(b); *In re* W.R.A., 200 N.C. App. 789 (2009).

18. G.S. 48-2-301.

19. G.S. 7B-1112.1; 48-3-203(d). *See also* 1 N.C. Div. of Soc. Servs., Child Welfare Services Manual Ch. VI, § 1301, at 5 (2009), http://info.dhhs.state.nc.us/olm/manuals/dss/csm-50/man/CSs1301.pdf.

Note that chapters in volume 1 of the North Carolina Division of Social Services Manual that were last amended before 2013 are referred to as the "Family Services Manual," and chapters that were amended in 2013 or later are referred to as the "Child Welfare Services Manual." For consistency in this book, all chapters will hereinafter be referred to as the "Child Welfare Services Manual."

20. Child Welfare Services Manual Ch. VI, § 1301 at 14–15, http://info.dhhs.state.nc.us/olm/manuals/dss/csm-50/man/CSs1301.pdf. Note that a county department may refer to its adoption committee by another name; the committee must consist of at least three members, one of whom is in a managerial position with the county department. The child's adoption social worker is a member of that child's adoption committee, but the child's court-appointed guardian ad litem is not. *See also* G.S. 7B-1112.1.

21. G.S. Chapter 7B is referred to as the "Juvenile Code."

to adopt the child.[22] State policy directs the adoption committee to select the child's current placement provider when the provider wishes to adopt the child, unless there is clear documentation that the placement is contrary to the child's welfare and best interests.[23] A current placement provider may be a paternal or maternal relative, court-approved non-relative, or licensed foster family.[24]

The North Carolina Division of Social Services' Child Welfare Services Manual directs a county department to consider a variety of factors when selecting a child's prospective adoptive parents. The factors[25] include

- the child's needs and the prospective parents' ability to meet those needs;
- if the prospective adoptive parents are the child's current placement providers who want to adopt the child, the length of time the child has been placed in their care, the benefits of allowing the child to remain in a familiar environment, and the child's ability to transition to a new home and form satisfactory relationships with a different family if the current providers are not selected as the child's prospective adoptive parents;
- the degree of bonding that has occurred between the child and the prospective adoptive parents;[26]
- whether siblings may be adopted together;
- compliance with the Multiethnic Placement Act,[27] and if the child is an "indian child,"[28] compliance with the Indian Child Welfare Act.[29]

---

22. G.S. 7B-1112.1. *See also* CHILD WELFARE SERVICES MANUAL Ch. VI, § 1301 at 5–6, http://info.dhhs.state.nc.us/olm/manuals/dss/csm-50/man/CSs1301.pdf.

23. CHILD WELFARE SERVICES MANUAL Ch. VI, § 1301 at 5–6, http://info.dhhs.state.nc.us/olm/manuals/dss/csm-50/man/CSs1301.pdf.

24. *Id.*

25. CHILD WELFARE SERVICES MANUAL Ch. VI, § 1301, at 5–9, http://info.dhhs.state.nc.us/olm/manuals/dss/csm-50/man/CSs1301.pdf.

26. Note that G.S. 7B-1110(a)(5) also addresses the quality of the relationship between the child and prospective adoptive parent.

27. Public Law No. 103-382, Part E created the Howard M. Metzenbaum Multiethnic Placement Act of 1994 (MEPA), which is an antidiscrimination law that applies to a child's placement by prohibiting states or agencies that receive federal funds from (1) discriminating on the basis of the adoptive or foster parent's and/or child's race, color, or national origin and (2) delaying or denying a child's placement solely on the basis of race, color, or national origin.

28. 25 U.S.C. § 1903(4) ("Indian child" is any unmarried person who is younger than 18 and is either a member of a federally recognized Indian tribe or is eligible for membership in a federally recognized Indian tribe and is the biological child of a member of a federally recognized Indian tribe); *see also id.* § 1903(8) (defining "indian tribe").

29. Indian Child Welfare Act (ICWA), 25 U.S.C. §§ 1901 through 1963 (additional procedures and standards are required for Indian children who are removed from their homes; the placement preference for foster care or a pre-adoptive home is with a member of an Indian tribe).

The adoption committee must also consider any input that is provided by the child's court-appointed guardian ad litem (GAL).[30]

The county department must notify the child's GAL and foster parents of its choice of the prospective adoptive parents within ten days of making the selection.[31] If the foster parents were not selected and they wish to adopt the child, they have a right to file a motion for a judicial review of the county department's selection with the district court.[32] The county department must include a form motion for judicial review in its notice to the foster parents when the foster parents are not selected as the child's prospective adoptive parents.[33] The child's GAL also has a right to file a motion for a judicial review of the county department's selection of the child's prospective adoptive parents.[34] The motion for judicial review must be filed in the abuse, neglect, or dependency proceeding within ten days of the department's notification.[35]

The district court review of the county department's selection is limited to determining whether the proposed placement is in the child's best interests.[36] The court must consider the recommendations of the county department and the child's GAL.[37] The foster parents have a right to be heard at the judicial review.[38] In determining the child's best interests, the court may consider the factors identified in the Child Welfare Services Manual. If the district court enters an order determining that the selected placement is not in the child's best interests, neither the Juvenile Code nor the Child Welfare Services Manual addresses what happens next. The statute governing the right to a judicial review does not authorize the district court to substitute its judgment for the county department's judgment and select different prospective adoptive parents.

---

30. CHILD WELFARE SERVICES MANUAL Ch. VI, § 1301, at 15. Note that the GAL is appointed in the abuse, neglect, or dependency proceeding pursuant to G.S. 7B-601. *See* G.S. 7B-1112.1 (The GAL has a right to request information from and consult with the county department concerning the selection process. If the GAL requests information about the process, the county department must provide that information within five business days.).

31. G.S. 7B-1112.1. Note that the statute refers to a "placement provider" and "foster parent" in different sentences, making it unclear if a placement provider who is not a foster parent is entitled to notice. The statute does not specify whether the notice must be in writing.

32. *Id.*

33. G.S. 7B-1112.1. *See* Form AOC-J-140, Motion for Review, www.nccourts.org/Forms/Documents/479.pdf (a county department may have created its own form motion). Note that because a county department must include a motion for judicial review with its notice to the child's foster parents, it is reasonable to conclude the notice to the foster parents must be in writing.

34. G.S. 7B-1112.1.

35. *Id.* Note that the statute does not specify if the time period is ten days from the sending or the receipt of the notice.

36. *Id.*

37. *Id.*

38. *Id.* Note that a foster parent's right to be heard does not make him or her a party to the abuse, neglect, or dependency proceeding.

To give the judicial review statute meaning, it is reasonable to conclude that the county department should select different prospective adoptive parents if the court finds that the selected prospective adoptive placement is not in the child's best interests. If the district court order included specific best interests of the child findings, including findings about the child's current placement, the adoption committee may consider those findings when making a new selection of prospective adoptive parents for the child.

Placement with the Prospective Adoptive Parents

A child who is the subject of an abuse, neglect, or dependency action and who has a permanent plan of adoption is likely to be placed in a prospective adoptive home by the county department. This type of adoptive placement is known as an "agency placement," as opposed to a "direct placement" that is made by the child's parents or guardian.[39]

An adoptive placement requires a pre-placement assessment.[40] The pre-placement assessment determines the suitability of the prospective adoptive parents and their home in general or for a specific child.[41] When a county department has placement responsibility for or custody of a child, the pre-placement assessment must include a criminal background check on the prospective adoptive parents and on any adults who reside in the home before the child may be placed in that home.[42]

If the county department selects the child's current placement provider as the prospective adoptive parent, even though the child has already been placed in that person's home, a pre-placement assessment for the child's adoption is still required.[43] It is possible that the individual had a general pre-placement assessment that was completed before the child was placed in his or her home. If so, the prior pre-placement assessment may be used so long as it has been completed or updated within eighteen months immediately preceding the child's placement in the home.[44]

If the county department selects a prospective adoptive parent who is not the child's current placement provider, the child will need to be placed in that home so that the

---

39. There are only two types of pre-adoptive placements under North Carolina law: a direct placement (G.S. 48-3-202) or an agency placement (G.S. 48-3-203). *See* G.S. 48-1-101(4) (agency includes county department); *see also id.* § 48-3-201(a) (persons with authority to place).

40. G.S. 48-3-301. *But see id.* § 48-3-301(b) (a pre-placement assessment is not required in a direct placement made by a parent or guardian to a relative specified by G.S. 48-3-301(b)).

41. G.S. 48-3-301 through -309 (pre-placement assessment procedures and content).

42. G.S. 48-3-203(d1); 48-3-309.

43. *See* G.S. 48-3-301.

44. G.S. 48-3-301(a).

prospective adoptive parents have standing to file the adoption petition.[45] The county department may not change the child's placement until (1) the ten-day time period for filing a motion for judicial review of its selection of the prospective adoptive parent has expired and (2) the child's guardian ad litem (GAL) or foster parent has not filed a motion for judicial review with the court.[46] Once the ten-day period to file a motion for judicial review has passed and a motion is not filed, the child may be moved to the selected prospective adoptive parent's home.[47] If the court in the abuse, neglect, or dependency action previously entered an order that designated a specific person with whom the child is placed, the county department will need to request a modification of that order before changing the child's placement.[48] If the court order granted placement authority with the county department, the department may move the child without first seeking permission from the court. Before the child is moved to his or her new placement, the county department must notify the child's GAL of its intent to change the child's placement.[49] If the GAL disagrees with the county department's plan to move the child, the GAL may file a motion for review of the child's change in placement in the abuse, neglect, or dependency proceeding.[50]

Notice of the Adoption Proceeding

The court does not issue a summons in an adoption proceeding.[51] Instead, within thirty days of filing the adoption petition, the petitioner must serve a notice of the filing of the adoption petition on a number of statutorily identified individuals, including

- the county department that placed the child;
- the child (if he or she is 12 or older); and
- a parent who has not consented to the adoption, executed a relinquishment, or had his or her parental rights terminated by court order.[52]

---

45. G.S. 48-2-301(a) (note that the court may waive placement for cause). *See also id.* § 48-3-201 (who may place a child for adoption).

46. G.S. 7B-1112.1.

47. *Id.*

48. *See* G.S. 7B-906.1(n); 7B-1000.

49. G.S. 7B-903.1(d). If emergency circumstances prevent the county department from first notifying the GAL of its intent to change the child's placement, the department must notify the GAL within seventy-two hours of moving the child to a new placement, unless a shorter period of time is required by local rules.

50. G.S. 7B-906.1(n); 7B-1000.

51. G.S. 48-2-401(g).

52. G.S. 48-2-401 (when the adoption petitioner has been informed that (1) a parent or guardian has filed an action to set aside his or her consent or relinquishment because of fraud or duress, (2) a person has legal or physical custody of the child, or (3) a person has a court-ordered right to visit or communicate with the child, the petitioner must provide

Notice must also be served on a man who to the actual knowledge of the adoption petitioner claims to be or is named as the child's biological or possible biological father; this includes any possible biological father who is unknown.[53] However, when a child is placed in the prospective adoptive home by a county department, and a father's or possible biological father's identity is unknown, rather than serve him with notice, a termination of parental rights action should be initiated.[54] A termination of parental rights action may be filed with the district court at the same time the adoption petition is filed with the clerk of superior court.[55] The termination of parental rights action may be commenced by filing a motion[56] in the abuse, neglect, or dependency action or by filing a petition[57] that initiates a separate action, which may be consolidated[58] with the abuse, neglect, or dependency action. The clerk of court shall stay the adoption proceeding until the termination of parental rights action has been decided by the district court.[59]

Notice does not need to be served on a possible biological father if he executed a consent, relinquishment, or notarized statement denying paternity or disclaiming any interest in the child;[60] had his rights terminated by court order; has been judicially determined not to be the child's father; or the court has ordered in a pre-birth determination proceeding[61] that his consent is not required.[62] A father or possible biological father may waive his right to the notice in open court or in writing.[63]

When a father or possible biological father is served with the notice that an adoption petition has been filed, he has thirty days after service, or if he was served by

---

notice to that parent or guardian and to those persons); *see also id.* § 48-2-402 (service of process is made pursuant to G.S. 1A-1, Rule 4).

53. G.S. 48-2-401(c)(3).

54. G.S. 48-2-402(c). Note that G.S. 7B-1103(a)(3), (4) limit a county department's standing to initiate a termination of parental rights action to when the county department has custody of the child through a court order or a parent's or guardian's properly executed relinquishment to the county department. *See* G.S. 48-3-701 through -707 (relinquishment).

55. G.S. 48-2-302(c).

56. G.S. 7B-1102; 7B-1106.1.

57. G.S. 7B-1104.

58. G.S. 7B-1102(c).

59. G.S. 48-2-402(c).

60. G.S. 48-2-401(c)(3). *See also id.* § 48-3-603(a)(5); Division of Social Services (hereinafter DSS) Form DSS-5118, Denial of Paternity, http://info.dhhs.state.nc.us/olm/forms/dss/dss-5118-ia.pdf. Only the man signs the denial; the mother's signature is not required.

61. G.S. 48-2-206.

62. G.S. 48-2-401(c)(3). (Note that notice is also not required to be served on a father or possible biological father when his consent to the adoption is not required because he was convicted of a sexual offense specified in G.S. 48-3-603(a)(9) that resulted in the child's conception.)

63. G.S. 48-2-406(a). A waiver in open court may be made by the person entitled to receive notice or by that person's authorized agent.

publication, forty days after the first publication of the notice, to file a response with the court.[64] He may assert that his consent to the child's adoption is required.[65] Whether his consent is required is a question of fact that requires the clerk to transfer the proceeding to the district court.[66] If the court concludes that his consent is not required, he is not a party to the proceeding.[67] Although not a party, he may present evidence as to whether the adoption is in the child's best interests.[68]

If the father or possible father fails to file with the court a timely response to the notice, his consent to the child's adoption is not required.[69] A petitioner may move for an order determining that the father's or possible father's consent to the adoption is not required because he failed to timely file a response to the notice.[70] The motion for such an order is not required, but by obtaining this order, the adoption petitioner will have confirmation from the court that he or she does not need to terminate the possible father's parental rights, since the court has determined that his consent is not necessary for the child's adoption to proceed.

The Impact of a Paternity Adjudication on Who Receives Notice

The adoption statute specifically states that notice is not required to be served on a man who has been determined not to be the child's father.[71] This means that a legal or putative father who was named in the abuse, neglect, or dependency proceeding and was adjudicated not to be the child's father is not entitled to notice of the adoption proceeding.

Similarly, an adjudication of paternity determines which man is entitled to receive notice that the adoption petition was filed. Collateral estoppel may bar a party who participated in or had a full and fair opportunity to litigate paternity in the abuse, neglect, dependency, or other proceeding that adjudicated paternity from now identifying someone other than the adjudicated father as a possible father who is entitled to notice of the adoption. Notice of the filing of the adoption petition should be limited to the adjudicated father. An exception may apply when the adoption petitioner is aware of a possible biological father who did not have a full and fair opportunity to participate in the prior proceeding that determined paternity. See chapter 4 for a full discussion of collateral estoppel.

---

64. G.S. 48-2-401(f); 48-2-402(b). *See id.* § 1A-1, Rule 4(j1).

65. G.S. 48-2-207(b).

66. *Id.*; *see* G.S. 48-2-601(a1); 1-301.2(b).

67. G.S. 48-2-207(d). *See also id.* § 48-1-101(11) ("party" defined).

68. G.S. 48-2-405.

69. G.S. 48-3-603(a)(7).

70. G.S. 48-2-207(a).

71. G.S. 48-2-401(c)(3).

If paternity has not been addressed in the underlying abuse, neglect, dependency, or other proceeding, a possible biological father is entitled to notice of the adoption petition, unless a statutory exception applies to him.[72]

Relinquishment, Consent, and Termination of Parental Rights

Before the county department may make an agency placement in the prospective adoptive home, the child's parent must have relinquished his or her rights over the child to the county department or the district court must have terminated his or her parental rights.[73] A mother, father, or possible biological father who executes a consent or relinquishment or had his or her parental rights terminated is not entitled to notice of the adoption petition being filed with the court.[74] Before an order for adoption can be entered, the petitioner must prove that he or she obtained the necessary consents to the adoption, relinquishments of parental rights, and/or termination of parental rights orders.[75]

Relinquishment

A relinquishment is executed for the purposes of a child's adoption and is a release of a parent's or guardian's rights over a child to a child-placing agency, which includes a county department.[76] The relinquishment is a permanent transfer of legal and physical custody of the child to the county department.[77] A parent's relinquishment must be in writing and signed under oath.[78]

---

72. *See id.*

73. G.S. 48-3-201(a)(1), (c), (d); 48-3-203(a) (a relinquishment transfers legal and physical custody of the child to the agency (see *id.* § 48-3-703(a)(5)). *Id.* § 48-3-701 (if the child's parents are married and living together, they must jointly relinquish their rights to the child; otherwise, one parent may execute a relinquishment to transfer custody to the department). G.S. 48-3-203(a) refers to termination of "the rights and duties of *a parent*" (emphasis added). *See also* G.S. 7B-1112(1).

74. G.S. 48-2-401(b)(1), (c)(3); 48-3-606(11); 48-3-703(a)(10); 7B-1112.

75. G.S. 48-2-304(b)(6) (an adoption petition must state that all necessary consents, relinquishments, or terminations of parental rights have been obtained and will be filed); 48-2-305(2) (petitioner must file required consent or relinquishment); 48-2-305(3) (petitioner must file certified copy of termination of parental rights order); 48-2-305(8) (petitioner must file document stating name of any individual whose consent, relinquishment, or termination of parental rights may be required but has not been obtained; these documents must be filed as soon as they are available). *See id.* § 48-3-601 (required consent); 48-3-603 (consent not required).

76. G.S. 48-3-701(a); 48-3-703(a)(5); 48-3-705. *See id.* § 48-1-101(4) ("agency" defined); 7B-600 (guardian).

77. G.S. 48-3-703(a)(5); 48-3-705(b), (c).

78. G.S. 48-3-702(a). *See* DSS Form DSS-1804, Relinquishment of Minor for Adoption by Parent or Guardian or Guardian Ad Litem of the Mother/Father, http://info.dhhs.state.nc.us/

A relinquishment to the county department should include an "affidavit of parentage"[79] that states the names, last known addresses, and marital statuses of the child's parents or possible parents.[80] This form is completed by the parent or guardian who is relinquishing the child to the county department. This affidavit of parentage is different from the affidavit of parentage (referred to in this book by the acronym AOP)[81] that is signed within ten days of the child's birth or is used for the purposes of establishing a child support obligation. The AOP should not be used for purposes of a relinquishment, as it does not contain all the information required by the adoption statute.[82]

Within seven calendar days following the day the relinquishment is executed, the parent or guardian may revoke his or her relinquishment in writing.[83] If the seventh day falls on a weekend or on a holiday when court is closed, the revocation period expires on the next business day.[84] A revocation divests the county department of legal and physical custody of the child and restores custody to the person who revoked the relinquishment if that person had physical custody of the child prior to executing the relinquishment.[85] If there is a court order of custody that is entered in the abuse, neglect, or dependency action, that custody order determines who has custody of the child upon the revocation of a relinquishment.

If a revocation is not made within the statutory time period, the relinquishment becomes irrevocable and may only be set aside for fraud, duress, or a motion made by the county department requesting that the relinquishment be voided because other necessary consents, relinquishments, or termination of parental rights cannot be obtained for the child's adoption.[86] A relinquishment may be rescinded by mutual agreement of the county department and the parent or guardian who executed the

---

olm/forms/dss/dss-1804-ia.pdf. Note that a parent's guardian ad litem (GAL) for purposes of a relinquishment must be appointed pursuant to G.S. 48-3-602 by the court presiding over the adoption proceeding when a parent has been adjudicated incompetent; this GAL is not the N.C. Rules of Civil Procedure Rule 17 GAL who was appointed to a respondent parent in the abuse, neglect, or dependency action pursuant to G.S. 7B-602(c) or in a termination of parental rights action pursuant to G.S. 7B-1101.1(c).

79. *See* DSS Form DSS-1809, Affidavit of Parentage, http://info.dhhs.state.nc.us/olm/forms/dss/dss-1809-ia.pdf.

80. G.S. 48-3-206.

81. See chapter 4 for a full discussion of the AOP.

82. The three different state form AOPs do not contain the marital statuses of the mother or father and do not contain any information about possible biological fathers.

83. G.S. 48-3-706(a). *See* DSS Form DSS-1805, Revocation of Relinquishment for Adoption by Parent, Guardian, or Guardian Ad Litem of the Mother/Father, http://info.dhhs.state.nc.us/olm/forms/dss/dss-1805-ia.pdf.

84. G.S. 48-3-706(a).

85. G.S. 48-3-706(b).

86. G.S. 48-3-705(a); 48-3-707(a)(1), (4); *see also id.* § 7B-909(b1).

relinquishment if the child has not been placed in a pre-adoptive home.[87] If the child has been placed in a pre-adoptive home and there has not been a final decree of adoption, the agreement of the pre-adoptive parent to rescind the relinquishment is also required.[88] A relinquishment may also be revoked after the statutory seven-day time period for revocation expires if the relinquishment provides for a revocation when the child will not be adopted by the prospective adoptive parent who is specifically identified in the written relinquishment.[89] In that case, a parent may revoke the relinquishment in writing within ten calendar days from when he or she receives notice from the county department that the adoption by the specified individual will not be completed.[90]

Consent to Adoption

A consent to the child's adoption is the individual's (or, in the case of a relinquishment, the county department's) voluntary agreement that the child will be adopted by a designated prospective adoptive parent.[91] Upon execution of the consent, custody of the child transfers to the prospective adoptive parent.[92] A consent must be in writing and signed under oath.[93] A consent may be revoked if the revocation is in writing and given to the person designated in the consent to accept a revocation within seven calendar days following the date the consent was executed.[94] If the seventh day falls on a weekend or on a holiday when court is closed, the revocation period expires on the next business day.[95] If a revocation of the consent is not made within the statutory time period, the consent is irrevocable and may only be set aside (1) upon a showing of fraud or duress, (2) upon a voluntary dismissal of the adoption with prejudice or a court's dismissal of the proceeding (provided that no appeal has been taken or the dismissal is affirmed), or (3) by mutual agreement of the prospective adoptive parent and the person who executed the consent.[96]

---

87. G.S. 48-3-707(a)(2).

88. G.S. 48-3-707(a)(3).

89. G.S. 48-3-704. (Note that G.S. 48-3-703(a)(5) allows for a relinquishment to identify a prospective adoptive parent that is selected by the agency and agreed to by the person executing the relinquishment.)

90. *Id.*

91. G.S. 48-3-605(c)(2), (d); 48-3-606(4).

92. G.S. 48-3-606(4); 48-3-607(b). Note that under G.S. 48-3-502(a), when a county department executes a consent, legal custody of the child remains with the county department until the adoption decree is final or the court orders legal custody to the prospective adoptive parent.

93. G.S. 48-3-605(a); 48-3-606.

94. G.S. 48-3-608(a). *See* DSS Form DSS-1806, Revocation of Consent to Adoption by Parent, Guardian, or Guardian ad Litem of the Mother/Father, http://info.dhhs.state.nc.us/olm/forms/dss/dss-1806-ia.pdf.

95. G.S. 48-3-608(a).

96. G.S. 48-3-607; 48-3-609.

Required Consents

There are several persons whose consent to a child's adoption is required, including the county department that placed the child; the child (if he or she is 12 or older); the child's guardian (if one is appointed); and, unless there has been a relinquishment or termination of parental rights, the child's mother and any man who may or may not be the child's biological father.[97] The consent statutes incorporate North Carolina laws on parentage by providing that consent is required from "any man who may or may not be the [child's] biological father" if

- he was married to the mother at the time the child was conceived or born;[98]
- he is the child's adoptive father;[99] or
- before an adoption petition was filed, he
  - legitimated the child,[100]
  - took the child into his home and openly held the child out as his biological child,[101] or
  - acknowledged his paternity and
    - is obligated to support the child through a written agreement or court order;
    - has provided in accordance with his financial means reasonable and consistent payments to support the mother during or after her pregnancy, the child, or both the mother and child, and has regularly visited and communicated with, or attempted to regularly visit and communicate with, the mother during or after her pregnancy, the child, or both the mother and child; or
    - married the mother before the child was placed for adoption or the mother relinquished her rights to the child.[102]

---

97. G.S. 48-3-601 (persons whose consent is required); 48-3-603 (persons whose consent is not required). Note that if the court finds that requiring the child's consent is not in the child's best interests, the court may waive the child's consent. *See also* DSS Form DSS-1801, Agency's Consent to Adoption, http://info.dhhs.state.nc.us/olm/forms/dss/dss-1801-ia.pdf; DSS Form DSS-1802, Consent to Adoption by Parent, Guardian, or Guardian ad Litem of the Mother/Father, http://info.dhhs.state.nc.us/olm/forms/dss/dss-1802-ia.pdf. Note that a parent's guardian ad litem (GAL) for purposes of consenting to an adoption must be appointed pursuant to G.S. 48-3-602 by the court presiding over the adoption proceeding when a parent has been adjudicated incompetent; this GAL is not the N.C. Rules of Civil Procedure Rule 17 GAL who was appointed to a respondent parent in the abuse, neglect, or dependency action or in a termination of parental rights proceeding pursuant to G.S. 7B-602(c) or 7B-1101.1(c); DSS Form DSS-1803, Consent of Child for Adoption, http://info.dhhs.state.nc.us/olm/forms/dss/dss-1803-ia.pdf.

98. G.S. 48-3-601(2)b.1., b.2. (applicable to a marriage that is or could be declared invalid).

99. G.S. 48-3-601(2)b.6.

100. G.S. 48-3-601(2)b.3.

101. G.S. 48-3-601(2)b.5.

102. G.S. 48-3-601(2)b.4.

The consent to adoption statute as applied to a man who may or may not be the child's biological father is much narrower in scope than the statute that determines who is entitled to receive notice that the adoption petition for the child was filed. The notice statute does not require the man to have taken any of the specified actions that are required in the consent statute.[103]

A possible biological father's consent is not required if

- he relinquished his parental rights,
- he had his parental rights terminated by court order,
- there is a judicial determination that he is not the child's father,
- there is a judicial determination that another man is the child's father,
- he was not married to the child's mother and after the child's conception he executed a notarized statement denying paternity or disclaiming any interest in the child,
- he failed to timely respond to the notice of the filing of the adoption petition, or
- he was convicted of first- or second-degree forcible rape, statutory rape of a child by an adult, or first-degree statutory rape and the child was conceived as a result of the rape.[104]

The Impact of an Adjudication of Paternity or Non-Paternity on Required Consents for an Adoption

If there is an adjudication of paternity in an abuse, neglect, dependency, or other judicial proceeding, then the consent of all possible biological fathers is not needed. Only the consent of the adjudicated father is necessary before the court may enter an order for adoption. The adjudication is a judicial determination that eliminates other men as the child's father or possible biological father. Similarly, an adjudication of a man's non-paternity eliminates the need to obtain his consent, even if he had previously been considered the child's legal father. The court's adjudication of non-paternity establishes that the man is not the child's biological or possible biological father. See chapter 6 for a discussion of the impact of a determination of non-paternity on a legal or putative father.

If the court did not address paternity in the abuse, neglect, dependency, or other proceeding, the court in the adoption proceeding must decide whether consent from each possible biological father is required. When a possible father does not file a timely response to the notice of the adoption petition, his consent to the adoption is not required,[105] but if he filed a timely response to the notice asserting that his consent to

---

103. *Compare* G.S. 48-2-401 (notice) *to* G.S. 48-3-601 (consent).
104. G.S. 48-3-603(a)(1), (2), (4), (5), (7), (9). *See id.* §§ 48-2-207(a); 14-27.21(c); 14-27.22(c); 14-27.23(d); 14-27.24(c).
105. G.S. 48-3-603(a)(7).

the adoption is required, the court must hold a hearing in the adoption proceeding to determine whether his consent is required.[106] Whether consent is required is a question of fact that must be heard by the district court.[107]

Applying the Adoption Consent Statute to a Man Who May or May Not Be the Child's Father

The adoption consent statute specifies when the consent of the child's father or possible biological father is required.[108] Unless the man is legally recognized as the child's father through either the marital presumption of a child's legitimacy or a previous adoption,[109] his consent will only be required if, before the adoption petition was filed, he assumed some of the burdens of parenthood by taking certain actions that are specified in the statute.[110] When determining if the man's consent is necessary, the court presiding over the adoption proceeding must decide if he strictly complied with required statutory elements set forth at Chapter 48, Section 3-601(2)b. of the North Carolina General Statutes (hereinafter G.S.).[111]

Interpreting G.S. 48-3-601(2)b.4.

There is a body of case law interpreting G.S. 48-3-601(2)b.4., which requires that, *before the adoption petition was filed*, the man

1. acknowledged his paternity;

2. has provided, in accordance with his financial means, reasonable and consistent payments for the support of the mother (during or after her pregnancy), the child, or the mother and child; and

3. regularly visited or communicated, or attempted to regularly visit or communicate, with the mother (during or after her pregnancy), the child, or both the mother and child.[112]

---

106. G.S. 48-2-207(b).

107. G.S. 48-2-601(a1); *See In re* Adoption of S.D.W., 367 N.C. 386, 389 (2014) ("The case was transferred from the Assistant Clerk of Court to the district court because of the existence of an issue of fact regarding . . . consent.").

108. G.S. 48-3-601.

109. G.S. 48-3-601(2)b.1., b.2., b.6. See chapter 4 for a discussion of the marital presumption.

110. *In re* Adoption of Anderson, 360 N.C. 271 (2006); *In re* Adoption of K.A.R., 205 N.C. App. 611 (2010). Note that G.S. 48-3-601 does not explicitly address a court adjudication of paternity.

111. Note that G.S. 48-3-601(2) applies to direct placement adoptions but G.S. 48-3-601(3)b. refers to agency placements and applies G.S. 48-3-601(2) to an individual who has not executed a relinquishment to the agency.

112. *In re* Adoption of Byrd, 354 N.C. 188 (2001); *Anderson*, 360 N.C. 271; *K.A.R.*, 205 N.C. App. 611; *see also* Lehr v. Robertson, 463 U.S. 248, 265 (1983) ("The legitimate state interests in facilitating the adoption of young children and having the adoption proceeding completed expeditiously that underlie the entire statutory scheme also justify a trial judge's

This statute does not require a formal *acknowledgment of paternity* prior to the filing of the adoption petition for a man to preserve his right to consent to the child's adoption. A man may acknowledge paternity through written or verbal assertions or conduct.[113] A verbal acknowledgment may be made to the child's mother, to others, or through a third party.[114] A man's acknowledgment of paternity must be unequivocal.[115] A request for genetic testing does not void his acknowledgment of paternity but, rather, reflects the possibility contemplated by the statute that he "may or may not be the biological father."[116]

In addition to acknowledging paternity, the man must, *within his financial means, provide reasonable and consistent support* for the mother and/or child before the adoption petition is filed.[117] The trial court has discretion to determine what constitutes reasonable and consistent payments that are within the father's financial means and may look to the child support guidelines for guidance.[118] The support must be real, tangible, and actually provided and not merely an expression of an intent to provide support.[119] The man cannot rely on others to provide support on his behalf.[120] A third-party payment does not relieve a father of his own support obligation.[121] He is also not relieved of his support obligation if the mother refuses to accept the support that he tenders to her.[122] The statute states that he provide support "for"—not "to"—the mother

determination to require all interested parties to adhere precisely to the procedural requirements of the statute.").

113. *Byrd*, 354 N.C. 188 (acknowledgment and stated desire to be part of the child's life was made to mother when she was pregnant).

114. *Id.*; *In re* Adoption of S.K.N., 224 N.C. App. 41 (2012) (father acknowledged paternity to his mother and his aunt, and his mother contacted the county department to inform it that her son believed he was the child's father).

115. *In re* Adoption of Shuler, 162 N.C. App. 328 (2004) (acknowledgment was not unequivocal when father identified himself at child's birth as the mother's "friend" and refused to have his name listed on the child's birth certificate, even though later he verbally acknowledged paternity).

116. *Byrd*, 354 N.C. 188 (after learning another man may be the child's father, conditional acknowledgment based on genetic testing did not void initial unequivocal acknowledgment of paternity); *S.K.N.*, 224 N.C. App. 41.

117. G.S. 48-3-601(2)b.4.II.

118. Miller v. Lillich, 167 N.C. App. 643 (2004); *In re* Adoption of K.A.R., 205 N.C. App. 611 (2010). *See* N.C. ADMIN. OFFICE OF THE COURTS, *Child Support Resources*, Child Support Guidelines, www.nccourts.org/courts/crs/childsupport.asp.

119. *Byrd*, 354 N.C. 188; *In re* Adoption of Anderson, 360 N.C. 271 (2006); *In re* Adoption of B.J.R., ___ N.C. App. ___, 767 S.E.2d 395 (2014).

120. *Byrd*, 354 N.C. 188.

121. *Id.*

122. *Anderson*, 360 N.C. 271 (the language of the statute requires "tangible means of support"; if attempted payments were sufficient, the statute would have expressly provided for attempts like it does when a man has "attempted to visit or communicate" with the mother and/or child).

and/or child, which requires him to provide support in alternative ways when a mother refuses his payments.[123] For example, he may open a bank account and make deposits that are for the mother and/or child;[124] pay medical bills for the mother's prenatal care or birthing expenses;[125] and/or purchase tangible items for the child, such as a car seat, crib and mattress, diapers, baby clothes, or the child's medication.[126]

The possible biological father who has acknowledged paternity must also *regularly visit or communicate with or attempt to visit or communicate with* the mother during or after her pregnancy, the child, or both the mother and child before the adoption petition is filed with the court. By engaging in such conduct, a possible biological father demonstrates that he is grasping or attempting to grasp the opportunity to develop a parent-child relationship.[127] A single visit with the child in a six-month period does not satisfy the requirement of the statute to regularly visit or communicate with the child.[128]

A father's consent is necessary when the court finds that he has satisfied all three prongs of the consent statute before the adoption petition was filed with the court.[129] Actions taken after genetic test results were available or paternity was adjudicated are not relevant under the consent statute if the actions occurred after the adoption petition was filed.[130] A possible biological father should not wait for the genetic test results to confirm his paternity before providing support for or visiting or communicating with the mother (during or after pregnancy) or with the child.[131]

It is not a defense that the biological father did not know that the child existed.[132] A man is expected to take efforts to discover the birth of his child who is born out of wedlock.[133] Ignorance of the law is also not a defense for failing to comply with the statutory requirements.[134] The components of the consent statute establish a bright-line rule for how a putative father demonstrates that he has assumed some of the burdens of parenthood.[135] The statutory framework incorporates the multiple purposes

---

123. *Id.*

124. *Id.*

125. Miller v. Lillich, 167 N.C. App. 643 (2004).

126. *Id.; In re* Adoption of K.A.R., 205 N.C. App. 611 (2010).

127. *In re* Adoption of B.J.R., ___ N.C. App. ___, 767 S.E.2d 395 (2014).

128. *Id.*

129. *In re* Adoption of Byrd, 354 N.C. 188 (2001); *K.A.R.*, 205 N.C. App. 611.

130. *B.J.R.*, ___ N.C. App. ___, 767 S.E.2d 395.

131. *Id.*

132. *In re* Adoption of S.D.W., 367 N.C. 386 (2014); *In re* Adoption of Clark, 95 N.C. App. 1 (1989), *rev'd on other grounds*, 327 N.C. 61 (1990).

133. *S.D.W.*, 367 N.C. 386 (putative father must grasp the opportunity to discover his child was born when the qualification of notice that the woman was pregnant and gave birth to his child is not beyond his control); *Clark*, 95 N.C. App. 1.

134. Lehr v. Robertson, 463 U.S. 248 (1983).

135. A Child's Hope, LLC v. Doe, 178 N.C. App. 96 (2006).

of "'establish[ing] a clear judicial process for adoptions, . . . promot[ing] the integrity and finality of adoptions, [and] structur[ing] services to adopted children, biological parents, and adoptive parents that will provide for the needs and protect the interests of all parties to an adoption, particularly adopted minors.' "[136] The statutory framework is also "designed to protect 'both the interests of biological fathers in their children and the children's interest in prompt and certain adoption procedures.' "[137]

After considering the three factors, if the court determines that the consent of "the man who may or may not be the biological father of the minor"[138] is not required, the adoption may proceed.[139] If the court determines that his consent is required and he does not provide it, the adoption cannot go forward until and unless his parental rights are terminated.[140]

Termination of Parental Rights

A termination of parental rights severs the legal relationship between a child and his or her parent.[141] A parent whose rights are terminated does not have a right to notice of the adoption proceeding or to object to or participate in the adoption proceeding.[142] Unless a statutory exception applies, when a parent has not relinquished his or her parental rights or consented to the child's adoption, the parent's rights must be terminated to achieve a child's permanent plan of adoption.[143] At each review and permanency planning hearing in an abuse, neglect, or dependency proceeding, the district court must

---

136. *In re* Adoption of Anderson, 360 N.C. 271, 276 (2006) (quoting G.S. 48-1-100(a)).

137. *S.D.W.*, 367 N.C. at 394 (quoting *Lehr*, 463 U.S. at 263).

138. G.S. 48-3-601(2)(b).

139. *See S.D.W.*, 367 N.C. 386; *In re* Adoption of Byrd, 354 N.C. 188 (2001); *In re* Adoption of B.J.R., ___ N.C. App. ___, 767 S.E.2d 395 (2014).

140. G.S. 48-2-207(c); *see id.* § 48-3-603(a)(1). Note that if paternity is raised as an issue at the termination of parental rights proceeding and the court adjudicates the possible biological father's non-paternity, his consent to the child's adoption will no longer be required pursuant to G.S. 48-3-603(a)(2).

141. G.S. 7B-1112. Note that until the child is adopted, the child retains the right to inherit from his or her parent whose rights were terminated. *See id.* § 48-1-106(c) (an adoption decree does not terminate the former parent's duty to pay child support arrearages owed by the former parent prior to the decree of adoption).

142. G.S. 7B-1112; 48-2-401(c)(3); 48-3-603(a)(1).

143. G.S. 48-2-207(c); 48-2-304(b)(6); 48-2-603(a)(4); 48-3-603(a)(1). Note that consent is not required from (1) a man who is not married to the child's mother and who after the child's conception executed a notarized statement denying paternity or disclaiming any interest in the child (G.S. 48-3-603(a)(5)), (2) a person who is served with a notice that the adoption petition was filed and does not timely respond to the notice (G.S. 48-3-603(a)(7)), (3) a man who does not timely respond to a notice of a pre-birth determination of consent (G.S. 48-3-603(a)(8)), and (4) a person who was convicted of specified sex offenses that resulted in the child's conception (G.S. 48-3-603(a)(9)).

consider "[w]hen and if termination of parental rights should be considered."[144] If the district court finds that a termination of parental rights is necessary to achieve the child's primary permanent plan of adoption, the county department must initiate a termination of parental rights proceeding within sixty days of entry of the court order that finds a termination of parental rights is needed.[145] The district court may order a different time period if it makes written findings as to why the county department cannot bring a termination of parental rights action within the statutorily proscribed sixty days.[146] When a termination of parental rights is needed as a precondition to the entry of the final decree of adoption, the district court will hear that action.[147]

When there is an underlying abuse, neglect, or dependency proceeding, a termination of parental rights action may be initiated by filing a motion in the abuse, neglect, or dependency proceeding or by filing a petition that commences a new action.[148] A county department has standing to initiate a termination of parental rights action only if it has custody of the child through a court order or a parent's or guardian's executed relinquishment to it.[149] A termination of parental rights action may be initiated by parties other than the county department. The child's guardian ad litem, court-appointed guardian, and parents each have standing to initiate a termination of parental rights action.[150] A person who the child has continuously resided with for two years immediately preceding the filing of a termination of parental rights action, a licensed child-placing agency to which the juvenile was relinquished for adoption, and an adoption petitioner also have standing to initiate a termination of parental rights action.[151] For purposes of an adoption, it is irrelevant who commenced the termination of parental rights action; it only matters that the order terminating parental rights is entered prior to the entry of the final decree of adoption.

---

144. G.S. 7B-906.1(d)(6). See chapter 6 for a discussion of review and permanency planning hearings.

145. G.S. 7B-906.1(m).

146. *Id.*

147. G.S. 7B-200(a)(4) (district court has exclusive jurisdiction over termination of parental rights proceeding); *see also id.* § 7B-1101; 7B-1102.

148. G.S. 7B-1102 (motion); 7B-1103(a); 7B-1104; *see also id.* § 7B-1106 (petition); 7B-1106.1 (motion). The termination of parental rights action may be consolidated with the abuse, neglect, or dependency action. *Id.* § 7B-1102(c). Note that if the termination of parental rights action is filed by motion, the court must have personal jurisdiction over the respondent parent.

149. G.S. 7B-1103(a)(3), (4); *In re* C.R.B., ___ N.C. App. ___, 781 S.E.2d 846 (2016).

150. G.S. 7B-1103(a)(1), (2), (6). Note that a parent may not terminate his or her own parental rights; the statute allows a parent to seek termination of the other parent's rights. *In re* Jurga, 123 N.C. App. 91 (1996).

151. G.S. 7B-1103(a)(4), (5), (7). *See In re* A.D.N., 231 N.C. App. 54 (2013) (interpreting "continuously resides with").

The Impact of a Paternity or Non-Paternity Adjudication on a Termination of Parental Rights Proceeding

If paternity has been determined in the abuse, neglect, dependency, or other proceeding, that father is the only man whose consent to the adoption is required.[152] A termination of his parental rights will be necessary if a statutory exception does not apply and he does not consent to the adoption or relinquish his rights.[153] There is not another possible biological father whose parental rights to the child must be terminated.

If a legal or putative father has been judicially determined not to be the child's father, he has no parental rights to the child, as he is no longer a legal father or putative father.[154] If a termination of parental rights motion or petition is filed naming a respondent who has been determined not to be the father, the district court should dismiss the action.[155] If the court does not dismiss the motion or petition, the respondent should consider filing a motion to dismiss because the order terminating his parental rights could have collateral consequences on his rights to his other children regardless of whether his other children are born before or after an order terminating his parental rights to this child is entered. One collateral consequence is that the involuntary termination of a parent's rights constitutes a portion of a ground necessary to terminate his parental rights to another child.[156] A second collateral consequence

---

152. G.S. 48-3-603(a)(2) (consent is not required from a man who may or may not be the child's biological father if another man has been judicially determined to be the child's father). There is a discrepancy between the statutory language for required exceptions to who must receive notice and who must consent to a child's adoption. While G.S. 48-2-401(c)(3) exempts service of notice on a man who has been judicially determined not to be the child's father, it does not have the companion language that is included in G.S. 48-3-603(a)(2) addressing when another man has been judicially determined to be the child's father. Notice may be required even though consent is not. Note that if the child has two fathers, i.e., a same-sex marriage and stepparent adoption by the husband spouse, the adoptive father's consent is required.

153. G.S. 48-3-603(a)(1) (termination of parental rights), (4) (relinquishment), (5) (notarized statement of man who is not married to child's mother denying paternity or disclaiming any interest in child), (7) (fails to timely respond to notice), (9) (conviction of certain sex crimes resulting in child's conception).

154. Lombroia v. Peek, 107 N.C. App. 745, 751 (1992) ("Mr. Lombroia's rights and responsibilities with regard to the minor child were finally determined when the Florida court found that he was not the father of the child."). *Cf. In re* Papathanassiou, 195 N.C. App. 278, 284 (2009) ("A determination that a petitioner in a legitimation action, and not the husband, is the biological father of the child terminates the husband's rights to the child, conferring them onto petitioner.").

155. *In re* J.S.L., 218 N.C. App. 610 (2012). G.S. 7B-1100 states the purposes of the termination of parental rights statutes and references biological and legal fathers. A man who has been judicially determined not to be the child's father is neither a biological nor a legal father.

156. G.S. 7B-1111(a)(9) (ground for termination of parental rights requires that the parent's rights to another child were involuntarily terminated by a court and the parent lacks the ability or willingness to establish a safe home). *See J.S.L.*, 218 N.C. App. 610.

applies when the parent has another child who is the subject of an abuse, neglect, or dependency action. In the abuse, neglect, or dependency action for the other child, the court must order as soon as the initial dispositional hearing in that action that the county department is not required to make reasonable efforts to reunify the child with his or her father if the court makes written findings that the father's rights to another child were involuntarily terminated.[157]

If paternity was not adjudicated in the abuse, neglect, dependency, or other action and the adoption petitioner has been informed of possible biological fathers, known and unknown, the adoption petitioner must determine whether a termination of his parental rights will be necessary for the adoption to proceed. If a known biological father satisfied the criteria set forth in the consent to adoption statute,[158] his parental rights must be terminated unless he consented to the adoption, relinquished his rights, or failed to timely respond to the notice that the adoption petition was filed.[159] An unknown possible father's rights must be terminated at the notice stage of an adoption action when the child has been placed with the prospective adoptive parent by the county department.[160] As a result of the termination of parental rights, his consent will not be required.[161]

When paternity has not been adjudicated, a possible biological father who is named as a respondent in the termination of parental rights action may raise paternity as an issue in that action.[162] If a party to the termination of parental rights proceeding requests genetic testing, the court must order the mother, child, and alleged respondent-father to submit to testing.[163] Genetic testing and a hearing on paternity may delay the termination of parental rights and accompanying adoption proceedings. If the court determines that the respondent father in the termination of parental rights proceeding is not the child's father, a termination of parental rights of a different respondent father whose consent to the adoption is required must occur before the child's adoption can proceed. If more than one respondent father is named in the termination of parental rights petition, the district court may conduct the hearing concerning the other respondent father's rights. If, however, the only named respondent father is the man who is adjudicated not to be the child's father, the action should

---

157. G.S. 7B-901(c)(2) (order at initial disposition); 7B-906.2(b) (order at permanency planning). See chapter 6 for a discussion of the initial dispositional hearing as well as an order that eliminates reasonable efforts for reunification between the child and his or her parent. *See* 42 U.S.C. § 671(a)(15)(D)(iii).

158. G.S. 48-3-601(2)b.

159. G.S. 48-3-603(a)(4), (5), (7).

160. G.S. 48-2-402(c).

161. G.S. 48-2-603(a)(1).

162. *J.S.L.*, 218 N.C. App. 610; *In re* L.D.B., 168 N.C. App. 206 (2005).

163. G.S. 8-50.1(b1); *see also J.S.L.*, 218 N.C. App. 610. See chapter 5 for a discussion of genetic testing and the hearing to adjudicate paternity.

be dismissed. A new termination of parental rights action must be commenced in the district court by the filing of a new petition or motion that names a different respondent father. A court cannot terminate the parental rights of a man, including an unknown father, who has not been named as a party in the termination of parental rights action.[164]

The Juvenile Code establishes a specific procedure that must be followed when a parental rights action only names an unknown father (i.e., "John Doe") as the respondent father. The district court must hold a preliminary hearing within ten days of the date on which the petition or motion is filed to try to determine the unknown father's name or identity.[165] Within thirty days of that preliminary hearing, the court must issue an order that either makes a finding identifying the child's father or, if the father remains unknown, ordering service by publication.[166] If a father is identified, he must be summoned to appear before the court, and he becomes a party without the need to amend the termination of parental rights petition or motion.[167] If a father is not identified at the preliminary hearing, the district court must order that the unknown father be served by publication for three consecutive weeks.[168]

Identifying a father and establishing paternity early on in the abuse, neglect, or dependency proceeding eliminates the need for a preliminary hearing to identify an unknown father in the termination of parental rights proceeding. A paternity adjudication also prevents the named respondent who has been determined to be the child's father from raising paternity as a defense to the termination of parental rights action. Having one man adjudicated as the child's father also (1) eliminates the possibility of bringing a termination of parental rights action that names multiple respondents, which may delay a child's permanency, especially if paternity is raised as an issue requiring genetic testing and a determination of paternity for the various named respondents; (2) uses additional court resources, including the need to appoint counsel to each respondent;[169] and (3) increases expenses incurred by the petitioner to serve multiple respondents.

Grounds for Termination of Parental Rights: G.S. 7B-1111(a)(5)

In the petition or motion to terminate parental rights, the petitioner or movant must allege facts sufficient to put the respondent on notice of at least one statutory ground for the termination of his parental rights.[170] There are eleven enumerated statutory

---

164. *L.D.B.*, 168 N.C. App. 206.

165. G.S. 7B-1105(a); *see also In re A.N.S.*, ___ N.C. App. ___, 767 S.E.2d 699 (2015).

166. G.S. 7B-1105(b), (d).

167. *In re M.M.*, 200 N.C. App. 248 (2009) (applying G.S. 7B-1104 and 7B-1105).

168. G.S. 7B-1105(d) (the court shall specify the contents of the notice that is most likely to identify the juvenile to the unknown parent).

169. G.S. 7B-1101.1(a), (a1).

170. G.S. 7B-1104(6). *See also In re B.S.O.*, ___ N.C. App. ___, 760 S.E.2d 59 (2014).

grounds to terminate parental rights.[171] One of the grounds is when the child is born out of wedlock and the father did not take specific actions to acknowledge paternity or support the child before the termination of parental rights action was filed.[172] Similar to the adoption statute that addresses when the consent of a man who may or may not be the child's biological father is required, the termination of parental rights statute authorizes the termination of a father's parental rights when he has not assumed responsibility for his child before the termination of parental rights action is filed.[173] But the two statutes do not mirror each other in establishing the steps a father must take to demonstrate that he has assumed the burdens of fatherhood.

The parental rights of a father of a child who is born out of wedlock may be terminated if he did not do one of the following *before the termination of parental rights action was filed:*

- File an affidavit of paternity with the Central Registry maintained by the North Carolina Department of Health and Human Services (hereinafter NC DHHS).[174]
- Legitimate the child through marriage or court action, or file a petition for the child's legitimation.[175]
- Establish paternity through a court action, which may be reflected by an amended birth certificate for the child, or execute an Affidavit of Parentage (AOP) when the child is born or as part of a child support services case.[176]
- Provide substantial financial support or consistent care for the child and mother.[177]

As with the consent to adoption statute, the termination of parental rights statute creates a bright-line rule requiring a father to strictly comply with the statutory elements set forth by the legislature.[178] A father's lack of knowledge of the child's existence is not a defense to a termination of parental rights based on this ground.[179] The statute

---

171. G.S. 7B-1111(a).

172. G.S. 7B-1111(a)(5).

173. A Child's Hope, LLC v. Doe, 178 N.C. App. 96 (2006).

174. G.S. 7B-1111(a)(5)a. *See* DSS Form DSS 6246, Affidavit of Paternity, http://info.dhhs.state.nc.us/olm/forms/dss/dss-6246-ia.pdf. Only the father signs this form. The Central Registry is not a putative father registry.

175. G.S. 7B-1111(a)(5)b., c.; *see also id.* § 49-12 (marriage); 49-10 and 49-12.1 (court action).

176. G.S. 7B-1111(a)(5)e. Note that the language says "establish[] paternity" but, as discussed in chapter 4, paternity is admitted but not judicially determined by a signed Affidavit of Parentage. Chapter 4 also discusses "other judicial proceeding[s]" that may determine paternity that are not specifically referenced in this statute.

177. G.S. 7B-1111(a)(5)d.

178. *A Child's Hope*, 178 N.C. App. 96.

179. *Id.*

reflects the legislature's intent not to make the future of a child who is born out of wedlock dependent on whether the father knows of the child's existence at the time the termination of parental rights action is filed.[180]

At the adjudicatory hearing to determine if a ground to terminate parental rights exists, the petitioner or movant (hereinafter "petitioner") has the burden of proof by clear, cogent, and convincing evidence.[181] The petitioner must prove that the father did not complete any of the actions required by the statute before the termination of parental rights action was filed.[182] A court order concluding that this ground has been proved by clear, cogent, and convincing evidence must include findings of fact addressing each of the statutorily required elements.[183]

The difficulty for a petitioner in proving the elements of this ground is that the petitioner must prove a negative.[184] It is possible that only the father will know if he filed an affidavit of paternity with the NC DHHS Central Registry. Perhaps to address this, the statute requires the petitioner make an inquiry to the Central Registry and authorizes the petitioner to admit into evidence the certified reply.[185] To prove that the father failed to legitimate the child (by marriage or court action) or establish paternity through a civil action, amended birth certificate, or execution of an AOP,[186] the petitioner may introduce testimony from the child's mother, respondent (via stipulations or cross-examination), or others with personal knowledge of the relevant facts. A petitioner may also introduce a certified copy of the child's birth certificate that does not name the respondent father.[187]

The petitioner must also prove that the respondent father did not provide "substantial financial support or consistent care" to the child and mother.[188] Neither "substantial financial support" nor "consistent care" is defined by the statute.[189] In interpreting "consistent care," the court of appeals in a recent case looked to the dictionary definition of consistency, which requires " 'regularity, or steady continuity throughout: showing no significant change, unevenness, or contradiction.' "[190] Applying that definition, the

---

180. *Id.* at 103.

181. G.S. 7B-1109(f); 7B-1111(b).

182. *In re* I.S., 170 N.C. App. 78 (2005).

183. *Id.* (court order did not contain findings for each subsection of G.S. 7B-1111(a)(5)a.).

184. *In re* J.K.C., 218 N.C. App. 22 (2012).

185. G.S. 7B-1111(a)(5)a. Note that if the reply states that the father did file an affidavit of paternity with the NC DHHS Registry before the termination of parental rights action was initiated, the petitioner or movant will not be able to prove the ground.

186. G.S. 130A-101(e)(2), (f) require that both the mother and putative father sign the AOP.

187. G.S. 8C-803(9) (hearsay exception, records of Vital Statistics), 8C-902(4) (self-authenticated certified copy of public record), 8C-1005 (public records).

188. G.S. 7B-1111(a)(5)e.; *I.S.*, 170 N.C. App. 78.

189. *In re* A.C.V., 203 N.C. App. 473 (2010).

190. *Id.* at 478 (quoting Webster's Third New International Dictionary Unabridged 484 (1976)).

court of appeals determined that the father did not provide "consistent care" to the mother when, during her pregnancy, he only made a few phone calls and attended some parenting classes and an ultrasound.[191] The court also found that the father did not provide "substantial financial support" to the mother or child when he purchased items for the baby that he kept at his home.[192] The court of appeals offered some guidance as to what would have constituted substantial financial support and consistent care when it stated, "it is reasonable to conclude that such language in the statute requires, at a minimum, that [the father] should have involved himself to the extent . . . requested . . . gas money, doctor co-pay reimbursement, and general financial support during [the mother's] pregnancy."[193]

The court of appeals has further held that in termination of parental rights actions the father must have provided substantial support directly *to* the mother and child.[194] This holding differs from the appellate opinions deciding whether a father's consent is required for the child's adoption. The court of appeals decisions are based on the different language of the statutes; the consent to adoption statute[195] requires that the father provided support "*for*" the mother or child, and the termination of parental rights statute[196] requires that the father provided support with respect "*to*" the mother or child. Another distinction between the consent to adoption and grounds to terminate parental rights statutes that has been identified by the court of appeals addresses the requirement that the father provide financial support. The termination of parental rights statute does not require the trial court to find that the father has an ability to pay; the petitioner need only prove that the respondent father did not provide substantial financial support and consistent care to the mother or child.[197] In contrast, the consent to adoption statute requires the court to consider the father's financial means when considering whether the father provided reasonable and consistent payments for the support of the mother and/or child.[198]

Best Interests of the Child

A termination of parental rights proceeding consists of two stages: an adjudication of a ground and the disposition.[199] A termination of parental rights cannot be based solely on the adjudication of a statutory ground. After the district court determines

191. *A.C.V.*, 203 N.C. App. 473.
192. *Id.*
193. *Id.* at 477–78.
194. *A.C.V.*, 203 N.C. App. 473.
195. G.S. 48-3-601(2)b.4.II.
196. G.S. 7B-1111(a)(5)d.
197. *In re* J.D.S., 170 N.C. App. 244 (2005); *In re* Hunt, 127 N.C. App. 370 (1997). *See* G.S. 7B-1111(a)(5)d.
198. G.S. 48-3-601(2)b.4.II.
199. *In re* Montgomery, 311 N.C. 101 (1984).

that a ground to terminate parental rights exists, the court must proceed to disposition and determine whether the termination of the respondent's parental rights is in the child's best interests.[200]

There is no burden of proof that a party must satisfy to prove a child's best interests.[201] Any party may introduce relevant evidence that supports his or her position regarding the child's best interests as those interests relate to the termination of the respondent's parental rights.[202] The district court exercises its discretion in determining whether the termination of the respondent's parental rights is in the child's best interests.[203]

Although the court exercises its discretion, it must consider six statutorily identified best interests of the child factors, and make written findings of those that are relevant.[204] The six factors are the child's age, the likelihood of the child's adoption, whether the termination of parental rights will aid in accomplishing the child's permanent plan, the bond between the child and parent, the quality of the relationship between the child and prospective adoptive parent, and any other relevant consideration.[205] If the court concludes that it is not in the child's best interests to terminate the respondent's parental rights, it must dismiss the petition or deny the motion.[206] If the court concludes that it is in the child's best interests to terminate the parental rights, the court should grant the petition or motion.

The Court's Decision and Its Impact on the Adoption Proceeding

If the court denies or dismisses the petition or motion for the termination of the parental rights of a person whose consent to the child's adoption is required, the adoption cannot proceed without that parent's consent, relinquishment, or subsequent termination of parental rights. If the court orders the termination of parental rights, a certified copy of the order must be filed in the adoption action.[207] The adoption may proceed once all the necessary consents, relinquishments, and terminations of parental rights are obtained.

---

200. G.S. 7B-1110.
201. *In re* Blackburn, 142 N.C. App. 607 (2002).
202. *See* G.S. 7B-1110(a).
203. *Blackburn*, 142 N.C. App. 607.
204. G.S. 7B-1110(a).
205. *Id.* Note that in *In re D.H.*, 232 N.C. App. 217 (2014), the court of appeals noted that the absence of an adoptive placement is not a bar to the termination of parental rights.
206. G.S. 7B-1110(b).
207. G.S. 48-2-304(b)(6); 48-2-305(3); 48-2-603(a)(4).

The Adoption Proceeding

If the adoption is uncontested, the clerk of superior court may order the adoption without a hearing or may schedule an uncontested hearing.[208] If the adoption is contested, it must be transferred to the district court.[209] An adoption is required to be decided after ninety days and before six months from the date on which the petition was filed, unless the court waives these time requirements for cause.[210]

Before an adoption hearing may begin, the court must find that proof of service of the notice that the petition was filed was made on the necessary persons or that a certified copy of a waiver of the notice by a required person has been filed with the court.[211] In addition to serving notice on parents whose consents are required but have not been obtained for the adoption, notice is required to be served on (1) the child if the child is 12 or older, (2) the county department that placed the child or that has a court order of legal custody of the child, and (3) anyone who the adoption petitioner has actually been informed of having a court order of custody, visitation, or communication rights with the child.[212] If the court determines that the notice was not served on an alleged father, the court must order that he be served with notice of the adoption hearing[213] and continue the hearing to allow for service of the notice.

Before the adoption may be ordered, the court must find that the notice of the filing of the petition was served on or properly waived by any person entitled to receive it.[214] The court must also find that each necessary consent, relinquishment, and termination of parental rights was obtained and filed with the court.[215] The court must review the pre-placement assessment and the report that was ordered by the court to assist it in determining if the adoption is in the child's best interests.[216] The court must determine

---

208. G.S. 48-2-601(a).

209. Johns v. Welker, 228 N.C. App. 177, 178, 181 (2013) ("As a contested adoption proceeding, it was transferred to District Court. . . . The district court has . . . jurisdiction over contested adoptions."). *See* G.S. 48-2-601(a1).

210. G.S. 48-2-601(b), (c); 48-2-603(a)(1).

211. G.S. 48-2-407; *see id.* § 48-2-401 (required notice); 48-2-406 (waiver of a notice). Although a certified copy of the waiver is required, G.S. 48-2-406(a) allows a person who is entitled to notice to waive the notice in open court personally or through an authorized agent.

212. G.S. 48-2-401(b)(1), (c)(1), (2), (4). (Note that G.S. 48-2-401 identifies other individuals who may be entitled to notice.)

213. G.S. 48-2-404.

214. G.S. 48-2-603(a)(3); 48-2-406 (waiver of notice).

215. G.S. 48-2-603(a)(4).

216. G.S. 48-2-603(a)(5); 48-3-301(c)(2); *see also id.* §§ 48-3-301 and 48-3-303 (pre-placement assessment); 48-2-501 and 48-2-502 (report: after an adoption petition is filed, the court orders the county department or other agency to complete and file a report with the court within sixty days of the order being mailed or delivered; the agency must interview each petitioner at his or her residence, interview the child, and observe the relationship between the child and petitioner(s); the report must address the suitability of the petitioner(s) and his or

that each petitioner is a suitable adoptive parent,[217] that there has been substantial compliance with the adoption statutes,[218] and that the adoption is in the child's best interests.[219]

If the court denies the adoption, custody of the child returns to the person or agency that had custody immediately before the adoption petition was filed.[220] If the petition is denied, the district court in the abuse, neglect, or dependency action continues to have jurisdiction, and a permanency planning hearing should be held to modify the child's permanent plans.

The Child's Adoption

If the petition is granted, the child has new parents, and the legal relationship between the child and his or her former parents is completely severed.[221] The child's name is changed to the name that is designated in the adoption decree.[222] A new birth certificate for the child will be created with the child's new name and parents' names.[223] The State Registrar must notify the register of deeds or other appropriate official to remove the child's original birth certificate from its records and forward it to the State Registrar.[224] The State Registrar must seal the child's original birth certificate and related documents.[225] The new birth certificate will only be on file and available from the State Registrar.[226]

The child is considered at law to be the legitimate child of his or her new parents.[227] The child's permanent plan has been achieved, and the abuse, neglect, or dependency proceeding automatically terminates.[228]

---

her home, raise any specific concerns about the child's best interests because of a substantial risk of harm to the child's well-being, and make a recommendation concerning the granting of the petition).

217. G.S. 48-2-603(a)(8).

218. G.S. 48-2-604(a)(11).

219. G.S. 48-3-502(b); 48-2-603(b); 48-2-606(a)(7).

220. G.S. 48-2-604(c).

221. G.S. 48-1-106(b), (c). *But see id.* § 48-1-106(d) (adoption by a stepparent does not sever the rights of the parent who is the stepparent's spouse).

222. G.S. 48-1-105; *see also id.* § 48-2-304(a)(4) (petition shall state the name by which the child is to be known if the adoption is granted).

223. G.S. 48-9-107(a).

224. G.S. 48-9-107(d).

225. G.S. 48-9-107(c).

226. G.S. 48-9-107(d).

227. G.S. 48-1-106(b).

228. G.S. 48-2-102(b).

Summary

For a child who is the subject of an abuse, neglect, or dependency proceeding and who has a primary permanent plan of adoption, there are two distinct but related court actions that are required: (1) the abuse, neglect, or dependency proceeding before the district court and (2) the adoption proceeding initiated before the clerk of superior court. A third action to terminate a parent's rights may also be necessary, although that proceeding may be part of or consolidated with the underlying abuse, neglect, or dependency proceeding in district court. These separate actions exist simultaneously and impact each other procedurally. The absence of a court adjudication of paternity or non-paternity may result in the need to serve notice on and possibly obtain consents or relinquishments from or termination of parental rights orders for multiple men who may be the child's biological father. A judicial determination of paternity limits who receives notice and who must consent, relinquish, or have his parental rights terminated for the adoption to proceed, thereby avoiding possible delays to the child's adoption. Ultimately, the child achieves permanency through his or her adoption.

Appendix A

Selected North Carolina General Statutes (G.S.) Specific to Child Welfare Proceedings

Abuse, Neglect, Dependency: G.S. Chapter 7B

§ 7B-100. Purpose.

This Subchapter shall be interpreted and construed so as to implement the following purposes and policies:

(1) To provide procedures for the hearing of juvenile cases that assure fairness and equity and that protect the constitutional rights of juveniles and parents;

(2) To develop a disposition in each juvenile case that reflects consideration of the facts, the needs and limitations of the juvenile, and the strengths and weaknesses of the family.

(3) To provide for services for the protection of juveniles by means that respect both the right to family autonomy and the juveniles' needs for safety, continuity, and permanence; and

(4) To provide standards for the removal, when necessary, of juveniles from their homes and for the return of juveniles to their homes consistent with preventing the unnecessary or inappropriate separation of juveniles from their parents.

(5) To provide standards, consistent with the Adoption and Safe Families Act of 1997, P.L. 105-89, for ensuring that the best interests of the juvenile are of paramount consideration by the court and that when it is not in the juvenile's best interest to be returned home, the juvenile will be placed in a safe, permanent home within a reasonable amount of time.

§ 7B-101. Definitions.

. . .

(3) Caretaker. - Any person other than a parent, guardian, or custodian who has responsibility for the health and welfare of a juvenile in a residential setting. A person responsible for a juvenile's health and welfare means a stepparent, foster parent, an adult member of the juvenile's household, an adult relative entrusted with the juvenile's care, any person such as a house parent or cottage parent who has primary responsibility for supervising a juvenile's health and welfare in a residential child care facility or residential educational facility, or

any employee or volunteer of a division, institution, or school operated by the Department of Health and Human Services. Nothing in this subdivision shall be construed to impose a legal duty of support under Chapter 50 or Chapter 110 of the General Statutes. The duty imposed upon a caretaker as defined in this subdivision shall be for the purpose of this Subchapter only.

. . .

(8) Custodian. - The person or agency that has been awarded legal custody of a juvenile by a court.

. . .

(9) Dependent juvenile. - A juvenile in need of assistance or placement because (i) the juvenile has no parent, guardian, or custodian responsible for the juvenile's care or supervision or (ii) the juvenile's parent, guardian, or custodian is unable to provide for the juvenile's care or supervision and lacks an appropriate alternative child care arrangement.

. . .

(18) Reasonable efforts. - The diligent use of preventive or reunification services by a department of social services when a juvenile's remaining at home or returning home is consistent with achieving a safe, permanent home for the juvenile within a reasonable period of time. If a court of competent jurisdiction determines that the juvenile is not to be returned home, then reasonable efforts means the diligent and timely use of permanency planning services by a department of social services to develop and implement a permanent plan for the juvenile.

. . .

(18b) Return home or reunification. - Placement of the juvenile in the home of either parent or placement of the juvenile in the home of a guardian or custodian from whose home the child was removed by court order.

. . .

§ 7B-200. Jurisdiction.

. . .

(b) The court shall have jurisdiction over the parent, guardian, custodian, or caretaker of a juvenile who has been adjudicated abused, neglected, or dependent, provided the parent, guardian, custodian, or caretaker has (i) been properly served with summons pursuant to G.S. 7B-406, (ii) waived service of process, or (iii) automatically become a party pursuant to G.S. 7B-401.1(c) or (d).

. . .

§ 7B-401.1. Parties.

(a) Petitioner. - Only a county director of social services or the director's authorized representative may file a petition alleging that a juvenile is abused, neglected, or dependent. The petitioner shall remain a party until the court terminates its jurisdiction in the case.

(b) Parents. - The juvenile's parent shall be a party unless one of the following applies:
   (1) The parent's rights have been terminated.
   (2) The parent has relinquished the juvenile for adoption, unless the court orders that the parent be made a party.
   (3) The parent has been convicted under G.S. 14-27.2 or G.S. 14-27.3 for an offense that resulted in the conception of the juvenile.

(c) Guardian. - A person who is the child's court-appointed guardian of the person or general guardian when the petition is filed shall be a party. A person appointed as the child's guardian pursuant to G.S. 7B-600 shall automatically become a party but only if the court has found that the guardianship is the permanent plan for the juvenile.

(d) Custodian. - A person who is the juvenile's custodian, as defined in G.S. 7B-101(8), when the petition is filed shall be a party. A person to whom custody of the juvenile is awarded in the juvenile proceeding shall automatically become a party but only if the court has found that the custody arrangement is the permanent plan for the juvenile.

(e) Caretaker. - A caretaker shall be a party only if (i) the petition includes allegations relating to the caretaker, (ii) the caretaker has assumed the status and obligation of a parent, or (iii) the court orders that the caretaker be made a party.

(e1) Foster Parent. – A foster parent as defined in G.S. 131D-10.2(9a) providing foster care for the juvenile is not a party to the case and may be allowed to intervene only if the foster parent has authority to file a petition to terminate the parental rights of the juvenile's parents pursuant to G.S. 7B-1103.

(f) The Juvenile. - The juvenile shall be a party.

(g) Removal of a Party. - If a guardian, custodian, or caretaker is a party, the court may discharge that person from the proceeding, making the person no longer a party, if the court finds that the person does not have legal rights that may be affected by the action and that the person's continuation as a party is not necessary to meet the juvenile's needs.

(h) Intervention. - Except as provided in G.S. 7B-1103(b), the court shall not allow intervention by a person who is not the juvenile's parent, guardian, custodian, or caretaker but may allow intervention by another county department of social services that has an interest in the proceeding. This section shall not prohibit the court from consolidating a juvenile proceeding with a civil action or claim for custody pursuant to G.S. 7B-200.

§ 7B-402. Petition.

(a) The petition shall contain the name, date of birth, address of the juvenile, the name and last known address of each party as determined by G.S. 7B-401.1, and allegations of facts sufficient to invoke jurisdiction over the juvenile. The petition may contain information on more than one juvenile when the juveniles are from the same home and are before the court for the same reason.

. . .

§ 7B-406. Issuance of summons.

. . .

(c) The summons shall advise the parent that upon service, jurisdiction over that person is obtained and that failure to comply with any order of the court pursuant to G.S. 7B-904 may cause the court to issue a show cause order for contempt.

. . .

§ 7B-407. Service of summons.

The summons shall be served under G.S. 1A-1, Rule 4(j) upon the parent, guardian, custodian, or caretaker, not less than five days prior to the date of the scheduled hearing. The time for service may be waived in the discretion of the court.

If service by publication under G.S. 1A-1, Rule 4(j1) is required, the cost of the service by publication shall be advanced by the petitioner and may be charged as court costs as the court may direct.

§ 7B-503. Criteria for nonsecure custody.

(a) When a request is made for nonsecure custody, the court shall first consider release of the juvenile to the juvenile's parent, relative, guardian, custodian, or other responsible adult. . . .

. . .

§ 7B-505. Placement while in nonsecure custody.

(a) A juvenile meeting the criteria set out in G.S. 7B-503 may be placed in nonsecure custody with the department of social services or a person designated in the order for temporary residential placement in:
   (1) A licensed foster home or a home otherwise authorized by law to provide such care; or
   (2) A facility operated by the department of social services; or
   (3) Any other home or facility, including a relative's home approved by the court and designated in the order.
(b) The court shall order the department of social services to make diligent efforts to notify relatives and any custodial parents of the juvenile's siblings that the juvenile is in nonsecure custody and of any hearings scheduled to occur pursuant to G.S. 7B-506, unless the court finds such notification would be contrary to the best

interests of the juvenile. The court shall order the department to make diligent efforts to notify relatives and other persons with legal custody of a sibling of the juvenile that the juvenile is in nonsecure custody and of any hearings scheduled to occur pursuant to G.S. 7B-506, unless the court finds the notification would be contrary to the best interests of the juvenile. In placing a juvenile in nonsecure custody under this section, the court shall first consider whether a relative of the juvenile is willing and able to provide proper care and supervision of the juvenile in a safe home. If the court finds that the relative is willing and able to provide proper care and supervision in a safe home, then the court shall order placement of the juvenile with the relative unless the court finds that placement with the relative would be contrary to the best interests of the juvenile.

(c) If the court does not place the juvenile with a relative, the court may consider whether nonrelative kin or other persons with legal custody of a sibling of the juvenile are willing and able to provide proper care and supervision of the juvenile in a safe home. The court may order the department to notify the juvenile's State-recognized tribe of the need for nonsecure custody for the purpose of locating relatives or nonrelative kin for placement. The court may order placement of the juvenile with nonrelative kin if the court finds the placement is in the juvenile's best interests.

(d) In placing a juvenile in nonsecure custody under this section, the court shall also consider whether it is in the juvenile's best interest to remain in the juvenile's community of residence. In placing a juvenile in nonsecure custody under this section, the court shall consider the Indian Child Welfare Act, Pub. L. No. 95-608, 25 U.S.C. §§ 1901, et seq., as amended, and the Howard M. Metzenbaum Multiethnic Placement Act of 1994, Pub. L. No. 103-382, 108 Stat. 4056, as amended, as they may apply. Placement of a juvenile with a relative outside of this State must be in accordance with the Interstate Compact on the Placement of Children, Article 38 of this Chapter. § 7B-506. Hearing to determine need for continued nonsecure custody.

§ 7B-506. Hearing to determine need for continued nonsecure custody.

. . .

(h) At each hearing to determine the need for continued custody, the court shall determine the following:

(1) Inquire as to the identity and location of any missing parent and whether paternity is at issue. The court shall include findings as to the efforts undertaken to locate the missing parent and to serve that parent, as well as efforts undertaken to establish paternity when paternity is an issue. The order may provide for specific efforts aimed at determining the identity and location of any missing parent, as well as specific efforts aimed at establishing paternity.

(2) Inquire about efforts made to identify and notify relatives as potential resources for placement or support and as to whether a relative of the juvenile is willing and able to provide proper care and supervision of the juvenile in a safe home. If the court finds that the relative is willing and able to provide proper care and supervision in a safe home, then the court shall order

temporary placement of the juvenile with the relative unless the court finds that placement with the relative would be contrary to the best interests of the juvenile. In placing a juvenile in nonsecure custody under this section, the court shall consider the Indian Child Welfare Act, Pub. L. No. 95-608, 25 U.S.C. §§ 1901, et seq., as amended, and the Howard M. Metzenbaum Multiethnic Placement Act of 1994, Pub. L. No. 103-382, 108 Stat. 4056, as amended, as they may apply. Placement of a juvenile with a relative outside of this State must be in accordance with the Interstate Compact on the Placement of Children set forth in Article 38 of this Chapter.

(2a) If the court does not place the juvenile with a relative, the court may consider whether nonrelative kin or other persons with legal custody of a sibling of the juvenile is willing and able to provide proper care and supervision of the juvenile in a safe home. The court may order the department to notify the juvenile's State-recognized tribe of the need for nonsecure custody for the purpose of locating relatives or nonrelative kin for placement. The court may order placement of the juvenile with nonrelative kin or other persons with legal custody of a sibling of the juvenile if the court finds the placement is in the juvenile's best interests.

. . .

§ 7B-600. Appointment of guardian.

(a) In any case when no parent appears in a hearing with the juvenile or when the court finds it would be in the best interests of the juvenile, the court may appoint a guardian of the person for the juvenile. The guardian shall operate under the supervision of the court with or without bond and shall file only such reports as the court shall require. The guardian shall have the care, custody, and control of the juvenile or may arrange a suitable placement for the juvenile and may represent the juvenile in legal actions before any court. The guardian may consent to certain actions on the part of the juvenile in place of the parent including (i) marriage, (ii) enlisting in the Armed Forces of the United States, and (iii) enrollment in school. The guardian may also consent to any necessary remedial, psychological, medical, or surgical treatment for the juvenile. The authority of the guardian shall continue until the guardianship is terminated by court order, until the juvenile is emancipated pursuant to Article 35 of Subchapter IV of this Chapter, or until the juvenile reaches the age of majority.

(b) In any case where the court has determined that the appointment of a relative or other suitable person as guardian of the person for a juvenile is the permanent plan for the juvenile and appoints a guardian under this section, the guardian becomes a party to the proceeding. The court may terminate the guardianship only if (i) the court finds that the relationship between the guardian and the juvenile is no longer in the juvenile's best interest, (ii) the guardian is unfit, (iii) the guardian has neglected a guardian's duties, or (iv) the guardian is unwilling or unable to continue assuming a guardian's duties.

. . .

§ 7B-602. Parent's right to counsel; guardian ad litem.

(a) In cases where the juvenile petition alleges that a juvenile is abused, neglected, or dependent, the parent has the right to counsel and to appointed counsel in cases of indigency unless that person waives the right. When a petition is filed alleging that a juvenile is abused, neglected, or dependent, the clerk shall appoint provisional counsel for each parent named in the petition in accordance with rules adopted by the Office of Indigent Defense Services and shall indicate the appointment on the juvenile summons or attached notice. At the first hearing, the court shall dismiss the provisional counsel if the respondent parent:

    (1) Does not appear at the hearing;

    (2) Does not qualify for court-appointed counsel;

    (3) Has retained counsel; or

    (4) Waives the right to counsel.

The court shall confirm the appointment of counsel if subdivisions (1) through (4) of this subsection are not applicable to the respondent parent.

    The court may reconsider a parent's eligibility and desire for appointed counsel at any stage of the proceeding.

(a1) A parent qualifying for appointed counsel may be permitted to proceed without the assistance of counsel only after the court examines the parent and makes findings of fact sufficient to show that the waiver is knowing and voluntary. The court's examination shall be reported as provided in G.S. 7B-806.

. . .

§ 7B-800. Amendment of petition.

The court, in its discretion, may permit a petition to be amended. The court shall direct the manner in which an amended petition shall be served and the time allowed for a party to prepare after the petition has been amended.

§ 7B-800.1. Pre-adjudication hearing.

(a) Prior to the adjudicatory hearing, the court shall consider the following:

. . .

    (2) Identification of the parties to the proceeding.

    (3) Whether paternity has been established or efforts made to establish paternity, including the identity and location of any missing parent.

    (4) Whether relatives, parents, or other persons with legal custody of a sibling of the juvenile have been identified and notified as potential resources for placement or support.

. . .

§ 7B-901. Initial dispositional hearing.

. . .

(b) At the dispositional hearing, the court shall inquire as to the identity and location of any missing parent and whether paternity is at issue. The court shall include findings of the efforts undertaken to locate the missing parent and to serve that parent and efforts undertaken to establish paternity when paternity is an issue. The order may provide for specific efforts in determining the identity and location of any missing parent and specific efforts in establishing paternity. The court shall also inquire about efforts made to identify and notify relatives, parents, or other persons with legal custody of a sibling of the juvenile, as potential resources for placement or support.

(c) If the disposition order places a juvenile in the custody of a county department of social services, the court shall direct that reasonable efforts for reunification as defined in G.S. 7B-101 shall not be required if the court makes written findings of fact pertaining to any of the following:

    (1) A court of competent jurisdiction has determined that aggravated circumstances exist because the parent has committed or encouraged the commission of, or allowed the continuation of, any of the following upon the juvenile:

        a. Sexual abuse.

        b. Chronic physical or emotional abuse.

        c. Torture.

        d. Abandonment.

        e. Chronic or toxic exposure to alcohol or controlled substances that causes impairment of or addiction in the juvenile.

        f. Any other act, practice, or conduct that increased the enormity or added to the injurious consequences of the abuse or neglect.

    (2) A court of competent jurisdiction has terminated involuntarily the parental rights of the parent to another child of the parent.

    (3) A court of competent jurisdiction has determined that (i) the parent has committed murder or voluntary manslaughter of another child of the parent; (ii) has aided, abetted, attempted, conspired, or solicited to commit murder or voluntary manslaughter of the child or another child of the parent; (iii) has committed a felony assault resulting in serious bodily injury to the child or another child of the parent; (iv) has committed sexual abuse against the child or another child of the parent; or (v) has been required to register as a sex offender on any government-administered registry.

(d) When the court determines that reunification efforts are not required, the court shall order a permanent plan as soon as possible, after providing each party with a reasonable opportunity to prepare and present evidence. The court shall schedule a subsequent hearing within 30 days to address the permanent plans in accordance with G.S. 7B-906.1 and G.S. 7B-906.2.

§ 7B-903. Dispositional alternatives for abused, neglected, or dependent juvenile.

(a)   The following alternatives for disposition shall be available to any court exercising jurisdiction, and the court may combine any of the applicable alternatives when the court finds the disposition to be in the best interests of the juvenile:

    (1)   Dismiss the case or continue the case in order to allow the parent, guardian, custodian, caretaker or others to take appropriate action.

    (2)   Require that the juvenile be supervised in the juvenile's own home by the department of social services in the juvenile's county or by another individual as may be available to the court, subject to conditions applicable to the parent, guardian, custodian, or caretaker as the court may specify.

    . . .

    (4)   Place the juvenile in the custody of a parent, relative, private agency offering placement services, or some other suitable person. If the court determines that the juvenile should be placed in the custody of an individual other than a parent, the court shall verify that the person receiving custody of the juvenile understands the legal significance of the placement and will have adequate resources to care appropriately for the juvenile.

    . . .

(a1)   In placing a juvenile in out-of-home care under this section, the court shall first consider whether a relative of the juvenile is willing and able to provide proper care and supervision of the juvenile in a safe home. If the court finds that the relative is willing and able to provide proper care and supervision in a safe home, then the court shall order placement of the juvenile with the relative unless the court finds that the placement is contrary to the best interests of the juvenile. In placing a juvenile in out-of-home care under this section, the court shall also consider whether it is in the juvenile's best interest to remain in the juvenile's community of residence. Placement of a juvenile with a relative outside of this State must be in accordance with the Interstate Compact on the Placement of Children.

    . . .

§ 7B-904. Authority over parents of juvenile adjudicated as abused, neglected, or dependent.

(a)   If the court orders medical, surgical, psychiatric, psychological, or other treatment pursuant to G.S. 7B-903, the court may order the parent or other responsible parties to pay the cost of the treatment or care ordered.

(b)   At the dispositional hearing or a subsequent hearing if the court finds that it is in the best interests of the juvenile for the parent, guardian, custodian, stepparent, adult member of the juvenile's household, or adult relative entrusted with the juvenile's care to be directly involved in the juvenile's treatment, the court may order the parent, guardian, custodian, stepparent, adult member of the juvenile's household, or adult relative entrusted with the juvenile's care to participate in medical, psychiatric, psychological, or other treatment of the juvenile. The cost of the treatment shall be paid pursuant to G.S. 7B-903.

(c) At the dispositional hearing or a subsequent hearing the court may determine whether the best interests of the juvenile require that the parent, guardian, custodian, stepparent, adult member of the juvenile's household, or adult relative entrusted with the juvenile's care undergo psychiatric, psychological, or other treatment or counseling directed toward remediating or remedying behaviors or conditions that led to or contributed to the juvenile's adjudication or to the court's decision to remove custody of the juvenile from the parent, guardian, custodian, stepparent, adult member of the juvenile's household, or adult relative entrusted with the juvenile's care. If the court finds that the best interests of the juvenile require the parent, guardian, custodian, stepparent, adult member of the juvenile's household, or adult relative entrusted with the juvenile's care undergo treatment, it may order that individual to comply with a plan of treatment approved by the court or condition legal custody or physical placement of the juvenile with the parent, guardian, custodian, stepparent, adult member of the juvenile's household, or adult relative entrusted with the juvenile's care upon that individual's compliance with the plan of treatment. The court may order the parent, guardian, custodian, stepparent, adult member of the juvenile's household, or adult relative entrusted with the juvenile's care to pay the cost of treatment ordered pursuant to this subsection. In cases in which the court has conditioned legal custody or physical placement of the juvenile with the parent, guardian, custodian, stepparent, adult member of the juvenile's household, or adult relative entrusted with the juvenile's care upon compliance with a plan of treatment, the court may charge the cost of the treatment to the county of the juvenile's residence if the court finds the parent, guardian, custodian, stepparent, adult member of the juvenile's household, or adult relative entrusted with the juvenile's care is unable to pay the cost of the treatment. In all other cases, if the court finds the parent, guardian, custodian, stepparent, adult member of the juvenile's household, or adult relative entrusted with the juvenile's care is unable to pay the cost of the treatment ordered pursuant to this subsection, the court may order that individual to receive treatment currently available from the area mental health program that serves the parent's catchment area.

(d) At the dispositional hearing or a subsequent hearing, when legal custody of a juvenile is vested in someone other than the juvenile's parent, if the court finds that the parent is able to do so, the court may order that the parent pay a reasonable sum that will cover, in whole or in part, the support of the juvenile after the order is entered. If the court requires the payment of child support, the amount of the payments shall be determined as provided in G.S. 50-13.4(c). If the court places a juvenile in the custody of a county department of social services and if the court finds that the parent is unable to pay the cost of the support required by the juvenile, the cost shall be paid by the county department of social services in whose custody the juvenile is placed, provided the juvenile is not receiving care in an institution owned or operated by the State or federal government or any subdivision thereof.

(d1) At the dispositional hearing or a subsequent hearing, the court may order the parent, guardian, custodian, or caretaker served with a copy of the summons pursuant to G.S. 7B-407 to do any of the following:

(1) Attend and participate in parental responsibility classes if those classes are available in the judicial district in which the parent, guardian, custodian, or caretaker resides.

(2) Provide, to the extent that person is able to do so, transportation for the juvenile to keep appointments for medical, psychiatric, psychological, or other treatment ordered by the court if the juvenile remains in or is returned to the home.

(3) Take appropriate steps to remedy conditions in the home that led to or contributed to the juvenile's adjudication or to the court's decision to remove custody of the juvenile from the parent, guardian, custodian, or caretaker.

(e) Upon motion of a party or upon the court's own motion, the court may issue an order directing the parent, guardian, custodian, or caretaker served with a copy of the summons pursuant to G.S. 7B-407 to appear and show cause why the parent, guardian, custodian, or caretaker should not be found or held in civil or criminal contempt for willfully failing to comply with an order of the court. Chapter 5A of the General Statutes shall govern contempt proceedings initiated pursuant to this section.

§ 7B-905.1. Visitation.

(a) An order that removes custody of a juvenile from a parent, guardian, or custodian or that continues the juvenile's placement outside the home shall provide for appropriate visitation as may be in the best interests of the juvenile consistent with the juvenile's health and safety. The court may specify in the order conditions under which visitation may be suspended.

(b) If the juvenile is placed or continued in the custody or placement responsibility of a county department of social services, the court may order the director to arrange, facilitate, and supervise a visitation plan expressly approved or ordered by the court. The plan shall indicate the minimum frequency and length of visits and whether the visits shall be supervised. Unless the court orders otherwise, the director shall have discretion to determine who will supervise visits when supervision is required, to determine the location of visits, and to change the day and time of visits in response to scheduling conflicts, illness of the child or party, or extraordinary circumstances. The director shall promptly communicate a limited and temporary change in the visitation schedule to the affected party. Any ongoing change in the visitation schedule shall be communicated to the party in writing and state the reason for the change.

   If the director makes a good faith determination that the visitation plan is not consistent with the juvenile's health and safety, the director may temporarily suspend all or part of the visitation plan. The director shall not be subject to any motion to show cause for this suspension but shall expeditiously file a motion for review.

   . . .

§ 7B-906.1. Review and permanency planning hearings.

(a) In any case where custody is removed from a parent, guardian, or custodian, the court shall conduct a review hearing within 90 days from the date of the dispositional hearing and shall conduct a review hearing within six months thereafter. Within 12 months of the date of the initial order removing custody, there shall be a review hearing designated as a permanency planning hearing. Review hearings after the initial permanency planning hearing shall be designated as subsequent permanency planning hearings. The subsequent permanency planning hearings shall be held at least every six months thereafter or earlier as set by the court to review the progress made in finalizing the permanent plan for the juvenile, or if necessary, to make a new permanent plan for the juvenile.

. . .

(d) At each hearing, the court shall consider the following criteria and make written findings regarding those that are relevant:

   (1) Services which have been offered to reunite the juvenile with either parent whether or not the juvenile resided with the parent at the time of removal or the guardian or custodian from whom the child was removed.

   (2) Reports on visitation that has occurred and whether there is a need to create, modify, or enforce an appropriate visitation plan in accordance with G.S. 7B-905.1.

   (3) Whether efforts to reunite the juvenile with either parent clearly would be futile or inconsistent with the juvenile's safety and need for a safe, permanent home within a reasonable period of time. The court shall consider efforts to reunite regardless of whether the juvenile resided with the parent, guardian, or custodian at the time of removal. If the court determines efforts would be futile or inconsistent, the court shall consider a permanent plan of care for the juvenile.

. . .

   (6) When and if termination of parental rights should be considered.

. . .

(e) At any permanency planning hearing where the juvenile is not placed with a parent, the court shall additionally consider the following criteria and make written findings regarding those that are relevant:

   (1) Whether it is possible for the juvenile to be placed with a parent within the next six months and, if not, why such placement is not in the juvenile's best interests.

   (2) Where the juvenile's placement with a parent is unlikely within six months, whether legal guardianship or custody with a relative or some other suitable person should be established and, if so, the rights and responsibilities that should remain with the parents.

   (3) Where the juvenile's placement with a parent is unlikely within six months, whether adoption should be pursued and, if so, any barriers to the juvenile's adoption.

(4)   Where the juvenile's placement with a parent is unlikely within six months, whether the juvenile should remain in the current placement, or be placed in another permanent living arrangement and why.

(5)   Whether the county department of social services has since the initial permanency plan hearing made reasonable efforts to implement the permanent plan for the juvenile.

(6)   Any other criteria the court deems necessary.

(f)   In the case of a juvenile who is in the custody or placement responsibility of a county department of social services and has been in placement outside the home for 12 of the most recent 22 months, or a court of competent jurisdiction has determined that the parent (i) has abandoned the child, (ii) has committed murder or voluntary manslaughter of another child of the parent, or (iii) has aided, abetted, attempted, conspired, or solicited to commit murder or voluntary manslaughter of the child or another child of the parent, the director of the department of social services shall initiate a proceeding to terminate the parental rights of the parent unless the court finds any of the following:

(1)   The permanent plan for the juvenile is guardianship or custody with a relative or some other suitable person.

(2)   The court makes specific findings as to why the filing of a petition for termination of parental rights is not in the best interests of the child.

(3)   The department of social services has not provided the juvenile's family with services the department deems necessary when reasonable efforts are still required to enable the juvenile's return to a safe home.

. . .

(k)   If at any time custody is placed with a parent or findings are made in accordance with subsection (n) of this section, the court shall be relieved of the duty to conduct periodic judicial reviews of the placement.

. . .

(n)   Notwithstanding other provisions of this Article, the court may waive the holding of hearings required by this section, may require written reports to the court by the agency or person holding custody in lieu of review hearings, or order that review hearings be held less often than every six months if the court finds by clear, cogent, and convincing evidence each of the following:

(1)   The juvenile has resided in the placement for a period of at least one year.

(2)   The placement is stable and continuation of the placement is in the juvenile's best interests.

(3)   Neither the juvenile's best interests nor the rights of any party require that review hearings be held every six months.

(4)   All parties are aware that the matter may be brought before the court for review at any time by the filing of a motion for review or on the court's own motion.

(5)   The court order has designated the relative or other suitable person as the juvenile's permanent custodian or guardian of the person.

The court may not waive or refuse to conduct a review hearing if a party files a motion seeking the review. However, if a guardian of the person has been appointed for the juvenile and the court has also made findings in accordance with subsection (n) of this section that guardianship is the permanent plan for the juvenile, the court shall proceed in accordance with G.S. 7B-600(b).

§ 7B-906.2. Permanent plans; concurrent planning.

(a) At any permanency planning hearing pursuant to G.S. 7B-906.1, the court shall adopt one or more of the following permanent plans the court finds is in the juvenile's best interest:

(1) Reunification as defined by G.S. 7B-101.

(2) Adoption under Article 3 of Chapter 48 of the General Statutes.

(3) Guardianship pursuant to G.S. 7B-600(b).

(4) Custody to a relative or other suitable person.

(5) Another Planned Permanent Living Arrangement (APPLA) pursuant to G.S. 7B-912.

(6) Reinstatement of parental rights pursuant to G.S. 7B-1114.

(b) At any permanency planning hearing, the court shall adopt concurrent permanent plans and shall identify the primary plan and secondary plan. Reunification shall remain a primary or secondary plan unless the court made findings under G.S. 7B-901(c) or makes written findings that reunification efforts clearly would be unsuccessful or would be inconsistent with the juvenile's health or safety. The court shall order the county department of social services to make efforts toward finalizing the primary and secondary permanent plans and may specify efforts that are reasonable to timely achieve permanence for the juvenile.

. . .

§ 7B-911. Civil child custody order.

(a) Upon placing custody with a parent or other appropriate person, the court shall determine whether or not jurisdiction in the juvenile proceeding should be terminated and custody of the juvenile awarded to a parent or other appropriate person pursuant to G.S. 50-13.1, 50-13.2, 50-13.5, and 50-13.7.

(b) When the court enters a custody order under this section, the court shall either cause the order to be filed in an existing civil action relating to the custody of the juvenile or, if there is no other civil action, instruct the clerk to treat the order as the initiation of a civil action for custody.

If the order is filed in an existing civil action and the person to whom the court is awarding custody is not a party to that action, the court shall order that the person be joined as a party and that the caption of the case be changed accordingly. The order shall resolve any pending claim for custody and shall constitute a modification of any custody order previously entered in the action.

If the court's order initiates a civil action, the court shall designate the parties to the action and determine the most appropriate caption for the case. The civil filing fee is waived unless the court orders one or more of the parties to pay the filing fee for a civil action into the office of the clerk of superior court. The order shall constitute a custody determination, and any motion to enforce or modify the custody order shall be filed in the newly created civil action in accordance with the provisions of Chapter 50 of the General Statutes. The Administrative Office of the Courts may adopt rules and shall develop and make available appropriate forms for establishing a civil file to implement this section.

(c) When entering an order under this section, the court shall satisfy the following:

    (1) Make findings and conclusions that support the entry of a custody order in an action under Chapter 50 of the General Statutes or, if the juvenile is already the subject of a custody order entered pursuant to Chapter 50, makes findings and conclusions that support modification of that order pursuant to G.S. 50-13.7.

    (2) Make the following findings:

        a. There is not a need for continued State intervention on behalf of the juvenile through a juvenile court proceeding.

        b. At least six months have passed since the court made a determination that the juvenile's placement with the person to whom the court is awarding custody is the permanent plan for the juvenile, though this finding is not required if the court is awarding custody to a parent or to a person with whom the child was living when the juvenile petition was filed.

§ 7B-1112.1. Selection of adoptive parents.

The process of selection of specific adoptive parents shall be the responsibility of and within the discretion of the county department of social services or licensed child-placing agency. In selecting the adoptive parents, any current placement provider wanting to adopt the child shall be considered. The guardian ad litem may request information from and consult with the county department or child-placing agency concerning the selection process. If the guardian ad litem requests information about the selection process, the county shall provide the information within five business days. The county department of social services shall notify the guardian ad litem and the foster parents of the selection of prospective adoptive parents within 10 days of the selection and before the filing of the adoption petition. If the guardian ad litem disagrees with the selection of adoptive parents or the foster parents want to adopt the juvenile and were not selected as adoptive parents, the guardian ad litem or foster parents shall file a motion within 10 days of the department's notification and schedule the case for hearing on the next juvenile calendar. The department shall not change the juvenile's placement to the prospective adoptive parents unless the time period for filing a motion has expired and no motion has been filed. The Department shall provide a copy of a motion for judicial review of adoption selection to the foster parents not selected. Nothing in this section shall be construed to make the foster parents a party to the proceeding solely based on receiving notification and the right to be heard by filing a motion. In hearing any motion, the court shall consider the recommendations of the agency and the guardian ad litem and other facts related to the selection of adoptive parents. The court shall then determine whether the proposed adoptive placement is in the juvenile's best interests.

§ 7B-2901. Confidentiality of records.

(a) The clerk shall maintain a complete record of all juvenile cases filed in the clerk's office alleging abuse, neglect, or dependency. The records shall be withheld from public inspection and, except as provided in this subsection, may be examined only by order of the court. The record shall include the summons, petition, custody order, court order, written motions, the electronic or mechanical recording of the hearing, and other papers filed in the proceeding. The recording of the hearing shall be reduced to a written transcript only when notice of appeal has been timely given. After the time for appeal has expired with no appeal having been filed, the recording of the hearing may be erased or destroyed upon the written order of the court.

　　The following persons may examine the juvenile's record maintained pursuant to this subsection and obtain copies of written parts of the record without an order of the court:

   (1) The person named in the petition as the juvenile;

   (2) The guardian ad litem;

   (3) The county department of social services; and

   (4) The juvenile's parent, guardian, or custodian, or the attorney for the juvenile or the juvenile's parent, guardian, or custodian.

　　. . .

Termination of Parental Rights: G.S. Chapter 7B

§ 7B-1105. Preliminary hearing; unknown parent.

(a) If either the name or identity of any parent whose parental rights the petitioner seeks to terminate is not known to the petitioner, the court shall, within 10 days from the date of filing of the petition, or during the next term of court in the county where the petition is filed if there is no court in the county in that 10-day period, conduct a preliminary hearing to ascertain the name or identity of such parent.

(b) The court may, in its discretion, inquire of any known parent of the juvenile concerning the identity of the unknown parent and may order the petitioner to conduct a diligent search for the parent. Should the court ascertain the name or identity of the parent, it shall enter a finding to that effect; and the parent shall be summoned to appear in accordance with G.S. 7B-1106.

(c) Notice of the preliminary hearing need be given only to the petitioner who shall appear at the hearing, but the court may cause summons to be issued to any person directing the person to appear and testify.

(d) If the court is unable to ascertain the name or identity of the unknown parent, the court shall order publication of notice of the termination proceeding and shall specifically order the place or places of publication and the contents of the notice which the court concludes is most likely to identify the juvenile to such unknown parent. The notice shall be published in a newspaper qualified for legal advertising in accordance with G.S. 1-597 and G.S. 1-598 and published in the counties directed by the court, once a week for three successive weeks. Provided, further, the notice shall:

(1) Designate the court in which the petition is pending;

(2) Be directed to "the father (mother) (father and mother) of a male (female) juvenile born on or about _____ (date) in _____ (County), (city) _____ (State) _____, respondent";

(3) Designate the docket number and title of the case (the court may direct the actual name of the title be eliminated and the words "In Re Doe" substituted therefor);

(4) State that a petition seeking to terminate the parental rights of the respondent has been filed;

(5) Direct the respondent to answer the petition within 30 days after a date stated in the notice, exclusive of such date, which date so stated shall be the date of first publication of notice and be substantially in the form as set forth in G.S. 1A-1, Rule 4(j1); and

(6) State that the respondent's parental rights to the juvenile will be terminated upon failure to answer the petition within the time prescribed.

Upon completion of the service, an affidavit of the publisher shall be filed with the court.

(e) The court shall issue the order required by subsections (b) and (d) of this section within 30 days from the date of the preliminary hearing unless the court shall determine that additional time for investigation is required.

(f) Upon the failure of the parent served by publication pursuant to subsection (d) of this section to answer the petition within the time prescribed, the court shall issue an order terminating all parental rights of the unknown parent.

§ 7B-1110. Determination of best interests of the juvenile.

(a) After an adjudication that one or more grounds for terminating a parent's rights exist, the court shall determine whether terminating the parent's rights is in the juvenile's best interest. The court may consider any evidence, including hearsay evidence as defined in G.S. 8C-1, Rule 801, that the court finds to be relevant, reliable, and necessary to determine the best interests of the juvenile. In each case, the court shall consider the following criteria and make written findings regarding the following that are relevant:

(1) The age of the juvenile.

(2) The likelihood of adoption of the juvenile.

(3) Whether the termination of parental rights will aid in the accomplishment of the permanent plan for the juvenile.

(4) The bond between the juvenile and the parent.

(5) The quality of the relationship between the juvenile and the proposed adoptive parent, guardian, custodian, or other permanent placement.

(6) Any relevant consideration.

. . .

§ 7B-1111. Grounds for terminating parental rights.

(a) The court may terminate the parental rights upon a finding of one or more of the following:

...

(5) The father of a juvenile born out of wedlock has not, prior to the filing of a petition or motion to terminate parental rights, done any of the following:

a. Filed an affidavit of paternity in a central registry maintained by the Department of Health and Human Services; provided, the petitioner or movant shall inquire of the Department of Health and Human Services as to whether such an affidavit has been so filed and the Department's certified reply shall be submitted to and considered by the court.

b. Legitimated the juvenile pursuant to provisions of G.S. 49-10, G.S. 49-12.1, or filed a petition for this specific purpose.

c. Legitimated the juvenile by marriage to the mother of the juvenile.

d. Provided substantial financial support or consistent care with respect to the juvenile and mother.

e. Established paternity through G.S. 49-14, 110-132, 130A-101, 130A-118, or other judicial proceeding.

...

(9) The parental rights of the parent with respect to another child of the parent have been terminated involuntarily by a court of competent jurisdiction and the parent lacks the ability or willingness to establish a safe home.

...

(11) The parent has been convicted of a sexually related offense under Chapter 14 of the General Statutes that resulted in the conception of the juvenile.

...

§ 7B-1112. Effects of termination order.

An order terminating the parental rights completely and permanently terminates all rights and obligations of the parent to the juvenile and of the juvenile to the parent arising from the parental relationship, except that the juvenile's right of inheritance from the juvenile's parent shall not terminate until a final order of adoption is issued. The parent is not thereafter entitled to notice of proceedings to adopt the juvenile and may not object thereto or otherwise participate therein:

(1) If the juvenile had been placed in the custody of or released for adoption by one parent to a county department of social services or licensed child-placing agency and is in the custody of the agency at the time of the filing of the petition or motion, including a petition or motion filed pursuant to G.S. 7B-1103(a)(6), that agency shall, upon entry of the order terminating parental rights, acquire all of the rights for placement of the juvenile, except as

otherwise provided in G.S. 7B-908(d), as the agency would have acquired had the parent whose rights are terminated released the juvenile to that agency pursuant to the provisions of Part 7 of Article 3 of Chapter 48 of the General Statutes, including the right to consent to the adoption of the juvenile.

(2) Except as provided in subdivision (1) above, upon entering an order terminating the parental rights of one or both parents, the court may place the juvenile in the custody of the petitioner or movant, or some other suitable person, or in the custody of the department of social services or licensed child-placing agency, as may appear to be in the best interests of the juvenile.

Interstate Compact on the Placement of Children: G.S. Chapter 7B

§ 7B-3800. Adoption of Compact.

The Interstate Compact on the Placement of Children is hereby enacted into law and entered into with all other jurisdictions legally joining therein in a form substantially as contained in this Article. It is the intent of the General Assembly that Article 37 of this Chapter shall govern interstate placements of children between North Carolina and any other jurisdictions not a party to this Compact. It is the intent of the General Assembly that Chapter 48 of the General Statutes shall govern the adoption of children within the boundaries of North Carolina.

. . .

Article III. Conditions for Placement.

(a) No sending agency shall send, bring, or cause to be sent or brought into any other party state any child for placement in foster care or as a preliminary to a possible adoption unless the sending agency shall comply with each and every requirement set forth in this Article and with the applicable laws of the receiving state governing the placement of children therein.

. . .

Adoption of Minors: G.S. Chapter 48

§ 48-1-100. Legislative findings and intent; construction of Chapter.

(a) The General Assembly finds that it is in the public interest to establish a clear judicial process for adoptions, to promote the integrity and finality of adoptions, to encourage prompt, conclusive disposition of adoption proceedings, and to structure services to adopted children, biological parents, and adoptive parents that will provide for the needs and protect the interests of all parties to an adoption, particularly adopted minors.

(b) With special regard for the adoption of minors, the General Assembly declares as a matter of legislative policy that:

  (1) The primary purpose of this Chapter is to advance the welfare of minors by (i) protecting minors from unnecessary separation from their original parents, (ii) facilitating the adoption of minors in need of adoptive placement by persons who can give them love, care, security, and support, (iii) protecting minors from placement with adoptive parents unfit to have responsibility for their care and rearing, and (iv) assuring the finality of the adoption; and

  (2) Secondary purposes of this Chapter are (i) to protect biological parents from ill-advised decisions to relinquish a child or consent to the child's adoption, (ii) to protect adoptive parents from assuming responsibility for a child about whose heredity or mental or physical condition they know nothing, (iii) to protect the privacy of the parties to the adoption, and (iv) to discourage unlawful trafficking in minors and other unlawful placement activities.

(c) In construing this Chapter, the needs, interests, and rights of minor adoptees are primary. Any conflict between the interests of a minor adoptee and those of an adult shall be resolved in favor of the minor.

(d) This Chapter shall be liberally construed and applied to promote its underlying purposes and policies.

§ 48-1-105. Name of adoptee after adoption.

When a decree of adoption becomes final, the name of the adoptee shall become the name designated in the decree.

§ 48-1-106. Legal effect of decree of adoption.

(a) A decree of adoption effects a complete substitution of families for all legal purposes after the entry of the decree.

(b) A decree of adoption establishes the relationship of parent and child between each petitioner and the individual being adopted. From the date of the signing of the decree, the adoptee is entitled to inherit real and personal property by, through, and from the adoptive parents in accordance with the statutes on intestate succession and has the same legal status, including all legal rights and obligations of any kind whatsoever, as a child born the legitimate child of the adoptive parents.

(c) A decree of adoption severs the relationship of parent and child between the individual adopted and that individual's biological or previous adoptive parents. After the entry of a decree of adoption, the former parents are relieved of all legal duties and obligations due from them to the adoptee, except that a former parent's duty to make past-due payments for child support is not terminated, and the former parents are divested of all rights with respect to the adoptee.

(d) Notwithstanding any other provision of this section, neither an adoption by a stepparent nor a readoption pursuant to G.S. 48-6-102 has any effect on the relationship between the child and the parent who is the stepparent's spouse.

  . . .

§ 48-2-102. Transfer, stay, or dismissal.

. . .

(b) If an adoptee is also the subject of a pending proceeding under Chapter 7B of the General Statutes, then the district court having jurisdiction under Chapter 7B shall retain jurisdiction until the final order of adoption is entered. The district court may waive jurisdiction for good cause.

§ 48-2-207. Necessity of consent post-petition.

(a) If any individual who is described in G.S. 48-3-601 or entitled to notice under G.S. 48-2-401(c)(3) is served with notice of the filing of the petition in accordance with G.S. 48-2-402 and fails to respond within the time specified in the notice, the court, upon motion by the petitioner, shall enter an order under G.S. 48-3-603(a)(7) that the individual's consent is not required for the adoption.

(b) The court shall hold a hearing to take evidence and determine whether an individual's consent to an adoption is required if any of the following:

   (1) Any individual described in G.S. 48-2-401(c)(3) who has been served with notice of the filing of the petition in accordance with G.S. 48-2-402 notifies the court within the time specified in the notice that he believes his consent to the adoption is required.

   (2) Any individual who has not been served with the notice of the filing of the petition intervenes in the adoption proceeding alleging that his or her consent to the adoption is required.

(c) If the court determines that the consent of any individual is required, the adoption cannot proceed until such individual's consent is obtained or such individual's parental rights are terminated. If the individual whose consent is required did not have physical custody of the minor immediately prior to the placement of the minor with the prospective adoptive parents, a finding that such individual's consent is required does not entitle such individual to physical custody of the minor.

(d) If the court determines that the consent of any individual described in G.S. 48-2-401(c)(3) is not required, such individual shall not be entitled to receive notice of, or to participate in, further proceedings in the adoption.

§ 48-2-401. Notice by petitioner.

(a) No later than 30 days after a petition for adoption is filed pursuant to Part 3 of this Article, the petitioner shall initiate service of notice of the filing on the persons required to receive notice under subsections (b), (c), and (d) of this section.

(b) In all adoptions, the petitioner shall serve notice of the filing on each of the following:

   (1) Any individual whose consent to the adoption is required but has not been obtained, has been revoked in accord with this Chapter, or has become void as provided in this Chapter.

. . .

(3) Any individual who has executed a consent or relinquishment, but who the petitioner has actually been informed has filed an action to set it aside for fraud or duress.

(4) Any other person designated by the court who can provide information relevant to the proposed adoption.

(c) In the adoption of a minor, the petitioner shall also serve notice of the filing on each of the following:

(1) A minor whose consent is dispensed with under G.S. 48-3-603(b)(2).

(2) Any agency that placed the adoptee.

(3) A man who to the actual knowledge of the petitioner claims to be or is named as the biological or possible biological father of the minor, and any biological or possible biological fathers who are unknown or whose whereabouts are unknown, but notice need not be served upon a man who has executed a consent, a relinquishment, or a notarized statement denying paternity or disclaiming any interest in the minor, a man whose parental rights have been legally terminated or who has been judicially determined not to be the minor's parent, a man whose consent to the adoption is not required under G.S. 48-3-603(a)(9) due to his conviction of a specified crime, or, provided the petition is filed within three months of the birth of the minor, a man whose consent to the adoption has been determined not to be required under G.S. 48-2-206.

(4) Any individual who the petitioner has been actually informed has legal or physical custody of the minor or who has a right of visitation or communication with the minor under an existing court order issued by a court in this State or another state.

. . .

(f) A notice required under this section must state that the person served must file a response to the petition within 30 days after service or, if service is by publication, 40 days after first publication of the notice, in order to participate in and to receive further notice of the proceeding, including notice of the time and place of any hearing.

. . .

§ 48-2-402. Manner of service.

(a) Service of the notice required under G.S. 48-2-401 must be made as provided by G.S. 1A-1, Rule 4, for service of process.

(b) In the event that the identity of a biological or possible biological parent cannot be ascertained and notice is required, the parent or possible parent shall be served by publication pursuant to G.S. 1A-1, Rule 4 (j1). The time for response shall be the time provided in the rule. The words "In re Doe" may be substituted for the title of the action in the notice as long as the notice contains the correct docket number. The notice shall be directed to "the unknown father [or mother] of" the adoptee, and the adoptee shall be described by sex, date of birth, and place of birth. The notice shall contain any information known to the petitioner that would allow an unknown parent or possible parent to identify himself or herself as the individual being addressed, such as the approximate date and place of conception, any name by which the other biological parent was known to the unknown parent or possible parent, and any fact about the unknown parent or possible parent known to or believed by the other biological parent. The notice shall also state that any parental rights the unknown parent or possible parent may have will be terminated upon entry of the order of adoption.

(c) In an agency placement under Article 3 of this Chapter, the agency or other proper person shall file a petition to terminate the parental rights of an unknown parent or possible parent instead of serving notice under subsection (b) of this section, and the court shall stay any adoption proceeding already filed, except that nothing in this subsection shall require that the agency or other proper person file a petition to terminate the parental rights of any known or possible parent who has been served notice as provided under G.S. 1A-1, Rule 4(j)(1) of the Rules of Civil Procedure.

§ 48-2-404. Notice of proceedings by court to alleged father.

If, at any time in the proceeding, it appears to the court that there is an alleged father of a minor adoptee as described in G.S. 48-2-401(c)(3) who has not been given notice, the court shall require notice of the proceeding to be given to him pursuant to G.S. 48-2-402.

§ 48-2-601. Hearing on, or disposition of, adoption petition; transfer of adoption proceeding; timing.

(a) If it appears to the court that a petition to adopt a minor is not contested, the court may dispose of the petition without a formal hearing.

(a1) If an issue of fact, an equitable defense, or a request for equitable relief is raised before the clerk, the clerk shall transfer the proceeding to the district court under G.S. 1-301.2.

(b) No later than 90 days after a petition for adoption has been filed, the court shall set a date and time for hearing or disposing of the petition.

(c) The hearing or disposition must take place no later than six months after the petition is filed, but the court for cause may extend the time for the hearing or disposition.

§ 48-2-603. Hearing on, or disposition of, petition to adopt a minor.

(a) At the hearing on, or disposition of, a petition to adopt a minor, the court shall grant the petition upon finding by a preponderance of the evidence that the adoption will serve the best interest of the adoptee, and upon finding the following:

(1) At least 90 days have elapsed since the filing of the petition for adoption, unless the court for cause waives this requirement.

(2) The adoptee has been in the physical custody of the petitioner for at least 90 days, unless the court for cause waives this requirement.

(3) Notice of the filing of the petition has been served on any person entitled to receive notice under Part 4 of this Article.

(4)   Each necessary consent, relinquishment, waiver, or judicial order terminating parental rights, has been obtained and filed with the court and the time for revocation has expired.

(5)   Any assessment required by this Chapter has been filed with and considered by the court.

(6)   If applicable, the requirements of the Interstate Compact on the Placement of Children, Article 38 of Chapter 7B of the General Statutes, have been met.

(7)   Any motion to dismiss the proceeding has been denied.

(8)   Each petitioner is a suitable adoptive parent.

(9)   Any accounting and affidavit required under G.S. 48-2-602 has been reviewed by the court, and the court has denied, modified, or ordered reimbursement of any payment or disbursement that violates Article 10 or is unreasonable when compared with the expenses customarily incurred in connection with an adoption.

(10)   The petitioner has received information about the adoptee and the adoptee's biological family if required by G.S. 48-3-205.

(10a) Any certificate of service required by G.S. 48-3-307 has been filed.

(11)   There has been substantial compliance with the provisions of this Chapter.

(b)   If the Court finds a violation of this Chapter pursuant to Article 10 or of the Interstate Compact on the Placement of Children, Article 38 of Chapter 7B of the General Statutes, but determines that in every other respect there has been substantial compliance with the provisions of this Chapter, and the adoption will serve the best interest of the adoptee, the court shall:

(1)   Grant the petition to adopt; and

(2)   Impose the sanctions provided by this Chapter against any individual or entity who has committed a prohibited act or report the violations to the appropriate legal authorities.

(c)   The court on its own motion may continue the hearing for further evidence.

§ 48-3-601. Persons whose consent to adoption is required.

Unless consent is not required under G.S. 48-3-603, a petition to adopt a minor may be granted only if consent to the adoption has been executed by:

. . .

(2)   In a direct placement, by:

    a.   The mother of the minor;

    b.   Any man who may or may not be the biological father of the minor but who:

        1.   Is or was married to the mother of the minor if the minor was born during the marriage or within 280 days after the marriage is terminated or the parties have separated pursuant to a written separation agreement or an order of separation entered under Chapters 50 or 50B of the General Statutes or a similar order of separation entered by a court in another jurisdiction;

2. Attempted to marry the mother of the minor before the minor's birth, by a marriage solemnized in apparent compliance with law, although the attempted marriage is or could be declared invalid, and the minor is born during the attempted marriage, or within 280 days after the attempted marriage is terminated by annulment, declaration of invalidity, divorce, or, in the absence of a judicial proceeding, by the cessation of cohabitation;

3. Before the filing of the petition, has legitimated the minor under the law of any state;

4. Before the earlier of the filing of the petition or the date of a hearing under G.S. 48-2-206, has acknowledged his paternity of the minor and

   I. Is obligated to support the minor under written agreement or by court order;

   II. Has provided, in accordance with his financial means, reasonable and consistent payments for the support of the biological mother during or after the term of pregnancy, or the support of the minor, or both, which may include the payment of medical expenses, living expenses, or other tangible means of support, and has regularly visited or communicated, or attempted to visit or communicate with the biological mother during or after the term of pregnancy, or with the minor, or with both; or

   III. After the minor's birth but before the minor's placement for adoption or the mother's relinquishment, has married or attempted to marry the mother of the minor by a marriage solemnized in apparent compliance with law, although the attempted marriage is or could be declared invalid; or

5. Before the filing of the petition, has received the minor into his home and openly held out the minor as his biological child; or

6. Is the adoptive father of the minor . . .

. . .

(3) In an agency placement by:

. . .

b. Each individual described in subdivision (2) of this section who has not relinquished the minor pursuant to Part 7 of Article 3 of this Chapter.

§ 48-3-603. Persons whose consent is not required.

(a) Consent to an adoption of a minor is not required of a person or entity whose consent is not required under G.S. 48-3-601, or any of the following:

(1) An individual whose parental rights and duties have been terminated under Article 11 of Chapter 7B of the General Statutes or by a court of competent jurisdiction in another state.

(2) A man described in G.S. 48-3-601(2), other than an adoptive father, if (i) the man has been judicially determined not to be the father of the minor to be adopted, or (ii) another man has been judicially determined to be the father of the minor to be adopted.

(3) Repealed by Session Laws 1997-215, s. 11(a).

(4) An individual who has relinquished parental rights or guardianship powers, including the right to consent to adoption, to an agency pursuant to Part 7 of this Article.

(5) A man who is not married to the minor's birth mother and who, after the conception of the minor, has executed a notarized statement denying paternity or disclaiming any interest in the minor.

(6) A deceased parent or the personal representative of a deceased parent's estate.

(7) An individual listed in G.S. 48-3-601 who has not executed a consent or a relinquishment and who fails to respond to a notice of the adoption proceeding within 30 days after the service of the notice or, if service is by publication, 40 days from the first publication of the notice.

(8) An individual notified under G.S. 48-2-206 who does not respond in a timely manner or whose consent is not required as determined by the court.

(9) (**See editor's note**) An individual whose actions resulted in a conviction under G.S. 14-27.21, G.S. 14-27.22, G.S. 14-27.23, or G.S. 14-27.24 and the conception of the minor to be adopted.

. . .

Appendix B

Selected North Carolina General Statutes (G.S.) and Administrative Code Provisions Related to Birth Certificates

Birth Certificates

North Carolina General Statutes

§ 130A-101. Birth registration.

. . .

(e) If the mother was married at the time of either conception or birth, or between conception and birth, the name of the husband shall be entered on the certificate as the father of the child, except as provided in this subsection. The surname of the child shall be the same as that of the husband, except that upon agreement of the husband and mother, or upon agreement of the mother and father if paternity has been otherwise determined, any surname may be chosen. The name of the putative father shall be entered on the certificate as the father of the child if one of the following conditions exists:

   (1) Paternity has been otherwise determined by a court of competent jurisdiction, in which case the name of the father as determined by the court shall be entered.

   (2) The child's mother, mother's husband, and putative father complete an affidavit acknowledging paternity that contains all of the following:

      a. A sworn statement by the mother consenting to the assertion of paternity by the putative father and declaring that the putative father is the child's natural father.

      b. A sworn statement by the putative father declaring that he believes he is the natural father of the child.

      c. A sworn statement by the mother's husband consenting to the assertion of paternity by the putative father.

      d. Information explaining in plain language the effect of signing the affidavit, including a statement of parental rights and responsibilities and an acknowledgment of the receipt of this information.

      e.   The social security numbers of the putative father, mother, and mother's husband.

      f.   The results of a DNA test that has confirmed the paternity of the putative father.

(f)   If the mother was unmarried at all times from date of conception through date of birth, the name of the father shall not be entered on the certificate unless the child's mother and father complete an affidavit acknowledging paternity which contains the following:

    (1)   A sworn statement by the mother consenting to the assertion of paternity by the father and declaring that the father is the child's natural father and that the mother was unmarried at all times from the date of conception through the date of birth;

    (2)   A sworn statement by the father declaring that he believes he is the natural father of the child;

    (3)   Information explaining in plain language the effect of signing the affidavit, including a statement of parental rights and responsibilities and an acknowledgment of the receipt of this information; and

    (4)   The social security numbers of both parents.

The State Registrar, in consultation with the Child Support Enforcement Section of the Division of Social Services, shall develop and disseminate a form affidavit for use in compliance with this section, together with an information sheet that contains all the information required to be disclosed by subdivision (3) of this subsection.

Upon the execution of the affidavit, the declaring father shall be listed as the father on the birth certificate, subject to the declaring father's right to rescind under G.S. 110-132. The executed affidavit shall be filed with the registrar along with the birth certificate. In the event paternity is properly placed at issue, a certified copy of the affidavit shall be admissible in any action to establish paternity. The surname of the child shall be determined by the mother, except if the father's name is entered on the certificate, the mother and father shall agree upon the child's surname. If there is no agreement, the child's surname shall be the same as that of the mother.

The execution and filing of this affidavit with the registrar does not affect rights of inheritance unless the affidavit is also filed with the clerk of court in accordance with G.S. 29-19(b)(2).

. . .

§ 130A-118. Amendment of birth and death certificates.

(a)   After acceptance for registration by the State Registrar, no record made in accordance with this Article shall be altered or changed, except by a request for amendment. The State Registrar may adopt rules governing the form of these requests and the type and amount of proof required.

(b)   A new certificate of birth shall be made by the State Registrar when:

    (1)   Proof is submitted to the State Registrar that the previously unwed parents of a person have intermarried subsequent to the birth of the person;

(2) Notification is received by the State Registrar from the clerk of a court of competent jurisdiction of a judgment, order or decree disclosing different or additional information relating to the parentage of a person;

(3) Satisfactory proof is submitted to the State Registrar that there has been entered in a court of competent jurisdiction a judgment, order or decree disclosing different or additional information relating to the parentage of a person; or

(4) A written request from an individual is received by the State Registrar to change the sex on that individual's birth record because of sex reassignment surgery, if the request is accompanied by a notarized statement from the physician who performed the sex reassignment surgery or from a physician licensed to practice medicine who has examined the individual and can certify that the person has undergone sex reassignment surgery.

(c) A new birth certificate issued under subsection (b) may reflect a change in surname when:

(1) A child is legitimated by subsequent marriage and the parents agree and request that the child's surname be changed; or

(2) A child is legitimated under G.S. 49-10 and the parents agree and request that the child's surname be changed, or the court orders a change in surname after determination that the change is in the best interests of the child.

. . .

§ 130A-119. Clerk of Court to furnish State Registrar with facts as to paternity of children born out of wedlock when judicially determined.

Upon the entry of a judgment determining the paternity of a child born out of wedlock, the clerk of court of the county in which the judgment is entered shall notify the State Registrar in writing of the name of the person against whom the judgment has been entered, together with the other facts disclosed by the record as may assist in identifying the record of the birth of the child as it appears in the office of the State Registrar. If the judgment is modified or vacated, that fact shall be reported by the clerk to the State Registrar in the same manner. Upon receipt of the notification, the State Registrar shall record the information upon the birth certificate of the child.

§ 49-13. New birth certificate on legitimation.

A certified copy of the order of legitimation when issued under the provisions of G.S. 49-10 shall be sent by the clerk of the superior court under his official seal to the State Registrar of Vital Statistics who shall then make the new birth certificate bearing the full name of the father, and change the surname of the child so that it will be the same as the surname of the father.

When a child is legitimated under the provisions of G.S. 49-12, the State Registrar of Vital Statistics shall make a new birth certificate bearing the full name of the father upon presentation of a certified copy of the certificate of marriage of the father and mother and change the surname of the child so that it will be the same as the surname of the father.

§ 48-9-107. New birth certificates [upon adoption].

(a) Upon receipt of a report of the adoption of a minor from the Division, or the documents required by G.S. 48-9-102(g) from the clerk of superior court in the adoption of an adult, or a report of an adoption from another state, the State Registrar shall prepare a new birth certificate for the adoptee that shall contain the adoptee's full adoptive name, sex, state of birth, and date of birth; the full name of the adoptive father, if applicable; the full maiden name of the adoptive mother, if applicable; and any other pertinent information consistent with this section as may be determined by the State Registrar. The new certificate shall contain no reference to the adoption of the adoptee and shall not refer to the adoptive parents in any way other than as the adoptee's parents.

(b) In an adoption by a stepparent, the State Registrar shall prepare a new birth certificate pursuant to subsection (a) of this section except:

   (1) The adoptive parent and the parent whose relation with the adoptee remains unchanged shall be listed as the adoptee's mother and father on the new birth certificate; and

   (2) The city and county of birth of the adoptee shall be the same on the new birth certificate as on the original certificate.

   The names of the adoptee's parents shall not be changed as provided in subdivision (1) of this subsection if the petitioner, the petitioner's spouse, the adoptee if age 12 or older, and any living parent whose parental rights are terminated by the adoption jointly file a request that the parents' names not be changed with the court prior to the entry of the adoption decree. The Division shall send a copy of this request with its report to the State Registrar or other appropriate official in the adoption of a minor stepchild, and the clerk of superior court shall send a copy with the documents required by G.S. 48-9-102(g) in the adoption of an adult stepchild.

   . . .

North Carolina Administrative Code (N.C.A.C.)

10A N.C.A.C. 41H, § .0301 GENERAL REQUIREMENTS

In addition to the requirements specified in 10A NCAC 41H .0104, no birth certificate shall be considered complete, correct, and acceptable for registration:

(1) that does not have the certifier's name typed or printed legibly under his signature,

(2) that does not supply all items of information called for thereon or satisfactorily account for their omission, and

(3) that contains any data relative to the putative father of a child born out of wedlock unless it is accompanied by the written consent of both parents under oath or a certified copy of a decree determining paternity.

10A N.C.A.C. 41H, § .0805 JUDICIAL DETERMINATION OF PATERNITY

For cases in which a court determines the paternity of an illegitimate child, the father's name shall be added and a copy of the amended certificate shall be forwarded to the register of deeds in the county where the birth occurred. In cases where the mother is married and the court determines the husband is not the father, the husband's name will be lined out, and if also determined by the court, the natural father's name will be added.

10A N.C.A.C. 41H, § .0909 AMENDMENTS TO BIRTH CERTIFICATES REQUIRING COURT ORDER

Unless otherwise provided by law or regulation, the following amendments may be made on a birth certificate only upon receipt of an order from a court of competent jurisdiction:
(1) change in the surname of the registrant,
(2) change in parentage.

10A N.C.A.C. 41H, § .1001 NEW CERTIFICATES OF BIRTHS FOLLOWING ADOPTIONS

(a) When a new certificate of birth is prepared by the State Registrar as prescribed in G.S. 48-29, all copies of the original certificate and all other information concerning the original certificate in the possession of any register of deeds shall be forwarded to the State Registrar, who shall file them in accordance with the provisions of G.S. 48-29. In the event such data have been computerized or otherwise automated, a paper copy of the identifying data shall be prepared and sent to the State Registrar. The automated data shall then be removed from the index or otherwise rendered unusable in a manner approved by the State Registrar.

(b) The record pertaining to an adoption shall not be sealed until after the adopting parents are furnished a full certified copy or until they or their legal representatives are notified of the information entered on the new certificate, so that errors can be identified or corrected prior to the sealing of the file. After the file is sealed, corrections and amendments shall be made in accordance with same rules which pertain to birth records of non-adopted persons, except that a copy of the adoption order will be required to correct the name.

10A N.C.A.C. 41H, § .1002 NEW CERTIFICATES OF BIRTH FOLLOWING LEGITIMATIONS

When a new certificate of birth is prepared by the State Registrar as prescribed in G.S. 49-13 and G.S. 130A-118, the register of deeds in the county where birth occurred shall send the original birth certificate to the State Registrar for filing in the sealed file and shall replace it with a copy of the new certificate prepared by the State Registrar.

10A N.C.A.C. 41H, § .1101 GENERAL

For all legitimations, a new birth certificate shall be prepared. The new birth certificate may reflect a new surname when the conditions of G.S. 130A-118(c) have been met. The new birth certificate shall reflect the mother's or father's surname unless otherwise directed by court order. A copy shall be forwarded to the register of deeds of the county of occurrence who shall return the original copy to the Vital Records Section. All materials pertaining to the legitimation shall be placed in a sealed file.

10A N.C.A.C. 41H, § .1102 LEGITIMATION BY SUBSEQUENT MARRIAGE

(a) Paragraphs (b) through (h) of this Rule establish the requirements for legitimations by subsequent marriage.

(b) If no name of the father is shown on the original certificate, affidavits of the mother and father on a form provided by the Vital Records Section, necessary information about the father and child, and proof of marriage are required.

(c) If the father's name appears on the original birth certificate and it is the man whom the mother married, only proof of marriage is required.

(d) If the father died before signing an affidavit, court determination of paternity or proof shall be required in lieu of the father's affidavit. Such proof may be hospital records, medical records, tax records, service records, or affidavits from close relatives of the father indicating that the man was the reputed father of the child.

(e) If the birth certificate shows a father other than the one the mother married, a court determination of paternity will be required.

(f) If the mother is legally married at the time of conception or birth, but claims that another man is the father and she later marries the natural father, a court determination of paternity shall be required in addition to proof of marriage.

(g) If the parents of an illegitimate child marry after the child reaches the age of six, additional proof of parentage shall be required such as school or medical records showing the child has used the surname of the father, hospital records or bills paid by the reputed father, or affidavits from relatives of the reputed father.

(h) For legitimating a child under G.S. 49-12 when another man's name appears on the birth record, proof must be submitted showing that the man named on the certificate is not the father of the child or a court order shall be required to remove the name of one man in order to add the name of another.

State of North Carolina, Administrative Office of the Courts, Records of the Clerks of Superior Court, Rules of Recordkeeping

Rule 12.19 – ORDERS DETERMINING PARENTAGE IN JUVENILE PROCEEDINGS

A juvenile proceeding may involve an adjudication affecting a child's parentage. When a judicial determination of parentage is entered in a juvenile proceeding, the court may issue a stand-alone Order that addresses the juvenile's parentage. The original stand-alone order should be placed in the new CVD file and a copy retained in the juvenile file. (See Rule 3.1B12(b).)

Rule 3.1B12

b. Orders Determining Parentage in Juvenile Proceedings

When a judicial determination of parentage is entered in a juvenile proceeding, the court may issue a stand-alone Order that addresses the juvenile's parentage for the sole purpose of creating a public record. The clerk shall create a new CVD file; no filing fees are required. The clerk shall send a certified copy of that Order to the State Registrar. This file should be microscanned. (See also Rule 12.19.)

Appendix C

Selected North Carolina General Statutes (G.S.) Related to Parentage

North Carolina General Statutes

§ 49-10. Legitimation.

The putative father of any child born out of wedlock, whether such father resides in North Carolina or not, may apply by a verified written petition, filed in a special proceeding in the superior court of the county in which the putative father resides or in the superior court of the county in which the child resides, praying that such child be declared legitimate. The mother, if living, and the child shall be necessary parties to the proceeding, and the full names of the father, mother and the child shall be set out in the petition. A certified copy of a certificate of birth of the child shall be attached to the petition. If it appears to the court that the petitioner is the father of the child, the court may thereupon declare and pronounce the child legitimated; and the full names of the father, mother and the child shall be set out in the court order decreeing legitimation of the child. The clerk of the court shall record the order in the record of orders and decrees and it shall be cross-indexed under the name of the father as plaintiff or petitioner on the plaintiff's side of the cross-index, and under the name of the mother, and the child as defendants or respondents on the defendants' side of the cross-index.

§ 49-11. Effects of legitimation.

The effect of legitimation under G.S. 49-10 shall be to impose upon the father and mother all of the lawful parental privileges and rights, as well as all of the obligations which parents owe to their lawful issue, and to the same extent as if said child had been born in wedlock, and to entitle such child by succession, inheritance or distribution, to take real and personal property by, through, and from his or her father and mother as if such child had been born in lawful wedlock. In case of death and intestacy, the real and personal estate of such child shall descend and be distributed according to the Intestate Succession Act as if he had been born in lawful wedlock.

§ 49-12. Legitimation by subsequent marriage.

When the mother of any child born out of wedlock and the reputed father of such child shall intermarry or shall have intermarried at any time after the birth of such child, the child shall, in all respects after such intermarriage be deemed and held to be legitimate and the child shall be entitled, by succession, inheritance or distribution, to real and personal property by, through, and from his father and mother as if such child had been born in lawful wedlock. In case of death and intestacy, the real and personal estate of such child shall descend and be distributed according to the Intestate Succession Act as if he had been born in lawful wedlock.

§ 49-12.1. Legitimation when mother married.

(a) The putative father of a child born to a mother who is married to another man may file a special proceeding to legitimate the child. The procedures shall be the same as those specified by G.S. 49-10, except that the spouse of the mother of the child shall be a necessary party to the proceeding and shall be properly served. A guardian ad litem shall be appointed to represent the child if the child is a minor.

(b) The presumption of legitimacy can be overcome by clear and convincing evidence.

(c) The parties may enter a consent order with the approval of the clerk of superior court. The order entered by the clerk shall find the facts and declare the proper person the father of the child and may change the surname of the child.

(d) The effect of legitimation under this section shall be the same as provided by G.S. 49-11.

(e) A certified copy of the order of legitimation under this section shall be sent by the clerk of superior court under his official seal to the State Registrar of Vital Statistics who shall make a new birth certificate bearing the full name of the father of the child and, if ordered by the clerk, changing the surname of the child.

§ 49A-1. Status of child born as a result of artificial insemination.

Any child or children born as the result of heterologous artificial insemination shall be considered at law in all respects the same as a naturally conceived legitimate child of the husband and wife requesting and consenting in writing to the use of such technique.

§ 50-11.1. Children born of voidable marriage legitimate.

A child born of voidable marriage or a bigamous marriage is legitimate notwithstanding the annulment of the marriage.

Paternity

§ 49-14. Civil action to establish paternity; motion to set aside paternity.

(a) The paternity of a child born out of wedlock may be established by civil action at any time prior to such child's eighteenth birthday. A copy of a certificate of birth of the child shall be attached to the complaint. The establishment of paternity shall not have the effect of legitimation. The social security numbers, if known, of the minor child's parents shall be placed in the record of the proceeding.

(b) Proof of paternity pursuant to this section shall be by clear, cogent, and convincing evidence.

(c) No such action shall be commenced nor judgment entered after the death of the putative father, unless the action is commenced either:

(1) Prior to the death of the putative father;

(2) Within one year after the date of death of the putative father, if a proceeding for administration of the estate of the putative father has not been commenced within one year of his death; or

(3) Within the period specified in G.S. 28A-19-3(a) for presentation of claims against an estate, if a proceeding for administration of the estate of the putative father has been commenced within one year of his death.

Any judgment under this subsection establishing a decedent to be the father of a child shall be entered nunc pro tunc to the day preceding the date of death of the father.

(d) If the action to establish paternity is brought more than three years after birth of a child or is brought after the death of the putative father, paternity shall not be established in a contested case without evidence from a blood or genetic marker test.

(e) Either party to an action to establish paternity may request that the case be tried at the first session of the court after the case is docketed, but the presiding judge, in his discretion, may first try any pending case in which the rights of the parties or the public demand it.

(f) When a determination of paternity is pending in a IV-D case, the court shall enter a temporary order for child support upon motion and showing of clear, cogent, and convincing evidence of paternity. For purposes of this subsection, the results of blood or genetic tests shall constitute clear, cogent, and convincing evidence of paternity if the tests show that the probability of the alleged parent's parentage is ninety-seven percent (97%) or higher. If paternity is not thereafter established, then the putative father shall be reimbursed the full amount of temporary support paid under the order.

(g) Invoices for services rendered for pregnancy, childbirth, and blood or genetic testing are admissible as evidence without requiring third party foundation testimony and shall constitute prima facie evidence of the amounts incurred for the services or for testing on behalf of the child.

(h) Notwithstanding the time limitations of G.S. 1A-1, Rule 60 of the North Carolina Rules of Civil Procedure, or any other provision of law, an order of paternity may be set aside by a trial court if each of the following applies:

(1) The paternity order was entered as the result of fraud, duress, mutual mistake, or excusable neglect.

(2) Genetic tests establish the putative father is not the biological father of the child.

The burden of proof in any motion to set aside an order of paternity shall be on the moving party. Upon proper motion alleging fraud, duress, mutual mistake, or excusable neglect, the court shall order the child's mother, the child whose parentage is at issue, and the putative father to submit to genetic paternity testing pursuant to G.S. 8-50.1(b1). If the court determines, as a result of genetic testing, the putative father is not the biological father of the child and the order of paternity was entered as a result of fraud, duress, mutual mistake, or excusable neglect, the court may set aside the order of paternity. Nothing in this subsection shall be construed to affect the presumption of legitimacy where a child is born to a mother and the putative father during the course of a marriage.

§ 49-16. Parties to proceeding.

Proceedings under this Article may be brought by:

(1) The mother, the father, the child, or the personal representative of the mother or the child.

(2) When the child, or the mother in case of medical expenses, is likely to become a public charge, the director of social services or such person as by law performs the duties of such official,

    a. In the county where the mother resides or is found,

    b. In the county where the putative father resides or is found, or

    c. In the county where the child resides or is found.

Criminal Nonsupport

§ 49-2. Nonsupport of child born out of wedlock by parents made misdemeanor.

Any parent who willfully neglects or who refuses to provide adequate support and maintain his or her child born out of wedlock shall be guilty of a Class 2 misdemeanor. A child within the meaning of this Article shall be any person less than 18 years of age and any person whom either parent might be required under the laws of North Carolina to support and maintain if the child were the legitimate child of the parent.

§ 49-5. Prosecution; death of mother no bar; determination of fatherhood.

Proceedings under this Article may be brought by the mother or her personal representative or, if the child is likely to become a public charge, the director of social services or such person as by law performs the duties of such official in said county where the mother resides or the child is found. Proceedings under this Article may be brought in the county where the mother resides or is found, or in the county where the putative father resides or is found, or in the county where the child is found. The fact that the child was born outside of the State of North Carolina shall not be a bar to proceedings against the putative father in any county where he resides or is found, or in the county where the mother resides or the child is found. The death of the mother shall in no wise affect any proceedings under this Article. Preliminary proceedings under this Article to determine the paternity of the child may be instituted prior to the birth of the child but when the judge or court trying the issue of paternity deems it proper, he may continue the case until the woman is delivered of the child. When a continuance is granted, the courts shall recognize the person accused of being the father of the child with surety for his appearance, either at the next session of the court or at a time to be fixed by the judge or court granting a continuance, which shall be after the delivery of the child.

§ 49-7. Issues and orders.

The court before which the matter may be brought shall determine whether or not the defendant is a parent of the child on whose behalf the proceeding is instituted. After this matter has been determined in the affirmative, the court shall proceed to determine the issue as to whether or not the defendant has neglected or refused to provide adequate support and maintain the child who is the subject of the proceeding. After this matter has been determined in the affirmative, the court shall fix by order, subject to modification or increase from time to time, a specific sum of money necessary for the support and maintenance of the child, subject to the limitations of G.S. 50-13.10. . . .

The court before whom the matter may be brought, on motion of the State or the defendant, shall order that the alleged-parent defendant, the known natural parent, and the child submit to any blood tests and comparisons which have been developed and adapted for purposes of establishing or disproving parentage and which are reasonably accessible to the alleged-parent defendant, the known natural parent, and the child. The results of those blood tests and comparisons, including the statistical likelihood of the alleged parent's parentage, if available, shall be admitted in evidence when offered by a duly qualified, licensed practicing physician, duly qualified immunologist, duly qualified geneticist or other duly qualified person. The evidentiary effect of those blood tests and comparisons and the manner in which the expenses therefor are to be taxed as costs shall be as prescribed in G.S. 8-50.1. In addition, if a jury tries the issue of parentage, they shall be instructed as set out in G.S. 8-50.1. From a finding on the issue of parentage against the alleged-parent defendant, the alleged-parent defendant has the same right of appeal as though he or she had been found guilty of the crime of willful failure to support a child born out of wedlock.

§ 14-322. Abandonment and failure to support spouse and children.

. . .

(d) Any parent who shall willfully neglect or refuse to provide adequate support for that parent's child, whether natural or adopted, and whether or not the parent abandons the child, shall be guilty of a misdemeanor and upon conviction shall be punished according to subsection (f). Willful neglect or refusal to provide adequate support of a child shall constitute a continuing offense and shall not be barred by any statute of limitations until the youngest living child of the parent shall reach the age of 18 years.

. . .

(f) A first offense under this section is a Class 2 misdemeanor. A second or subsequent offense is a Class 1 misdemeanor.

Declaratory Judgment Actions

§ 1-253. Courts of record permitted to enter declaratory judgments of rights, status and other legal relations.

Courts of record within their respective jurisdictions shall have power to declare rights, status, and other legal relations, whether or not further relief is or could be claimed. No action or proceeding shall be open to objection on the ground that a declaratory judgment or decree is prayed for. The declaration may be either affirmative or negative in form and effect; and such declarations shall have the force and effect of a final judgment or decree.

§ 1-254. Courts given power of construction of all instruments.

Any person interested under a deed, will, written contract or other writings constituting a contract, or whose rights, status or other legal relations are affected by a statute, municipal ordinance, contract or franchise, may have determined any question of construction or validity arising under the instrument, statute, ordinance, contract, or franchise, and obtain a declaration of rights, status, or other legal relations thereunder. A contract may be construed either before or after there has been a breach thereof.

§ 1-255. Who may apply for a declaration.

Any person interested as or through an executor, administrator, trustee, guardian or other fiduciary, creditor, devisee, heir, next of kin, or cestui que trust, in the administration of a trust, or of the estate of a decedent, a minor, an incompetent person, or an insolvent person, may have a declaration of rights or legal relations in respect thereto:

(1) To ascertain any class of creditors, devisees, heirs, next of kin or others; or

(2) To direct the executors, administrators, or trustees to do or abstain from doing any particular act in their fiduciary capacity; or

(3) To determine any question arising in the administration of the estate or trust, including questions of construction of wills and other writings.

(4) To determine the apportionment of the federal estate tax, interest and penalties under the provisions of Article 27 of Chapter 28A.

§ 1-260. Parties.

When declaratory relief is sought, all persons shall be made parties who have or claim any interest which would be affected by the declaration, and no declaration shall prejudice the rights of persons not parties to the proceedings. In any proceeding which involves the validity of a municipal ordinance or franchise, such municipality shall be made a party, and shall be entitled to be heard, and if the statute, ordinance or franchise is alleged to be unconstitutional, the Attorney General of the State shall also be served with a copy of the proceeding and be entitled to be heard.

Appendix D

Genetic Marker Testing, G.S. 8-50.1

§ 8-50.1. Competency of blood tests; jury charge; taxing of expenses as costs.

    (a)   In the trial of any criminal action or proceeding in any court in which the question of parentage arises, regardless of any presumptions with respect to parentage, the court before whom the matter may be brought, upon motion of the State or the defendant, shall order that the alleged-parent defendant, the known natural parent, and the child submit to any blood tests and comparisons which have been developed and adapted for purposes of establishing or disproving parentage and which are reasonably accessible to the alleged-parent defendant, the known natural parent, and the child. The results of those blood tests and comparisons, including the statistical likelihood of the alleged parent's parentage, if available, shall be admitted in evidence when offered by a duly qualified, licensed practicing physician, duly qualified immunologist, duly qualified geneticist, or other duly qualified person. Upon receipt of a motion and the entry of an order under the provisions of this subsection, the court shall proceed as follows:

        (1)   Where the issue of parentage is to be decided by a jury, where the results of those blood tests and comparisons are not shown to be inconsistent with the results of any other blood tests and comparisons, and where the results of those blood tests and comparisons indicate that the alleged-parent defendant cannot be the natural parent of the child, the jury shall be instructed that if they believe that the witness presenting the results testified truthfully as to those results, and if they believe that the tests and comparisons were conducted properly, then it will be their duty to decide that the alleged-parent is not the natural parent; whereupon, the court shall enter the special verdict of not guilty; and

        (2)   By requiring the State or defendant, as the case may be, requesting the blood tests and comparisons pursuant to this subsection to initially be responsible for any of the expenses thereof and upon the entry of a special verdict incorporating a finding of parentage or nonparentage, by taxing the expenses for blood tests and comparisons, in addition to any fees for expert witnesses allowed per G.S. 7A-314 whose testimonies supported the admissibility thereof, as costs in accordance with G.S. 7A-304; G.S. Chapter 6, Article 7; or G.S. 7A-315, as applicable.

    (b)   Repealed by Session Laws 1993, c. 333, s. 2.

(b1) In the trial of any civil action in which the question of parentage arises, the court shall, on motion of a party, order the mother, the child, and the alleged father-defendant to submit to one or more blood or genetic marker tests, to be performed by a duly certified physician or other expert. The court shall require the person requesting the blood or genetic marker tests to pay the costs of the tests. The court may, in its discretion, tax as part of costs the expenses for blood or genetic marker tests and comparisons. Verified documentary evidence of the chain of custody of the blood specimens obtained pursuant to this subsection shall be competent evidence to establish the chain of custody. Any party objecting to or contesting the procedures or results of the blood or genetic marker tests shall file with the court written objections setting forth the basis for the objections and shall serve copies thereof upon all other parties not less than 10 days prior to any hearing at which the results may be introduced into evidence. The person contesting the results of the blood or genetic marker tests has the right to subpoena the testing expert pursuant to the Rules of Civil Procedure. If no objections are filed within the time and manner prescribed, the test results are admissible as evidence of paternity without the need for foundation testimony or other proof of authenticity or accuracy. The results of the blood or genetic marker tests shall have the following effect:

(1) If the court finds that the conclusion of all the experts, as disclosed by the evidence based upon the test, is that the probability of the alleged parent's parentage is less than eighty-five percent (85%), the alleged parent is presumed not to be the parent and the evidence shall be admitted. This presumption may be rebutted only by clear, cogent, and convincing evidence;

(2) If the experts disagree in their findings or conclusions, the question of paternity shall be submitted upon all the evidence;

(3) If the tests show that the alleged parent is not excluded and that the probability of the alleged parent's parentage is between eighty-five percent (85%) and ninety-seven percent (97%), this evidence shall be admitted by the court and shall be weighed with other competent evidence;

(4) If the experts conclude that the genetic tests show that the alleged parent is not excluded and that the probability of the alleged parent's parentage is ninety-seven percent (97%) or higher, the alleged parent is presumed to be the parent and this evidence shall be admitted. This presumption may be rebutted only by clear, cogent, and convincing evidence.

Appendix E

Selected North Carolina General Statutes (G.S.) Related to Child Support

§ 110-132. Affidavit of parentage and agreement to motion to set aside affidavit of parentage.

(a) In lieu of or in conclusion of any legal proceeding instituted to establish paternity, the written affidavits of parentage executed by the putative father and the mother of the dependent child shall constitute an admission of paternity and shall have the same legal effect as a judgment of paternity for the purpose of establishing a child support obligation, subject to the right of either signatory to rescind within the earlier of:

(1) 60 days of the date the document is executed, or

(2) The date of entry of an order establishing paternity or an order for the payment of child support.

In order to rescind, a challenger must request the district court to order the rescission and to include in the order specific findings of fact that the request for rescission was filed with the clerk of court within 60 days of the signing of the document. The court must also find that all parties, including the child support enforcement agency, if appropriate, have been served in accordance with Rule 4 of the North Carolina Rules of Civil Procedure. In the event the court orders rescission and the putative father is thereafter found not to be the father of the child, then the clerk of court shall send a copy of the order of rescission to the State Registrar of Vital Statistics. Upon receipt of an order of rescission, the State Registrar shall remove the putative father's name from the birth certificate. In the event that the putative father defaults or fails to present or prosecute the issue of paternity, the trial court shall find the putative father to be the biological father as a matter of law.

(a1) Paternity established under subsection (a) of this section may be set aside in accordance with subsection (a2) of this section or in accordance with G.S. 50-13.13.

(a2) Notwithstanding the time limitations of G.S. 1A-1, Rule 60 of the North Carolina Rules of Civil Procedure, or any other provision of law, an affidavit of parentage may be set aside by a trial court after 60 days have elapsed if each of the following applies:

(1) The affidavit of parentage was entered as the result of fraud, duress, mutual mistake, or excusable neglect.

(2) Genetic tests establish that the putative father is not the biological father of the child.

The burden of proof in any motion to set aside an affidavit of parentage after 60 days allowed for rescission shall be on the moving party. Upon proper motion alleging fraud, duress, mutual mistake, or excusable neglect, the court shall order the child's mother, the child whose parentage is at issue, and the putative father to submit to genetic paternity testing pursuant to G.S. 8-50.1(b1). If the court determines, as a result of genetic testing, the putative father is not the biological father of the child and the affidavit of parentage was entered as a result of fraud, duress, mutual mistake, or excusable neglect, the court may set aside the affidavit of parentage. Nothing in this subsection shall be construed to affect the presumption of legitimacy where a child is born to a mother and the putative father during the course of a marriage.

(a3) A written agreement to support the child by periodic payments, which may include provision for reimbursement for medical expenses incident to the pregnancy and the birth of the child, accrued maintenance and reasonable expense of prosecution of the paternity action, when acknowledged as provided herein, filed with, and approved by a judge of the district court at any time, shall have the same force and effect as an order of support entered by that court, and shall be enforceable and subject to modification in the same manner as is provided by law for orders of the court in such cases. The written affidavit shall contain the social security number of the person executing the affidavit. Voluntary agreements to support shall contain the social security number of each of the parties to the agreement. The written affidavits and agreements to support shall be sworn to before a certifying officer or notary public or the equivalent or corresponding person of the state, territory, or foreign country where the affirmation, acknowledgment, or agreement is made, and shall be binding on the person executing the same whether the person is an adult or a minor. The child support enforcement agency shall ensure that the mother and putative father are given oral and written notice of the legal consequences and responsibilities arising from the signing of an affidavit of parentage and of any alternatives to the execution of an affidavit of parentage. The mother shall not be excused from making the affidavit on the grounds that it may tend to disgrace or incriminate her; nor shall she thereafter be prosecuted for any criminal act involved in the conception of the child as to whose paternity she attests.

(b) At any time after the filing with the district court of an affidavit of parentage, upon the application of any interested party, the court or any judge thereof shall cause a summons signed by him or by the clerk or assistant clerk of superior court, to be issued, requiring the putative father to appear in court at a time and place named therein, to show cause, if any he has, why the court should not enter an order for the support of the child by periodic payments, which order may include provision for reimbursement for medical expenses incident to the pregnancy and the birth of the child, accrued maintenance and reasonable expense of the action under this subsection on the affidavit of parentage previously filed with said court. The court may order the responsible parents in a IV-D establishment case to perform a job search, if the responsible parent is not incapacitated. This includes IV-D cases in which the responsible parent is a noncustodial mother or a noncustodial father whose affidavit of parentage has been filed with the court or when paternity is not at issue for the child. The court may further order the responsible parent to participate in the work activities, as defined in 42 U.S.C. § 607, as the court deems appropriate.

The amount of child support payments so ordered shall be determined as provided in G.S. 50-13.4(c). The prior judgment as to paternity shall be res judicata as to that issue and shall not be reconsidered by the court.

§ 110-132.1. Paternity determination by another state entitled to full faith and credit.

A paternity determination made by another state:

(1) In accordance with the laws of that state, and

(2) By any means that is recognized in that state as establishing paternity
    shall be entitled to full faith and credit in this State.

§ 110-132.2. Expedited procedures to establish paternity in IV-D cases.

(a) In a IV-D court action, a local child support enforcement office may, without obtaining a court order, subpoena a minor child, the minor child's mother, and the putative father of the minor child (including the mother's husband, if different from the putative father) to appear for the purpose of undergoing blood or genetic testing to establish paternity. A subpoena issued pursuant to this section must be served in accordance with Rule 4 of the North Carolina Rules of Civil Procedure. Refusal to comply with a subpoena may be dealt with as for contempt of court, and as otherwise provided under law. A party may contest the results of the genetic or blood test. If the results are contested, the agency shall, upon request and advance payment by the contestant, obtain additional testing.

(b) A person subpoenaed to submit to testing pursuant to subsection (a) of this section may contest the subpoena. To contest the subpoena, a person must, within 15 days of receipt of the subpoena, request a hearing in the county where the local child support enforcement office that issued the subpoena is located. The hearing shall be before the district court and notice of the hearing must be served by the petitioner on all parties to the proceeding. Service shall be in accordance with Rule 4 of the North Carolina Rules of Civil Procedure. The hearing shall be held and a determination made within 30 days of the petitioner's request for hearing as to whether the petitioner must comply with the subpoena to undergo testing. If the trial court determines that the petitioner must comply with the subpoena, the determination shall not prejudice any defenses the petitioner may present at any future paternity litigation.

§ 110-133. Agreements of support.

In lieu of or in conclusion of any legal proceeding instituted to obtain support from a responsible parent for a dependent child born of the marriage, a written agreement to support the child by periodic payments executed by the responsible parent when acknowledged before a certifying officer or notary public or the equivalent or corresponding person of the state, territory, or foreign country where the acknowledgment is made and filed with and approved by a judge of the district court in the county where the custodial parent of the child resides or is found, or in the county where the noncustodial parent resides or is found, or in the county where the child resides or is found shall have the same force and effect, retroactively and prospectively, in accordance with the terms of the agreement, as an order of support entered by the court, and shall be enforceable and subject to modification in the same manner as is provided by law for orders of the court in such cases. A responsible parent executing a written agreement under this section shall provide on the agreement the responsible parent's social security number.

§ 110-134. Filing of affidavits, agreements, and orders; fees.

All affidavits, agreements, and resulting orders entered into under the provisions of G.S. 110-132 and G.S. 110-133 shall be filed by the clerk of superior court in the county in which they are entered. The filing fee for the institution of an action through the entry of an order under either of these provisions shall be in an amount equal to that provided in G.S. 7A-308(a)(18).

§ 52C-4-401. Establishment of support order.

. . .

(b) The tribunal may issue a temporary child support order if the tribunal determines that such an order is appropriate and the individual ordered to pay is any of the following:
  (1) A presumed father of the child.
  (2) Petitioning to have his paternity adjudicated.
  (3) Identified as the father of the child through genetic testing.
  (4) An alleged father who has declined to submit to genetic testing.
  (5) Shown by clear and convincing evidence to be the father of the child.
  (6) An acknowledged father as provided by Chapter 110 of the General Statutes.
  (7) The mother of the child.
  (8) An individual who has been ordered to pay child support in a previous proceeding and the order has not been reversed or vacated.

. . .

§ 52C-4-402. Proceeding to determine parentage.

A tribunal of this State authorized to determine parentage of a child may serve as a responding tribunal in a proceeding to determine parentage of a child brought under this Chapter or a law or procedure substantially similar to this Chapter.

Case Index

North Carolina Cases

A

A Child's Hope, LLC v. Doe, 178 N.C. App. 96 (2006)   *134, 140, 141*

Adams v. Tessener, 354 N.C. 57 (2001)   *19, 20, 21*

B

Batcheldor v. Boyd, 119 N.C. App. 204 (1995)   *8, 49, 51, 66*

Blake v. Norman, 37 N.C. App. 617 (1978)   *60*

Bluebird Corp. v. Aubin, 188 N.C. App. 671 (2008)   *63*

Bowman v. Howard, 182 N.C. 662 (1921)   *49*

Brondum v. Cox, 292 N.C. 192 (1977)   *83*

Burton v. City of Durham, 118 N.C. App. 676 (1995)   *61, 63, 70*

Byerly v. Tolbert, 250 N.C. 27 (1959)   *7, 47*

C

Carter v. Carter, 232 N.C. 614 (1950)   *48, 49*

Chambers v. Chambers, 43 N.C. App. 361 (1979)   *49*

Cole v. Cole, 74 N.C. App. 247 (1985)   *47, 88*

Columbus County *ex rel.* Brooks v. Davis, 163 N.C. App. 64 (2004)   *86*

County of Rutherford *ex rel.* Child Support Enforcement Agency v. Whitener, 100 N.C. App. 70 (1990)   *70*

D

David N. v. Jason N., 359 N.C. 303 (2005)   *20*

Devane *ex rel.* Robinson v. Chancellor, 120 N.C. App. 636 (1995)   *64, 65, 68, 70*

Dowd v. Johnson, ___ N.C. App. ___, 760 S.E.2d 79 (2014)   *33*

Duncan v. Duncan, 366 N.C. 544 (2013)   *62*

E

Eakett v. Eakett, 157 N.C. App. 550 (2003)   *21, 115*

Estroff v. Chatterjee, 190 N.C. App. 61 (2008)   *6*

Eubanks v. Eubanks, 273 N.C. 189 (1968)   *7, 30, 47, 70*

G

Greenlee v. Quinn, 255 N.C. 601 (1961)   *48*

Guilford County *ex rel.* Gardner v. Davis, 123 N.C. App. 527 (1996)   *53, 65*

Gunter v. Gunter, 228 N.C. App. 138 (2013)   *43*

H

Helms v. Landry, 363 N.C. 738 (2009)   *54*

Helms v. Landry, 194 N.C. App. 787 (2009)   *8, 54*

Hill *ex rel.* Hill v. West, 189 N.C. App. 189 (2008)   *62, 67*

Hussey v. Cheek, 31 N.C. App. 148 (1976)   *61, 70*

Table of Statutes, Regulations, and Policy Manuals

North Carolina General Statutes

North Carolina Session Laws

North Carolina Administrative Code (N.C.A.C.)

Rules of Recordkeeping (Administrative Office of the Courts, Records of the Clerks of Superior Court)